RELIANCE

WKNIFE

SNOWDRIFT

EAT SLAVE
LAKE

Fort Resolution

TAZIN
LAKE

Fort
Smith

Camsell Portage

URANIUM CITY

LAKE
ATHABASKA

Fond
Du Lac

Fort
Chipewyan

Stony
Rapids

Black
Lake

Embarras Portage

Fort Mac Kay

rt McMurray

La Loche

Anzac

Jim Rheaume

ARCTIC JOURNAL

BW Brown

ARCTIC JOURNAL

Bern Will Brown

NOVALIS

© Novalis, Saint Paul University, Ottawa, Canada, 1998

Editor: Chris Humphrey

Cover: design by Christiane Lemire, photos by Bernard Willett Brown;
  cover portrait of Bern Will Brown by Jim Laragy, *Democrat & Chronicle,*
  Rochester, N.Y., 1986.

Interior paintings and photographs: Bernard Willett Brown

Layout: Gilles Lépine

Novalis
  49 Front St. East, 2nd Floor, Toronto, Ontario   M5E 1B3
  1-800-387-7164 or (416) 363-3303

Printed in Canada

Canadian Cataloguing-in-Publication Data

Brown, Bernard Will, 1920-
Arctic journal

Includes index.

ISBN 2-89088-901-7

  1. Brown, Bernard Will, 1920– 2. Missionaries–
Canada, Northern–Biography. 3. Oblates of Mary
Immaculate–Canada, Northern–Biography. I. Title.

BV2813.B76A3 1997   266'.2719   C97-901166-3

NOVALIS

CONTENTS

FOREWORD

The year was 1967, and I had only just been appointed Commissioner of the North West Territories. It was Canada's Centennial, and celebrations were going on all over the nation. It was during this period that I first met Bern Will Brown, the leader of a crew of N.W.T. Voyageurs taking part, along with crews from throughout Canada, in the hundred-day, 3,283-mile Centennial Voyageur Canoe Pageant.

Affectionately known as "The Padre of the Logs," Bernard has lived in Northern Canada for some fifty years, while pursuing a rich life, first as a missionary and builder of churches, missions and cabins, and also as a trapper, photographer, artist, pilot and writer, not to mention a multitude of other services to his community and friends.

During my fifteen years associated with the Territories I spent a lot of time visiting and travelling with Bernard. While dropping into Nahanni and Colville Lake, I noticed the innovating style of the A-frame log churches that he built, and I marvelled at the speed and the very low cost at which he had completed them.

On a visit to Colville Lake during the Christmas holidays in 1965, I was surprised to see his collection of ten thousand pictures depicting life on the land. Several years later, on one of my regular visits to the settlement, I noticed a painting that he had done from one of his slides and I asked him if he would sell it to me. As a missionary, he had painted a number of beautiful pictures for several of the churches he had served, and I don't think that it ever occurred to him what they would be worth, or that, indeed, he should sell any of his work.

After much persuasion on my part, he agreed not only to sell me the painting, but to loan the photo he had used to develop the idea for the painting. I recall saying to him, "Bernard, you have a keen eye for detail, and, if you ever decided to commit to canvas what you have seen and learned from many years of living off the land with the Dene and Inuit of the Arctic, you could and would be making a great contribution to the people of this vast land and also mankind." I knew of no other person in the North at that time who had lived as long on the land as he had, with those magnificent people of the Arctic, and who possessed the God-given ability to record for posterity an authentic impression of life in the Arctic.

Bernard was not in the North for personal gain, and it took some time before he would agree. Of course, the rest is history. His picture of his powerful huskies and his companion, Philip Stenne, was unbelievably three-dimensional. It was used on the cover of the 1970 Centennial Report of the North West Territories Government and on the Hodgsons' annual Christmas card that year. During my twenty-eight years producing annual reports, never did I receive as many compliments for our format as that year.

I knew a good thing when I saw it, and during each visit to Colville Lake I would buy as many of Bern's paintings as I could for the N.W.T. Government. Some were given to distinguished visitors; the majority, however, adorn the walls of government offices or are in The Prince of Wales Heritage Centre in Yellowknife.

In 1975 I took HRH The Prince of Wales to Colville Lake to meet Bernard and his wife Margaret in order to show him what it was like living close to the land. The idea behind developing the Colville Lake settlement by the then Father Bernard Brown

PREFACE

In my northern travels spanning half a century I've met and talked with many men who had led amazingly interesting lives. Yet none of them ever wrote down their experiences, and so carried them to the grave. I often regretted that: we've all lost part of our history.

From the day I arrived in the North in 1948 I've faithfully kept a daily journal which now fills up our fire-proof safe. If this log Mission burns down, these pages at least will be saved. Hearing of this, many visitors have encouraged me to write a book, and finally they have convinced me. I am under no illusion that my life in the North really warrants an account in print, especially when I think of all those who preceded me and lived significant lives that ought to be recorded.

My reactions to the people, places and events of my northern experiences are entirely my own. I have not been influenced by the Church, the government or any individuals. No ghost-writer has altered my original impressions. I write what I think.

Since high school days I've been an avid and consistent reader of northern books and now have a library of nearly six hundred volumes on the North. They are still my favourite and almost exclusive reading material. This form of self-education equipped me with a very good background when I first came into the country, and has made my life a lot more interesting since.

Many northern books, however, frustrate and disappoint me because they lack details. Some authors, because they don't know or because they are trying to speed up the narrative, leave out names of people and places, times, distances, techniques employed, and so forth. I've tried to write the kind of book on the North that I like to read.

One of my big regrets was that I didn't bring my camera with me when I arrived in the North. I had no idea that the northern scene would change so rapidly, so drastically. I could have recorded on film a way of life that has now almost disappeared. Perhaps this text will help keep some of it alive. I did gradually get into photography, but very sparingly. I missed a lot of great opportunities.

If we could control the date of our birth, I think that, for the sake of this narrative, I would wish that I had been born twenty years earlier. As it was, I got in just too late to see the stern-wheeler *Distributor* plying the Mackenzie River. On the other hand, I thank God that I was on time to witness dog-team travel before it gave way to the motor toboggan, or "snowmobile." My arrival coincided with the opening of the first day school, which precipitated government welfare and the slow disintegration of life on the land for the natives.

I was lucky to belong to an organization that would assign me to a variety of postings spread over a vast area of the North, from the Crees in the south to the Eskimos in the north. I thereby became a witness to many people and places. If I had remained in one location all these years, I doubt that I would have had enough experiences to fill this book.

So what you are about to read is a journal of what I've seen and done in the first seven years in the North of Canada, my experiences written as candidly and truthfully as I know how.

1

GETTING THERE

It was six hours since I had left Fort Norman, North West Territories, heading north on the broad, frozen expanse of the Mackenzie River. The settlement had still been asleep at 6 a.m. when I pulled out. I was glad there were no eyes to witness my embarrassment when my toboggan overturned coming down the steep bank, throwing me into the snow. Luckily I'd clung to the head-rope, so I didn't lose my dog-team. As usual, these five huskies were keen to run at the start, but they didn't know that we had fifty-three hard miles ahead of us, with no trail to follow, or they would have conserved their energy. All my previous trips with them had been close to the settlement.

The lead dog, Fox, picked his way across the mile-wide river around broken ice slabs pushed up by the current at freeze-up time. This rough ice was hard on the oak sled boards. Once we had crossed to the west side of the river the going became easier, as the protected water here had been free of moving ice when it froze. We more or less followed the shore, occasionally cutting across to the many small willow-covered islands. At this latitude in January it's not really daylight until 11 a.m., but the dogs seem to run better at night anyway. It may be the wolf blood in them.

About noon I stopped for lunch, but we weren't near any brush I could use to kindle a fire. I sat on the curved head of the toboggan and pulled a huge ham sandwich from inside my shirt. Brother Médard had made it for me that morning and had advised me to keep it next to my wool undershirt so it wouldn't freeze. Nonetheless, it was frozen so stiff that I gave up gnawing on it and gave it to the dogs. I had better luck chewing on a dried whitefish. The temperature was forty-four degrees below zero, Fahrenheit.

After our ten-minute lunch break, we continued on with Fox breaking trail in about six inches of powdered snow. Having just passed a major landmark called Bear Rock, I estimated we were now ten miles out of Fort Norman, with twenty-five left to go before we would reach Pat Tourangeau's cabin where I hoped to spend the night. By 2 p.m. the hazy sun had disappeared, leaving us in semi-darkness. The dogs were tiring, which meant that I had to get off the sled more often to run behind and crack the whip.

As the miles lengthened my hopes of getting to that heated cabin faded. I began to worry about spending the night in the open without a tent or stove. Fox was weary, too, and began wandering off course. I had to keep correcting him with shouts of *"Cha"* for left and *"Gee"* for right. Precious time and energy were being wasted on this zigzag course. My spirits dropped with the temperature. Realizing at last that yelling directions at my leader was futile, I got off the sled, put on my snowshoes and started walking ahead of the team. I had to rethink this arrangement when Fox, eager to keep up, began stepping on the backs of my snowshoes and tripping me. I solved this problem by swinging a willow switch behind me, keeping him at a respectful distance.

We were now moving in a straight line – but at a much reduced pace – through a curtain of falling snow that enveloped us in a cold gloom and drastically limited visibility. I had to keep that vague left bank of the river in sight or we could end up travelling in circles without knowing it. As it was, we seemed to be moving in an eerie void with no horizon, land and sky blending in a solid whiteout. Only the harness bells and creaking snowshoes penetrated the silence.

I shuffled on, mile after mile, ever wary of stepping into over-flow that would be invisible until I got my feet wet; moose-hide mukluks absorb water like blotters. The fear of thin ice was uppermost in my mind. We were walking on snow-covered ice, beneath which flowed one of the world's greatest rivers; where the current was swift the ice could be thin. I kept straining my eyes hoping to spot a faint light from a cabin window up ahead, but it never materialized out of the mist.

This was my first trip by dog-team of any consequence and it was turning out like nothing I had expected. Now that I was on my feet walking, the cold didn't bother me, intense as it was. In fact, I soon overheated and my breath rimmed my wolverine parka hood in heavy frost. Still, after a few hours my legs were getting tired and I was hungry.

Worse than the physical discomforts, however, were the doubts and fears that preyed upon my mind. Was I really sure of the route I was taking? Could I have passed that cabin without seeing its light? Had they left and was the cabin now unoccu-pied? Could one actually get lost on this frozen river? If I didn't reach the cabin, could I make it through the night on this open trail? Questions like these occupied my mind as we plodded on, mile after mile.

My rest periods became more frequent. When I took time out to sit and rest on the head of the toboggan the dogs flopped down too, and every time I resumed the march it became harder to get the dogs up on their feet to follow me. By 7 p.m. I had to give in to fatigue and admit to myself that we weren't going to make it to the cabin; we would be forced to spend the night right where we were. The logical place to make camp was above the riverbank among the trees, but the banks were so high and steep that climbing them was impossible. My only alternative was a ravine which cut a gap in those insurmountable walls and seemed to offer some protection. When we got there I found the mouth of this ravine blocked by a ten-foot drift of snow, over which we tumbled in the dark. The dogs landed on top of each other, precipitating the first dog fight of the day. I had a hard time breaking it up even with the help of the whip handle. This added exertion left me panting as I sat on the end of a drift log, contemplating the dismal prospects of the campsite in which I was to spend the night.

Taking my axe from the sled I splintered kindling off the drift log, the only piece of firewood in sight. Still wearing my snowshoes I tramped down the snow and carefully arranged my precious kindling in the shape of a teepee, which I then lit. By the light of the feeble flames reflecting off the white walls of snow surrounding us, I unharnessed the dogs and chained them to the small green willows that stuck up through the snow. Next I placed my supper of a frozen whitefish and bannock near the fire to thaw. Returning from the sled with my arms full of gear I was dismayed to see my supper disappearing in great gulps down the throat of Mustache, the wheel dog. Another mistake: I had chained him too close to the fire. I moved him back without scolding him, thinking that if I had been in his place I'd have done the same. Then I set out another fish and bannock.

The fire was heating up steadily and I was beginning to luxuriate in its warmth as I sat close to it on my bedroll. Then, just as I extended my bare hands toward the welcome warmth and gazed into its crackling embers, I got the "Uh – Oh!" impression that it might be sinking. It was. As I watched, fascinated yet powerless, my precious source of heat and light gradually hissed its way below the surface of the snow and out of sight like some doomed ship at sea, leaving me in the dark again with a half-frozen supper. It was another lesson on life in the North: never build a fire on top of snow!

Not knowing how far I might have to dig down to solid ground, but estimating it would be farther than I could dig with a snowshoe – and not having much firewood anyway – I had to do without that essential part of any night on the trail. After gnawing at what grub was partially thawed, I turned to the next item of business: preparing a bed for the night.

How I envied the huskies: they had gulped down their frozen fish and were now contentedly curled up in the snow, snug as bugs in a rug. As for me, I lacked a tent for shelter or even spruce boughs to insulate me from the snow. The only hope I had of passing the night in any degree of comfort was that my as-yet-untried eiderdown sleeping bag would really be "proof against cold down to forty below," as the four-star guarantee claimed. Using a snowshoe for a shovel I dug out a niche in the wall of snow. That it resembled one of those tombs in the catacombs wasn't reassuring.

I spread the sleeping bag out on this icy shelf anyway and climbed in, parka, mukluks and all. One more mistake to add to my list of follies: my clothes were damp from melting snow and perspiration. Nevertheless I zipped the bag to the very top and pulled my head inside. As I lay there trying to sleep I could feel an ominous cold creeping up from my feet. I couldn't help mentally reviewing stories I had read of people in the Far North succumbing to sleep in the cold, never to awaken. So, though I prayed for sleep, I began to fear it. My sleeping bag became a shivering bag.

During that painful night I had plenty of time to review the events of the day that had ended in my present predicament. I asked myself if this was to be the life ahead of me at age twenty-eight. Did I know what I was getting into when I volunteered for the northern missions? Would the oil refinery workers and air force personnel at Norman Wells ever guess what it had cost me to come and conduct a service for them? Wasn't my left foot getting numb, or maybe frozen?

With the first faint glow of approaching dawn I was up and harnessing the dogs. I gave no thought to a fire or breakfast. I felt only a compelling urge to get away from the frigid ravine. And then, as I led the team down onto the river's ice again, I saw what appeared to be a dim light from a cabin window a half mile across on the opposite shore. It couldn't be! But it was. Throughout that miserable night I had been less than a mile away from the comforts of a warm cabin.

It wasn't just one tough break that had produced this adventure. My lack of experience in driving dogs – and a poor team at that, as I later found out – my lack of knowledge of the route and of camping out in winter alone, all had combined to produce this nightmare trip. I should not have been sent out on this trip without a veteran companion. I was learning the hard way.

As soon as my team caught the sound of the Tourangeau dogs barking they fairly flew over the snow toward them. At that moment a Canadian Pacific DC-3 airliner passed low over us on its landing approach to the Norman Wells airport twelve miles away. I could see faces in the windows and imagined their comments:

"Look down there, a dog-team, probably a trapper . . ."

"This cold doesn't bother that breed."

Would they have believed anyone who said: "You're wrong. That's a young missionary priest from New York State who's been in the country less than three months. He just spent the night in a snow bank across the river and nearly froze to death!"

❄ ❄ ❄

I was born in 1920 in Rochester, New York, and raised with two younger brothers nine miles north on the shore of Lake Ontario. Our home, named "Hearthcliff," sat on a bluff fifty feet above the beach. My mother, of French and Swiss stock, was extremely devout and made it a habit to attend daily mass. My father, of English and Irish ancestry, was also one of three brothers. He was attracted to the outdoors and loved fishing and hunting. Living only a few feet from the water, we learned to swim early in life. We also had a canoe, a sailboat and an outboard motor. By age twelve I was running a muskrat trap line and catching the odd skunk! I took a mail order course in taxidermy.

About this time in my life I got very interested in art, for which I was showing some talent. My parents had me enrol in a Saturday class for beginners where I began with graphite sketches, then pen and ink, water colour, and finally oil. I liked it so much that I was spending every spare minute in my room painting. Some of those early works still survive.

As soon as I could handle a high-powered rifle, Dad took me with him on his annual fall deer hunts in the Adirondack Mountains. In the summer of 1936, when my brother Justin was fourteen and I a year-and-a-half older, we spent forty-six days paddling seven hundred miles in Ontario, Canada. The following summer we used a birch-bark canoe on a trip farther north in the Province of Quebec. When I got into high school I began reading all the books about the Far North in the Rochester Public Library. I also enrolled in night school classes at the Mechanics Institute where I learned sketching from life. I was told I had a natural talent for art.

Like most boys my age, I wasn't sure what I wanted to do with my life. For some time I thought I might follow in the footsteps of my uncle, Dr. William Paul Brown, a medical doctor. So I hitch-hiked up to Dartmouth College in Hanover, New Hampshire, and spent a week with a pre-med student. I was attracted to this college because of its ski team, but I soon found out that if I pursued a medical course I would have little or no time to ski!

In my last year in high school Dad had me enrol in a special civilian flying course conducted by the U.S. Army at the University of Rochester. Their long-range plan was to have flying instructors ready in case the United States joined World War II. Although I did get my private license that year and then went on the following year to take their advanced acrobatic course, flying as a career didn't appeal to me.

During my four years of high school at Aquinas Institute, one of the Basilian Fathers who ran it suggested to me privately that I might be a candidate for the priesthood. Prompted no doubt by Mom's example and by her words, the idea had been germinating in my mind. One day Dad surprised me by saying that if he had to do it all over again he would have become a priest! Luckily for me he didn't. Still, the very atmosphere in our family was conducive to the idea. We five often said the rosary together especially if we were driving in the car. We never missed Sunday

mass. Several relatives were priests or nuns. As a remote preparation – just in case I decided that way – I signed up for both Latin
and Greek in high school.

To get an idea of what might be involved I wrote to the Jesuits, who were in charge of the Catholic missions in Alaska, asking
them how long their scholastic course took to prepare a person
for priesthood. Their answer was staggering: a minimum of thirteen years after high school graduation! This meant that I would
already be in my thirties before going north as a Jesuit. The idea
was preposterous. Then I found out that a French order called
the Oblates of Mary Immaculate had charge of all the Catholic
missions in the Canadian Far North. So I wrote to them. Their
answer was a bit more reasonable. They required their candidates to take two years of college in Buffalo, a year of novitiate in
Massachusetts, two years of philosophy in Newburgh, New
York, and four years of theology in Washington, D.C., culminat-
ing in ordination, for a total of nine years after high school.
Although this course was four years shorter than the Jesuits', I
would still be twenty-seven before I could hope to get into the
North. These two religious organizations controlled all access to
the northern Catholic missions on our continent. There was no
alternative.

My big problem was my inherent hatred of school. I was
close to finishing twelve years behind a desk and the very
thought of suffering another nine years seemed beyond my
endurance. I disliked school work so much I absolutely refused
to carry books home to do homework except just prior to final
exams when I crammed for a couple of nights. Luckily I managed
to pass all my grades without failing.

On one of our hunting trips into the Adirondacks I met Nelse
Defendorf at Keene Valley, who told me of a recent winter's trapping in Alaska. He spoke of workers needed in Ketchikan,
Alaska, to man pressure hoses to wash down gold – no prior
experience necessary. This idea so fired my imagination that I
talked a classmate, Bernard Gallagher, into joining me after graduation for a trip to Alaska.

In that summer of 1939, as we started hitchhiking west with fifty dollars between us, America was in the dying throes of the Depression. Near Erie, Pennsylvania, a mini-hurricane left the roads blocked with fallen trees and we got a week's work as loggers. From Indianapolis we delivered a new school bus to Fort Scott, Kansas. At Cheyenne, Wyoming, we worked at the annual Frontier Days Rodeo prodding stock into chutes and later, on horseback, herding cattle back to their home ranch. From there we took a job chauffeuring a party through Yellowstone Park. We picked cherries in the State of Washington for Japanese-American farmers and finally bummed a ride with a trucker into Seattle. We had less than a dollar between us, but we had successfully reached the west coast.

Our plan now was to accept any kind of work on a ship heading for Alaska or, failing that, to stow away. As it happened there was a longshoremen's strike tying up all northbound ships along the Seattle waterfront. After three nights spent in this sleazy dock area we were so hungry and discouraged we hitch-hiked to the site of the Grand Coulee Dam being built on the Columbia River and got some work shovelling gravel. Our dreams of Alaska were fading behind us.

As the summer wore on and the longshoremen's strike was still unsettled, we decided to head back east for home. En route we spent an exciting week with the Flathead Indians on a reserve in northern Montana. A couple of young bucks our age took a liking to us and let us use two of their horses to corral some of their buffalo with them.

From there we found so few cars on the roads we were forced to ride the rails. We boarded one of a string of boxcars with 129 Depression hard-luck types who were following the harvests for work. I was surprised to see women among them. This train kept rolling on day and night for three days, stopping only briefly now and then to take on coal or water. Luckily we met two professional hoboes named Lefty and Dick who took us under their wing and showed us some tricks of the trade. First of all, they had us climb up on top of a car loaded with lumber. By lying flat up there we went undetected when the railroad police, called bulls, drove everyone else off the train. They would all run ahead and again reboard as the train pulled out. We were left undisturbed, but we had to suffer a lot of traffic from fellow travellers who were moving back and forth over the cars to get to those that held ice for refrigeration. This melting ice was their only source of drinking water. And when there was no side wind the engine smoke blew over us in a shower of black cinders.

Later in the week, when the train began stopping at small towns, Lefty and Dick showed us how to go into a restaurant, order a meal and then, before it was served, go into their wash-room, clean up and leave by the back door. Then we would work both sides of a street asking housewives for specific items of food for a stew we would cook up at the local hobo jungle. When we finally arrived at Minneapolis we tried to wash up using the trickle of water leaking from the refrigeration cars. Evidently we didn't do a very good job because when we tried to get into the local YMCA they refused us as being too dirty. We hitch-hiked from there back to Rochester. It was the end of August and, although we hadn't accomplished our objective, we were a little wiser for having wrestled with life in the raw and having come out unscathed.

So now I found myself back home with my future unre-solved, but I was in time to enter the juniorate class at the Oblate College in Buffalo if I so desired. My parents were urging me to give it a try. I finally phoned them and told them I was coming. For some reason I didn't want to admit to my buddies that I was entering a junior seminary, so I told them I was going to the Air Cadet College in Pensacola. Deep down I felt that I wouldn't per-severe in the Oblate Juniorate and I didn't want to burn any bridges behind me. On the other hand I thought that I might regret it later in life if I didn't at least give the religious life a try. I said my goodbyes and hitch-hiked to Buffalo.

I found myself in the juniorate with six other candidates, but before the year was out I was the sole survivor! This was a sur-prise, as I thought I would be the first to leave. I got home for the summer and continued my flying. In Buffalo again for my second year of college I had three new classmates, older men who had quit the business world to study for the priesthood. We four went through the next eight years together.

Once we began our novitiate in Tewksbury, Massachusetts, the following year, we could no longer go home for visits. Clad in cassocks, we entered the very strict phase of our training, a strictness that would persist right up to ordination. Our days were regulated by bells that woke us in the early morning, called us to chapel, to classroom, to work, to meals and back to chapel again. Our mail was censored both coming and going. We had no spending money, no newspapers or radio and smoking was forbidden under pain of instant dismissal. The next year, when we were taking our two years of philosophy in Newburgh, we met some of the army cadets from the military academy at West Point who admitted that our regimen was far stricter than theirs.

From the outset I had been very open about the fact that I had joined the Oblates to go north. I was accepted under this understanding with the promise that I had "a good chance" of getting this assignment if I persevered. Oddly enough I was the only candidate wanting to go in that direction. The rest of my classmates had their sights set on warmer climes.

Initially my superiors merely smiled at my unusual preference for the North. Yet as the years ground on and I persisted in my resolve I was looked upon as being odd. When I got down to my final year of theology in Washington some became downright hostile. I couldn't understand this attitude in view of their wide use of the Arctic in pictures to attract recruits.

"Brother, be sensible," said my superior as I sat stiffly before him in his office a few months before ordination. "You simply don't realize what this foolish idea of yours could lead to. The Oblates working in that frozen field are all Frenchmen. They're different from us. Very puritanical. I've heard they wear cassocks even in the shower! They speak only French. You wouldn't be able to talk to them or know what they were saying about you. And have you thought about those long winter nights that last for six months? Nothing to do? No one to talk to? You'd go stark, raving mad."

The pressure was on and every means was used to get me to change my mind about going north before I wrote my mandatory letter to the Superior General in Rome indicating my preference in a world-wide field of possible assignments. When my superior suspected that his harangues were not producing the desired effect on me he attempted to reduce my hopes to zero by adding that he would send an accompanying letter along with mine with an emphatic veto! It seemed as though I had run up against another type of longshoremen's strike blocking my way to the North.

At this point in my life my spirits were at a low ebb. As a good religious I had been trained to accept any assignment given to me by my superiors. In fact I had taken a vow of obedience to do just that. I knew deep down that I would honour this vow, but the idea of spending my life in Japan or Brazil or even in the States seemed as difficult a future to contemplate as would be that of submitting to nine additional years in classrooms. Possible, but painful. The focus of my dreams had never wavered from a life in the North.

And then, like an answer to prayer, my liberating angel appeared in the person of Bishop Joseph Trocellier, O.M.I. He was head of the Western Arctic's Mackenzie Vicariate and happened to visit our scholasticate. I lost no time in getting an interview with him and expressing my views. The result was that he not only encouraged me to persevere in my plans to go to the North, but promised that he would write his own letter to the Superior General requesting my services in his area of the North West Territories. The battle had been won and I could approach ordination with an untroubled mind. Although this did not dispel a frosty atmosphere around the scholasticate, I was at peace. I was heading north.

2

THE NORTH AT LAST

What a great feeling of liberation it was to get away from the grey walls of that institution. My youngest brother, Thomas, drove down to Washington in his car and took me back to Rochester for my first visit home in seven years. As we rode along, side by side, reviewing the news of the past few years, he suddenly informed me of a momentous decision: he had decided to join my religious congregation!

This was a complete surprise as I thought he was happily engaged in a profitable plastics business. After he had graduated from the Merchant Marine Academy at King's Point, New York, he spent several years on ships in the South Pacific and when he returned home Dad had helped him start his own business called "Tom Brown Associates." And now he was telling me he wanted to quit this lucrative career to follow in my footsteps! I had to admire his enthusiasm in tackling the long ordeal I had just completed. Without wanting to discourage him, I had to admit that I couldn't go through it again. Besides, I had been driven by a great desire to go north which motivated me and which he didn't share.

During the previous year our middle brother, Justin, had paid me a visit at the scholasticate to tell me of his desire to join the Christian Brothers and devote his life to teaching. He had graduated from the Merchant Marine Academy at St. Mateo on the west coast and after his tour of duty on supply ships in the

South Pacific had enrolled in the Mackay School of Mines in Reno, Nevada. He had spent a winter mining near Fairbanks, Alaska, and had a pilot's licence from the U.S. Navy.

When we talked over his qualifications I thought he would be a valuable addition to the Oblate Brothers in the North who were operating all kinds of transportation along the Mackenzie River. I advised him to forget the Christian Brothers and contact Bishop Trocellier. Once he did this he was quickly accepted and sent up to Fort Resolution in the North West Territories to begin his novitiate. So Justin actually got into the North ahead of me. Now, with our younger brother planning to join us, it looked like all three of us would soon be members of the same religious family.

That summer passed very pleasantly amid family and friends at Hearthcliff. We often sat out on the front lawn evenings, watching the boats come into port at sunset and the northern lights begin to appear across the lake over Canada. I imagined them reflecting off the land of ice and snow that would soon be my new home.

My hitchhiking days were over. When I left Rochester at the end of that summer I was driving a new two-ton truck loaded with medical supplies for the northern missions. After a week I reached the end of the road north at Edmonton. From there I continued via the Northern Alberta Railway (NAR) with the truck on a flatcar and myself in the Pullman. This train, dubbed "the muskeg express" by locals, was an adventure in itself. Rolling cautiously on narrow gauge tracks and pulled by a venerable steam locomotive, it took two days to reach the end of steel at Waterways. Much of the roadbed lay on spongy muskeg and derailments due to tipping were frequent. The single coach car in which we travelled was lit by kerosene lamps swinging overhead and heated by a pot-bellied, coal-burning stove. Bunks were folded up out of the way during the day.

The cast of characters riding that train fit into the scene perfectly: Indian women with babies tied in blankets on their backs, grizzled trappers in mackinaws, moccasin-clad bush people who carried either half-pound tins of Ogden Fine Cut Tobacco to roll cigarettes, or empty tins for cuspidors if they were chewing Copenhagen Snuff.

Also on board was a fellow Oblate missionary, Father Pat Mercredi, born at Fort Chipewyan and now serving several mission stations along our route. When he heard that I was interested in art he just had to show me the paintings he had done on the walls of his church at the settlement of Philomena. It was dark at midnight when we reached that spot and we were already in our bunks, but Father Pat had the engineer make an unscheduled stop so we could scramble up the bank and with the aid of a flashlight see his paintings. The friendly conductor gave us ten minutes and then a blast from the locomotive whistle sent us scurrying back down to our car. The muskeg express resumed its clickety-clack progress north into the night. Actually I was less impressed with the missionary's artwork than I was with his ability to stop and hold a train.

Arriving at Waterways, Alberta, we were met by a truck which took us the final three miles to Fort McMurray and the mission. This NAR rail line was supposed to go on to McMurray, but some said it was never completed so that they could still charge "construction rates." The area didn't impress me too favourably. The most southern mission in the Mackenzie Vicariate, it was not nearly northern enough in its atmosphere for me. I was to become very familiar with it when, ten years later, I would spend four years here.

While my truck and its precious load of medical supplies went on north from here via a Northern Transportation Company barge, I was given a lift by a commercial fisherman, George McInnes, in his Anson aircraft. I was seated on my suitcase in the tail of the plane when I happened to notice that this tail section was held by only three bolts. I inched forward beyond that dividing crack and got out my rosary, although if the tail did separate it wouldn't help any to be in any other part of the plane. At any rate, on a wing and a prayer we landed in Fort Smith. I had reached the North West Territories at last.

Fort Smith was the unofficial capital of the Territories, the seat of the civil administration with offices for all government departments. It was also the headquarters of the vast Mackenzie Vicariate which stretched as far north as people lived, and the home base of Bishop Joseph Trocellier, O.M.I., who presided over it. His enclave was a small community in itself, with the mission building housing about twenty Oblates, the convent accommodating some sixteen Grey Nuns of Montreal, the cathedral church, a three-storey hospital, two schools, warehouses and garages, stables, an ice house and even a morgue! Twenty miles out of town was St. Bruno's cattle ranch. Fifteen miles down river was the Brothers' sawmill.

The dedicated Grey Nuns cared for the sick – mostly natives suffering from tuberculosis – taught school, did the cooking and laundry, the sewing and a host of other tasks that kept them occupied from early morning until late at night. And they did it all with a smile while dressed in their uncomfortable starched habits. When they did finally retire to their tiny rooms in the hospital attic they often suffered through sleepless winter nights due to the cold. One of the nuns told me she always took the small rug off the floor and put it on her bed before retiring.

For their part the Brothers kept busy operating the large farm that enabled this whole complex to be self-supporting. They had milk cows and beef cattle, horses, chickens and turkeys. They cut enough cordwood to heat all the buildings and they milled enough lumber to put up all their buildings in Fort Smith and many others farther north. This was the supply depot for all the missions down river. During the short summer these Brothers used their boat, the *Sant'Anna,* and its barge to move all the supplies needed to operate the various missions down to the Arctic Coast. At Tuktoyaktuk they transferred freight to their forty-ton schooner, *Our Lady of Lourdes,* for distribution to coastal missions. A nightly short wave radio "sched" linked all the missions to this control centre at Fort Smith and requests for aid never stopped pouring in.

As soon as I arrived I was greeted by Oblate missionaries scurrying about in black soutanes with felt shoes sticking out the bottoms and bushy beards sprouting at the tops. The priests could be distinguished from the Brothers by the size of the crucifix stuck in their cinctures. Those of the Brothers were smaller.

"Comment ça va?" and "Bienvenue!" greeted me from every side as I started using my untried high school French. I was taken immediately into the bishop's office where he sat plump and jovial behind his pectoral cross and, through a haze of pipe smoke, queried me in a thick French accent about my trip. His immediate concern was the whereabouts of my new truck and its load of supplies. I assured "His Excellency" it was safe aboard a barge which would land in two weeks' time – barring a sudden freeze-up. The short interview over, I was shown to an even shorter room on the third floor where I lugged my suitcase and unpacked. I had no idea if I were moving in for good or merely passing through, but at least I had my foot in the door to the real North.

I had entered a world unlike any I had known before and hour by hour I was discovering its secrets. One thing I quickly learned was that the bishop was not the boss in that house; it was a bell hung strategically in the main stairwell which invariably snapped one to attention when it spoke. It had a spring-loaded clapper activated by a rope on the ground floor, and it spoke with an urgent firehouse clang that could stop a conversation in mid-sentence – or a deep sleep in mid-snore. The mission personnel's day was regulated by it from its first four-alarm summons to prayer at 4:50 a.m., until it sounded for night prayers at 8:30. Nobody liked it, but everyone respected and obeyed it.

Not assigned to any duties except to say mass at the convent in the early morning, I found my days free to walk around and get acquainted. I had played the guitar since I was a kid, so I became popular in the TB ward from the minute I first yodelled a cowboy tune. And over at school I got instant recognition the minute I started drawing animals on the blackboard. I even wandered next door to visit the Mercredi family. My Dad was a great one for visiting people and I think I inherited that trait.

Our Oblate community assembled for meals three times a day in the basement refectory of the hospital. This ritual was presided over by the bishop, who sat at the head of the table, said the grace and blessed our food. Following a short reading from Scripture the bishop then gave us his *"tu autem Domine miserere nobis,"* which was a signal we were allowed to talk during this meal. We all answered, *"Deo Gratias"* – Thank God – and dug in with gusto amid some encouraging *bon appétit*'s. We ate all the courses out of our soup bowls "to save on water" – dishwater, I guessed. Following the meal we trooped into chapel together for a short prayer and following supper we congregated in the mission's upstairs recreation hall. There I was quickly initiated into the card game called cribbage, which I was told was a sine qua non of life in the North. They were right. It is *the* northern card game and I have been playing it ever since.

My International truck arrived in Fort Fitzgerald and I drove it over the sixteen-mile portage road to Fort Smith and helped unload it into one of the vast warehouses. Every day we watched fascinated as the local RCMP, the Royal Canadian Mounted Police, drove a two-ton truck into our pasture with a load of prisoners to dig up and carry away sod. They said that they were making a nine-hole golf course near their barracks. I couldn't help but think of the description of that game given me by Bishop Turquetil of Hudson Bay who had ordained me. "Golf," he said, "is a game with a three-foot stick with a small white ball at one end, and a damn fool at the other."

The members of the mission at Fort Smith didn't participate in any outdoor games as such, but on the big feast days we all piled into a freight truck and drove out to the Brothers' wood shack for a picnic. No one saw any need to take up golf. The seasonal buffalo hunt would be considered a sport by many, but to us it simply meant a lot of hard work – not the pulling of the trigger – but the skinning and butchering. Some of those brutes weighed over two thousand pounds. We weren't hunting for ourselves but for the children in our hostels and the patients in our hospitals and we needed a lot of meat to be sent as far north as Aklavik. I helped a little by bringing down an old bull with my .270 Winchester, an ordination gift.

Hunting the sharp-tailed grouse on their fall migration south, however, proved to be more of a challenge. You could pick them out of the tops of dead spruce with a .22, if you were a good shot. I can remember unloading fifty at the hospital kitchen and feeling relieved that it would be the Sisters' job, and not the hunters', to pluck them.

Father Mansoz was the oldest veteran at the mission and we were celebrating his seventy-fifth birthday. Following the banquet I was sitting with him in his room puffing on one of the White Owl cigars that were traditionally passed out. I had not acquired the tobacco habit yet and I put the question to this wise old missionary as to whether or not I should smoke? He replied that he thought maybe if I smoked a pipe it would provide some soothing companionship later on during the hard times and added, "Zer har zo mini tings ve kin not do, zee?" Then he got to reminiscing about his life in the North and how it had passed so unbelievably fast, saying, as he gazed out the window, "Zo mini tings to do yet. But zey tell me too hold now. Me, I feel just start, but zey say zit quiet, you do nuf already." Some forty-five years separated us and yet he predicted I too would be seventy-five before I realized it. He was right.

October's gold had given way to November's white. In spite of the similarities to the scholasticate I had just left I caught myself beginning to like this place – not everything, that's true. I really was not getting enough sleep, and I was getting very little out of the daily spiritual reading in French. The food was monotonous, either buffalo or whitefish, which showed little inspiration in its preparation. What compensated for these drawbacks, however, was the uplifting spirit of the place. One could not help but notice the open, generous and friendly atmosphere that hung over this religious community like a benediction. They were poor and it showed, but that didn't dampen their enthusiasm.

Our quarters were cramped, often cold and dark, but no one complained about it. No one expected anything better, so no one was disappointed. Everyone had his own job to do and took a special pride in doing it well for the common good. There didn't appear to be any weak links in the chain, no discord, no problems that couldn't be solved.

In short, it was a small, insular community of happy, dedicated religious people living a communal life in the ideal sense of that word. Few in the outside world knew we even existed and unfortunately that existence was to be short-lived. Fifty years later they would all be gone, the mission turned into a museum, and most of the other buildings torn down. Looking at that empty space today one might find it hard to imagine the activity that once flourished there.

On the 4th of November I was back in the bishop's office and he was saying, "Fadder Brown, I'm a not a certaine justa yet where I'm a gonna puta you, but ina meantime how you likea visit your brudder Justin ata Fort Res (Fort Resolution)?" The bishop had gone through the Italian scholasticate at San Georgio and had a very musical combination of Italian and French accents.

The following morning found me aboard the Canadian Pacific Airline's DC-3 for the eighty-mile hop over to Fort Resolution on the shore of Great Slave Lake and to a reunion with the younger brother who had beaten me into the North by a year. I found him out behind the mission with a sledge hammer and wedges, splitting four-foot lengths of firewood. We had a month to fill each other in on our recent experiences, but to do this we were allowed no special visiting privileges. Justin was going through his year of strict novitiate training prior to taking his first vows. We got together where and when we could.

The Fort Resolution mission was a smaller version of the one I had just left at Fort Smith, with the addition of a large boarding school for native children. The Chipewyan Indians living there were still following their traditional lifestyle of hunting and trapping. Here I was excited to see my first dog-teams in action. I joined Justin and his Oblate community in most of their daily religious exercises. The one that started the day at 5:15 in their dimly lit chapel is the most memorable. The usual prayers were followed by the standard half-hour of meditation, during which one of the good Brothers behind us demonstrated various types of northern snoring, outstanding for both variety and volume.

During the day when I couldn't be with my brother I took advantage of the chance to visit around the settlement. Fred Camsell, less well-known brother of Charles,* was the Postmaster. He told me of his yearly trips to Winnipeg for an education when he was a boy, and of his going to work for the Hudson Bay Company at Fort Rae in 1889. Joe Lirette was a "free-trader" and told me of wolves he had killed that weighed over 200 pounds.

Perhaps the most notorious local character was another trader by the name of George Pinsky. One of his little trade tricks was to give change to his customers – who paid with paper money – by tearing off a smaller portion of the bill to insure that the balance would be returned to his store. As a result a lot of the local bills were either sewn or taped together. I kept one as a souvenir. George sold me a half-dozen oranges at a fabulous price and invited me to return in the evening for a game of bridge. I never did get back to join in a bridge game and Justin didn't get to eat the oranges, as he was scrupulously observing one of the rules that forbids eating between meals and that directs that all gifts be shared with the community.

While at Res I was invited by the superior, Father Mokwa, to spend a couple of nights at the Brothers' wood camp ten miles away and act as chaplain. This occasioned my first ride in a dogsled capably driven by Brother Petrin. I was amazed at both the power and speed of these draught animals and the intelligent way their leader obeyed the voice commands of the driver behind me.

---

* Charles Camsell, born at Fort Liard, N.W.T., in 1876, was Deputy Minister of Mines and from 1935 to 1946 he was Commissioner of the N.W.T. He was also the Chief Factor of the Hudson Bay Company.

When we pulled up in front of the rough-hewn log cabin bunk-house, out came a big, burly French-Canadian in a stocking cap and full beard. "My soul, comment ça va?" he shouted, and I knew I was meeting the most widely known and best-loved Brother in the Territories – the loud, jovial, cross-eyed Brother Henri Latreille, known simply as "Frère Hon-ri."

For the next two days that cabin rocked with his outrageous stories and laughter as he cooked for a half-dozen wood-cutters. Following my early morning mass for the crew, I was free to help the Brother with his many chores. He chopped the firewood needed to heat the cabin and fuel the cook stove and introduced me to the standard northern torture instrument called a Swede saw. He also had me help him visit a gill net set under the ice and to appreciate losche liver, one of the special northern delicacies, comparable to moose nose and beaver tail. We also checked the snares he had set for snowshoe rabbits.

To add excitement to these experiences we were visited one night by a pack of timber wolves who were trying to get at our sled dogs. They kept up a frightful chorus of howls as they circled our cabin in the dark. I would have been a hero if I had shot one and driven them off, but although I stayed up half the night I could not get one in my rifle's telescopic sight.

Back with Brother Justin at the Res mission I was full of enthusiasm after my brief bush experience and eager for more. We speculated on what the future held in store for each of us in this wild and exciting Northland and whether we couldn't manage to be stationed together after he had finished his novitiate and made his profession. What we couldn't have anticipated at the time was the accident that would befall him the following spring. While he was repairing the church roof, his safety rope broke and he fell thirty feet, breaking both ankles and injuring his spinal column. The local doctor put him in a cast, but when gangrene set in he was sent to Edmonton where he spent the next three months in hospital. It ended in his having to leave the North and give up his plans of becoming an Oblate Lay Brother. He never expressed any bitterness over this turn of events, accepting it all as the will of God. Dad, with his characteristic humour, would later tell people that he had two sons who were priests and one who fell away from the church!

Back in Fort Smith I was again in the bishop's office recounting my visit with my brother when he suddenly interrupted my small talk with something important. "Fadder Brown, I tink I finda justa spot for you – Forta Norman. Lots ah missionaries starta dere. Watta you tink?" I thought it was a great idea and heartily accepted my first official "obedience" in the Mackenzie Vicariate.

Although I had to leave the bustling mission at Fort Smith behind me, I had been lucky to experience it firsthand at its glorious peak.

3

FORT NORMAN

On December 3rd, 1948, I was on board Canadian Pacific Airlines (CPA) DC-3 Mainliner, piloted by Captain Ken Dewer, as it winged its way north over the frozen Mackenzie River with stops at Hay River, Fort Simpson and Wrigley. It was dark when we finally landed at Norman Wells, the northern terminus of the line, and stepped out into minus forty-five degrees Fahrenheit. While the ground crew scurried about putting wing covers on the aircraft for the overnight stay the local RCMP escorted the stewardess away and we, the passengers, were taken to the CPA boarding house capably run by a matronly woman known affectionately as "Ma."

The next day I made the final flight to my destination, Fort Norman, aboard a Waco biplane flown by local bush pilot Mike Zubko. We sat down on skis in deep snow on Plane Lake a mile behind the settlement where Father Jean Denis, O.M.I., my new Superior, met me with his dog-team. After we had thrown my baggage into his sled he offered to let me drive the team back to the mission. Borrowing his heavy mitts, I stood behind grasping the sled handles while he rode in the cariole. Careening down that steep, twisting trail into town, I fell off not once but twice, to his great amusement. Evidently dog mushing was not as easy as it looked.

Brother Médard, blood-brother of Frère Henri, welcomed me warmly when we got to the mission. Not as tall or as overpowering as his older brother, the clean-shaven Médard was more rotund, but he had the same jolly manner, the same heavy Quebec French accent.

As soon as I had my parka off (as was the custom in those days, I wore my cassock underneath), I was given a tour of the building. The first thing I noticed was the height of the door jambs. Those early Frenchmen who had built it must have been very short, as they had allowed only a five-and-a-half-foot clear-ance for the doors. My two companions could walk through them erect, but I had to be careful to duck my six-foot frame. This two-storey mission had been built in the last century of squared spruce logs dovetailed at the corners, chinked with mud and straw and covered inside and out with hand-hewn boards. Once the logs had been covered on both sides in this way you could not see if the chinking was falling out, and to a great extent it had. The mission had been whitewashed on the outside, apparently to make it resemble a proper frame building. Inside, the boards lin-ing the walls ran vertically and were painted – pink!

I was taken across the common room where accordion doors opened to reveal the chapel hidden behind them, unheated except during services. To the right of this were two smaller rooms, the first being a seldom-used parlour, the second the room of Father Denis. Along the left side was the room of Brother Médard and the kitchen. This opened up in back to a closed-in porch which he called a *tambour*, where he stacked his kindling. There was a second floor containing a library and three bed-rooms, but this area was left empty and unheated during the cold months. To gain access to it, you had to go through the ground floor confessional, an arrangement I could never understand.

Out behind the mission there was a carpenter's workshop, a privy, several warehouses and a small garage for the tractor – all built of logs, of course – and five doghouses, to each of which a dog was chained. A hundred feet to the north of the mission stood the church dedicated to St. Teresa of Avila. It had been built of the same spruce logs, but its interior displayed the inspired work of many missionaries over many years. It becomes more impressive when one considers that all the lumber used had to be whipsawed from logs, then planed by hand. The altar and the two doors leading to the sacristy contained intricate fretwork that was truly marvellous. All of the walls were decorated with designs and pictures painted right on the boards with a mixture of local fish oil and coloured powder from France. The Gothic windows contained glass that had been three years in shipment from Montreal by York boats over perilous portages.

This building was a living monument to the missionaries who had laboured here over the span of nearly a century, beginning in 1859 with Father Henri Grollier. The one who spent the most time on it, however, was Father Xavier Ducot, who had arrived in 1876 with only two axes, three saws and eight nails! He spent forty years here. When in 1964 I heard that it was to be demolished, I tried my best to avert such a tragedy, wrote to the Superior General in Rome and volunteered to shore it up and skid it back out of the way to preserve it. Alas, my ideas of preservation were out-voted and it was torn down.

Like almost all settlements in the Territories, Fort Norman had grown around a trading post, in this case one placed strategically at the confluence of the Bear and Mackenzie Rivers. An imposing 1,750-foot outcrop of limestone called Bear Rock rises steeply from the Mackenzie a few miles down river. To the west the first ranges of the Rockies loom on the horizon.

The whites in town numbered about twenty-five and represented the same organizations found in most northern settlements. Besides the Church and the Hudson Bay Company, there were civil servants working as police officers, and one or more nurses, school teachers, game officers and Indian agents. Fort Norman was unique, however, in that it employed nearly a dozen men working for the Royal Canadian Corps of Signals who had handled communications up and down the Mackenzie River since the end of World War II.

There were some 200 natives living at the Fort, sometimes in town and sometimes out in the bush. They called themselves *Dene,* meaning simply, "the men." When they were met by

Alexander Mackenzie in 1789 they were dressed in clothing made entirely from the skins of the snowshoe rabbit, so he named them Hareskins, or the Hare tribe. Apparently when this type of clothing gets infested with lice it is almost impossible to delouse. The Eskimos noticed this when they first met them and called them *Iklilik*, "the lousy ones," a name they still use, although I doubt the Hare Indians are aware of it. Father Emile Petitot, who travelled extensively among this tribe in the 1860's, described them as a talkative people, "homely and friendly as children."

Although this tribe was still to some degree dependent upon their traditional hunting and trapping for a livelihood, their mobility had been curtailed the previous year when the government put up the first of many day schools. Previously their children had been educated in the mission-run boarding schools in Fort Providence and Aklavik. The problem with a day school was that the mothers would have to stay home to take care of the children instead of accompanying their husbands on their trap lines. Then the men did not go out as far or stay out as long, with a resulting loss of the fur harvest. When the people predicted this outcome the Department of Education told them not to worry because they would be given rations to compensate. Thus there began the era of crippling welfare in the North West Territories.

In the bush the people lived in tents, but in town most of them had constructed log cabins which were strung along a flat bench of land below the mission and the barracks. Each family had its dog-team tied outside. All had been baptized Christian in the previous century, with the exception of one old man who still practised the ancient rites of the medicine man whenever he could secure a client. Respiratory infections were endemic and many were carrying active tuberculosis. Death was common. Life was harsh and often brief, but the Church held out a promise of a better life to come and the missionaries who carried this message were held in high esteem.

Back at the mission I was assigned the parlour as my bedroom and lost no time in moving in. Even at midday I needed the light of a Coleman gas lamp in order to work, as the single-paned window was darkened by an inch of frost. A wind charger mounted outside was connected to a bank of six-volt wet batteries in the root cellar under the kitchen floor. These were perpetually undercharged, however, so electric lights were used only on special occasions.

On the morning following my arrival I was roused from sleep by the Brother clanging a hand-held brass bell and singing out the traditional *"Benedicamus Domino"* – Let us bless the Lord! – to which I managed an unenthusiastic *"Deo Gratias"* – Thank God! I struggled to unzip myself from my sleeping bag. Swinging my feet out onto an icy linoleum floor I fumbled with a match and lit a candle. Through a cloud of condensation from my breath my wrist-watch told me it was 4:50 a.m. The water in my basin was frozen solid. Thoughts like "we could probably be living just as comfortably in a tent" raced through my mind. I quickly dressed in my cassock and moved out into the common room where the heater, having been goaded by a can of fuel oil that Brother used to saturate the wood, was roaring its defiance at the cold.

I was just beginning to feel some heat when Father Denis rushed out of his room and opened the chapel doors. A new wave of frosty air swept across the room. The cold be damned! We three got down on our knees to recite the traditional Oblate morning prayers in French, followed by the breviary in Latin. At fifteen-minute intervals Brother rang another bell, mounted outside, to call the faithful to morning mass. Several old cronies shuffled in and sat on the floor by the stove in silence.

Following the mass and the thanksgiving afterwards the chapel doors were closed behind us and I was introduced to the pious old souls who had braved the forty-five-below temperature to honour their God while the rest of the town slept. We shook hands, but I couldn't communicate with them. It was readily apparent that I would be practically useless here as a missionary until I could speak the language. And, as my companions were speaking French, I would need to master that language as well.

Our early morning spiritual exercises were followed by breakfast, presided over by Brother Médard in the small kitchen. It consisted of porridge and home-made bread. I soon got into the routine of spending the rest of the morning studying the Hareskin language, tutored by Father Denis. Lunch followed the Angelus at noon, after which I got some exercise outdoors, either hunting ptarmigan on snowshoes or driving the dogs to bring in a load of firewood.

At five in the afternoon the chapel doors were again opened so that we could pray the rosary together before the Blessed Sacrament. At six we took our third meal of the day in the kitchen, after which we played either cribbage or chess. Night prayer at 9 p.m. capped our day. Brother stoked the fire with a couple of large logs and we retired. We were following a schedule that was identical in every detail in all the forty-some missions throughout the Vicariate and very close to the one that had regulated my life for the past nine years. Our Oblate predecessors had been doing the same things at the same hours in this same house since way into the last century. It was, as Tevye said in *Fiddler on the Roof*, "Tradition!"

Others before me had studied the Hareskin language, but, oddly enough, they had left no grammar behind them. During my scholastic years I had studied French, Latin, Greek and Hebrew, all with the aid of grammars. Now I had to make my own. It was particularly difficult because, with the exception of a dozen words taken from the French, this language in no way resembled any I had studied. In only one way was I helped, and that was in the construction of their sentences which followed the Latin: the object came first, followed by the adjectives and adverbs, with the verb at the end.

The first sentence that I memorized was *"Dene ke'en tanedi?"* "How do you say that in Hareskin?" Armed with this one question I spent many an hour visiting the natives and marking down the names of anything I could point to. The nouns were hard enough to memorize, but the verbs were murder. One reason for this was that the verbs changed with the particular type of action described; for example, if you said you were going on foot or by boat or by aircraft, the verb for "going" changed with each mode of travel.

Another difficulty for the missionary was the absence of words to describe abstract ideas, especially those needed to explain Christianity. *Grace* was translated as "that which makes a man's heart strong." *Sacrament* came across as "God's medicine." For a newcomer like myself it was extremely difficult to separate a sentence into individual words. The problem was caused by a combination of the language's own elision and poor enunciation by the native speaker. One particular woman was the exception to this rule and when she visited the mission Father Denis would say, "Now just listen to her speak. You can hear every word."

And there are a lot of them. Father Petitot, who was the most gifted linguist to work among these people, estimated they may have some 600,000 words! He was also convinced that a language so rigidly structured, so grammatically correct as this could not possibly have been invented by an illiterate race of nomads. God created the earth, why couldn't God create a language, he argued. Later the renowned ethnologist Diamond Jenness summed up his study of eleven native Canadian tongues by saying: "The most primitive Indians of Canada, those of the Mackenzie River Valley, possessed the most complex language."

The French language was infinitely easier – no comparison – and aided by Brother Médard I made rapid progress in it. Trouble arose, however, from the fact that the brand of French he was speaking, the Quebec patois, was unacceptable to a Frenchman from France like Father Denis. This occasioned some heated arguments during meals and prompted our superior to keep a French dictionary on the table. At one meal Brother asked me, "Comment vous dites 'steam' – en Anglais?" (How do you say 'steam' in English?). I answered, "*Vapeur*," and Father Denis threw up his hands in despair! One thing he couldn't stand was *Franglais*.

Once the Mackenzie River is frozen over, it becomes a poor place to set a gill net for fish, and that makes Fort Norman a difficult place to get dog food during the winter. Brother resorted to all kinds of tricks to keep the five mission dogs fed, like never putting soap in the dishwater so he could mix rolled oats in it later for dog food!

The nearest fish lake, called Taketue, lay twelve miles to the east and Brother had built a tiny, two-bunk log cabin there years before. He used to walk there on snowshoes to visit a gill net he had set under the ice. Now he suggested we drive the dogs up there and set a net.

When we arrived there the first thing we did was cut the two longest green spruce poles we could find. After trimming them neatly we tied them end-to-end, making a single pole forty feet long. Laying this pole on top of the ice where the net was to be set, we cut holes through the ice at both ends. Then we moved the pole on in a straight line from the second hole and cut a third. Finally we had a series of holes forty feet apart spanning the two-hundred-foot length of the net.

Next we tied the end of a long cord to our pole, which we then pushed through the first hole and under the ice toward the second hole. It was like pulling thread under cloth with a needle. The ice was thin enough that we could see the pole, so we had little difficulty using a forked stick to push the pole from hole to hole until we pulled it out at the last one. Now we had the cord under the ice from the first to the last hole, and all we had to do was attach the net to one end and pull it under. Brother had the net piled neatly at the first hole with rocks for weights attached to one side of the net and floats attached to the other. While I pulled on the cord he paid out the net, one side of which immediately sank to the bottom so that the net was in a vertical position. We secured both ends to a cord tied to a rock on the bottom and a forked green willow above the ice. The job took us about an hour and a half and worked without a hitch. It is one of those northern jobs that can be learned easily if one has a veteran to demonstrate how. We retired to the snug cabin and spent the evening playing chess.

The next morning we pulled out the net to see what we had caught. We opened the two end holes with the long-handled ice chisel and tied the long cord, called a *te-klu*, to one end of the net. Then we pulled the net out onto the ice dragging the *te-klu* back under the ice in its place. After taking a couple dozen whitefish and pike from the net we reset it by pulling it back with the *te-klu*. We piled snow around each end hole to minimize freezing, put the *te-klu* back in the cabin and left for home. During the winter we tried to visit this net once a week and, as I got more proficient at it, I went out alone sometimes and returned to the mission the same day. It was a welcome break from studying.

❈ ❈ ❈

Soon Christmas, the big feast of the winter, was upon us. Because the mass (*Christ*-mass) is celebrated at midnight, the natives gave it the name *Tewe-yati* – "the night we pray." A few teams came from as far away as Fort Franklin on Great Bear Lake, some eighty miles east. They usually brought haunches of Barren Land caribou and large trout, food that was scarce around Fort Norman.

Others came in from the foothills of the Rockies to the west and were known as the Mountain Indians. I happened to be out on snowshoes one afternoon hunting ptarmigan along the river-bank when I ran into one of those families coming in for Christmas. They were covered with frost and moving painfully slowly when they stopped to shake my hand. Leading the procession was the father with a child on his back and a rifle in his hand, breaking trail on snowshoes. His wife was following in her traditional position about five paces back with the baby of the family wrapped in a blanket on her back. She was followed by two teenage daughters on snowshoes that were trimmed on the front tips with ptarmigan feet, good luck amulets.

Next in line was a team of four pitifully thin dogs straining in tattered harness ahead of a heavily loaded birch toboggan driven by two teenage boys. Bringing up the rear was another team of three dogs driven by the eldest son. When I asked him if he had a lot of meat he pulled back the canvas cover of his sled to reveal two children in their sheepskin parkas, asleep. As we stood there trying to communicate in the few words of their language I knew, the dogs curled up and the snow started drifting over them. It took a couple of cracks of the dog whip to bring them to their feet again to resume the last mile of their five-day trek into the settlement. I stood there fascinated as they got under way again, the sleds creaking along and a fog of ice crystals enveloping them. Gradually they dissolved in the distance and the wind went to work erasing their track, an apt symbol of their unrecorded passage through time. We can only guess where they came from as the drifting snows of a thousand cruel winters have wiped out the trails behind them. The Holy Family itself, en route to Bethlehem, couldn't have had a tougher trip than the one this family took to celebrate Christmas.

For two days before the big feast the Brother kept a roaring fire going in the big church to thaw it out. I paced the floor of the mission's common room, memorizing a sermon in English for the Midnight Mass which traditionally attracted all the whites in town. Father Denis would deliver another in the native tongue. When that night arrived and I was on my feet speaking, some might have misconstrued a few tears in my eyes as an expression of overwhelming emotion when, in fact, my feet were slowly freezing in tight Christmas moccasins. In spite of the temperature inside, the old church was crowded to the walls and the congregational singing was enough to raise the roof.

Three days later the children's Christmas tree party was held in the mission and some seventy adults crowded into that room to watch the fun. I had some fun myself watching an old-timer turn one of our electric lights off and on while exclaiming, "Monla duye," which could be loosely translated as "Those white men are amazing." A few days later, at midnight on New Year's

Eve, with the temperature slipping to sixty below, the town erupted in crackling gunfire in the traditional salute to the New Year – 1949.

On the 4th of January I had the rare pleasure of doing something strictly ministerial, performing a baptism. By now it was becoming obvious to me that such occasions would be few and far between. I could keep myself busy all right, but not doing things that are considered priestly. So why all the years of theology? To prepare me for what? The endless stream of native visitors who occupied Father Denis' day in idle conversation were not discussing theological problems. They were talking about hunting, trapping and the weather. I wondered to myself if I could stand a lifetime of such banal conversations? Where were the challenges of yesteryear, when our missionaries wrestled with the devil himself to win pagan souls to Christ? Now ministry seemed to have evolved into a simple holding pattern to maintain the status quo. Pioneer men of the cloth in the last century had rounded up and branded all the sheep. All that remained for their successors was to keep the flock from straying. We were all well aware of the privations and hardships of our black-robed predecessors, but surely they must have been compensated for their trials by the satisfaction of seeing their spiritual achievements? Perhaps I was arriving on the scene a hundred years too late?

❊ ❊ ❊

Why is it that the North seems to be so populated with the type of person we call a "character"? Perhaps there are just as many in Edmonton or New York, but they are lost in the crowd. Perhaps it's the free spirit of the North that encourages people to be eccentric. Whatever the reason, I was running into an unusually large number of characters in the Territories.

Some of the most noteworthy characters have worked for the Hudson Bay Company. Among these were the three Gaudet brothers whose combined service among the Hareskins spanned a century. Now only Tim survived and he was spending his retirement years at Fort Norman. Tall, but slightly stooped, with a handlebar mustache drooping under a strawberry nose and with a heavy gold watch chain swinging from his vest, Tim represented the stereotypical HBC veteran. He often came to the mission at night to engage us in a game of rummy. His distinctly different French-Canadian accent must have resembled that spoken by the authentic *coureurs de bois* who in the early years manned the Company's York boats.

Besides possessing the skills needed by a successful trader, Tim was also skilled in the arts of bush life, like snowshoe-making. Everyone working in the bush needs several different sizes of snowshoes. I needed a pair, but I wanted to learn to make my own. So Tim guided me through all the phases of construction, from the proper selection of a white birch sapling, through the splitting, cutting and bending stages, to the final insertion of the *babiche* (webbing). The project was so successful that I went on to make several pairs. One pair, six feet, six inches long and used in deep snow, is now over forty-five years old and I'm still using them. The satisfaction I got from walking on shoes I had made was worth all the labour involved. Some years later I was invited to teach this skill in a high school workshop – to young natives!

In the opening chapter I described my first painful dogsled trip to Norman Wells. After Easter I made a second one, but in the meantime I had learned to handle the dogs better. The days were longer and I made it to Pat Tourangeau's cabin with no trouble. Now he, his wife Cecilia and their eight kids were living in their log warehouse, because the timbers holding the sod roof of their main cabin were rotting and they feared they would collapse. Pat was prevented from making these repairs on doctor's orders to take it easy, following the results of a chest X-ray that indicated he might have TB.

In fact he stayed indoors all that winter doing light housework while his robust wife took his dog-team and ran his trap line, even shooting a moose. Late in the spring Pat received a second letter from the Department of Health apologizing for an error. They had read the wrong X-ray and there was absolutely nothing wrong with Pat! Upon receipt of this news the first thing Cecilia did was to pin Pat to the floor to demonstrate how strong she had become during his winter hibernation. And then she ordered him outside to tackle the wood pile.

On the following morning of my trip I hitched up at Pat's cabin and ran the remaining twelve miles into Norman Wells, where I was again welcomed by the Imperial Oil refinery manager, K. Murray Mackenzie. The refinery itself was mostly dormant during the winter, with a skeleton crew keeping essential units heated but processing little crude. Although only forty-odd air miles separated Norman Wells from Fort Norman, their atmosphere and living styles were worlds apart. Here at Norman Wells I was quartered in a modern frame bungalow, steam-heated to around ninety degrees. The first thing I did was to remove my wool underwear. I ate T-bone steaks in the mess hall and my dogs ate almost as well. There was no wake-up bell and everyone spoke English. I held a daily service in the recreation hall and spent the rest of the day visiting the employees and their families.

Another character emerged from this group in the person of Hamar Nelson, a bachelor and part-time employee. Essentially a loner used to trapping and prospecting, Hamar was forced into the company of fellow humans from time to time to earn a new grubstake. When he emigrated from Scandinavia he landed on the shores of Hudson Bay and from there he moved west alone with his dog-team across the Barrens. He claimed that all he took with him for dog feed when he left Baker Lake was a sack of arctic hare skins and a case of tallow. Every night he would heat some tallow and dip a hare skin in it for each dog. When he passed Coppermine the Eskimos there dubbed him "The Lone Traveller."

He did a lot of prospecting in the mountains west of Norman Wells. He would disappear into those hills in the late fall and nobody would hear anything of him until he reappeared again in the spring. He would paddle in on a raft or a skin boat with a few sled dogs. He wouldn't tell anyone where he had been nor show his rock specimens. While recuperating at the Wells he would go back to work for the refinery. Depending on his physical condition he would go on some strange diets, sometimes eating nothing but vegetables for a few weeks, then straight meat and then again, all liquid.

I greatly admired this northern veteran and took advantage of my visits to the Wells to learn basic survival techniques from him. He showed me how to crimp the ends of a tent's stove pipe sections so that an eddy was created in the draught to trap the sparks. Then they didn't fly out the top and burn holes in the tent. He was the first person I had met in the North who knew how to build an igloo and I wasn't satisfied until we went down on the river and he demonstrated their construction. I'd go down every afternoon with a snow knife and build one until I got it right. No doubt there were some people watching who thought I was as odd as my instructor.

Back at the mission in Fort Norman I again tackled the study of the Dene language, which became more interesting as I began to put words together to form intelligible sentences. The closest satellite community to the Fort was at Willow Lake about thirty miles north-east, where a half-dozen of the Norman natives had built cabins. One of these Hareskins with the improbable name of Colin Campbell had a cabin there in which his wife had died the previous year. Following native custom he moved out of it and I was able to buy it for the mission for fifty dollars. I went up there by dogs, spent a few nights, and made plans to convert it into a chapel. Another project that emerged from the melting snowdrifts was an eighteen-foot round-bottomed cabin cruiser that had been lying out behind the mission for years. I decided to re-caulk its hull, overhaul its twenty-horsepower inboard Kermath engine and launch it as soon as we had open water.

Day by day, as the sun rose higher, the snow banks sank lower and ice on the inside of the mission's windows lost its grip on the glass and fell off, letting in that blessed sunshine. Our spirits rose with the temperature. Soon we could see patches of bare sand on Windy Island a mile across the river, followed by the cheery sight of ducks and geese landing there. When the west wind carried their raucous clatter across to us, how it activated our salivary glands!

Father Denis and I waited till the town was asleep one night and then we stole across with the dog-team pulling the toboggan loaded with a light canoe. Arriving at the open water near the islands we put the dogs in the canoe, ferried them to dry ground and tied them up. We were surrounded by migrating waterfowl who seemed to sense the range of our shotguns.

There was a flock of several hundred Canadian honkers on open water to the west of our island and I decided that the only way to get into range was to paddle upstream above them and then, lying unseen in the bottom of the canoe, drift down into their midst. This plan worked perfectly right up to the point where I could hear their cackling all about me, but when I tried to extricate myself from under the thwarts I was seized with the worst charley horse of my life. Before I could regain control of my leg muscles there wasn't a bird left within range. In fact I didn't bag my first goose until we had expended all our shotgun shells on ducks. Luckily I brought a goose down with my .22 as it flew over.

There was no darkness that night, neither was there any sleep for us. Yet when we retreated across the river before the town woke up we carried with us enough birds to brighten our table for the next month.

The term *break-up* means little to the person who has never passed a year in the North, but to those who have, it is a magic word that separates winter from summer and denotes everything that breathes new life into the land. The month was May and the white-knuckled grip of winter was finally broken. The smell of spruce permeated the balmy air as small birds reappeared in their branches and sang their cheery songs. People left their parkas at home and put on rubber boots to get out of their dark cabins and into the sun to greet one another. As Thoreau observed, "the winter of man's discontent was thawing as well as the earth."

The winter's drifts of snow melted and ran down to the river, quickly lifting its burden of ice forty feet above its winter level. Finally one day, without trumpet or fanfare, this whole frozen surface of the mighty Mackenzie began to move north. The break-up had begun! And as word raced from cabin to cabin the whole population assembled along the bank to watch in fascination. The spectacle was irresistible, drawing even the recluses we had scarcely seen all winter. Everyone was in a festive mood, greeting neighbours with words that meant, "Hurrah! We've survived another one!"

What dynamic forces of nature were at work before our astonished eyes: chunks of ice the size of houses, churning and tumbling, gouging tons of earth from the bank we were standing on. After the first day of ice had passed a more interesting spectacle hove into view: huge spruce trees, some standing upright in the press of ice, marched by in stately review, followed by intact cabins that must have slid down some crumbling cutbank, and then someone's scow, undamaged, on top of a huge cake of ice. The crowd cheered! It was like watching a parade and no one wanted to go home in case he should miss something.

Gradually the amount of ice began to thin out, but its place was taken by more trees and logs. Finally the floating ice completely disappeared and was replaced by a sea of wood stretching from bank to bank. We saw pass by huge, hundred-foot timbers that must have come all the way from the Liard River or even the Peace from above Fort Smith. All were on their way to the salt waters of the Arctic Ocean where wind and tide would scatter them from Herschel Island on the west to Cape Parry on the east. The show went on night and day for nearly a week before the river could free itself of this burden of ice and wood. And then, suddenly one morning, we awoke to find it reflecting a clear, blue sky without a stick to mar its glassy surface. The break-up was over. It was summer.

4

A Visit
to the Eskimos

"The banana boat is coming!" The cry went around town the day after the ice went out. And sure enough, there she was, rounding the bend up river, Captain Streeper's *Stewart Lake* from Fort Nelson. Always the first boat to arrive after break-up, it was carrying a load of fresh food which he sold right off the deck. The captain did a land-office business for a day and then shoved off and followed the retreating ice down river, stopping at each settlement.

The passing of the *Stewart Lake* indicated that all was clear up river, so we could embark on the annual harvest of firewood. Brother and I launched the mission's twenty-two-foot freighter canoe, which was pushed by a nine-horsepower motor called in the North a "kicker." We went up river twenty-five miles to drift back collecting logs as we went. We were looking for long, straight logs that would make a good raft. They were found stranded on small islands and sandbars by the recent high water. We would go ashore with the Swede saw, cut off the root end and roll them into the water, where we lashed them together. Soon we had a stable log platform upon which we put our tent and cook stove.

It was great to be out working in the sun except for one draw-
back – the mosquitoes. Justin and I had encountered mosquitoes
on our canoe trips in Eastern Canada, but nothing like this. Their
size and ferocity were remarkable enough, but their sheer
number was unbelievable. They followed us around in a cloud
and if the citronella juice we were using discouraged them from
biting, nothing prevented them from penetrating our eyes and
mouths. Head nets might have helped if we had had them. All
we could do was drape our kerchiefs over our heads. Brother
didn't seem to be bothered by them as I was, so I supposed that
one built up some immunity to them over years of exposure. At
least in our tent at night our mosquito bars (nets we hung over
our sleeping bags) protected us from them. In spite of this nui-
sance we brought back a raft of about thirty cords of wood,
enough to heat the mission and church for another year. We
landed them at the foot of the village and from there Brother
skidded them up into the mission yard with his tractor.

Having completed this job, I was free to launch the refur-
bished cabin cruiser I had re-christened the *Nayuka* – Northern
Lights – and to give it a shakedown cruise. From what I heard, it
had been built in Vancouver and given to Bishop Breynat to be
used to visit the missions along the Mackenzie. I soon learned
why he had abandoned it at Fort Norman some twenty-five
years earlier. Its barrel shape not only made it tippy, but it drew
a lot of water, a disadvantage in navigating a river full of sandbars. The inboard engine, however, seemed to run fine, so I
decided to use it to visit my outpost mission at Norman Wells. A
twenty-two-year-old native, Alphonse Menako, joined me as
first mate.

We had a good trip down river to Norman Wells where I was
surprised to find that the Royal Canadian Air Force had moved
in, swelling the population by two hundred souls. They were
part of the 408 Squadron at Rockcliffe, near Ottawa, and were
occupied photographing all of the Western Arctic to correct the
existing maps. They gave me a Quonset hut (which got its name
from Quonset, Rhode Island, where they were prefabricated),

across from the new canteen and dining room. I divided it into a chapel and living quarters behind. The Imperial Oil refinery was now operating at full capacity, so the town was abuzz with activity. With aircraft taking off and landing continuously, trucks roaring up and down the dirt roads, people coming and going, Norman Wells was a far cry from the sleepy Fort Norman I had just left.

Genial Wing Commander Roy Woods, in charge of the Air Force personnel, enlisted my help to keep his men occupied on the days when bad weather prevented them from flying. One thing we did was start a leather craft shop. We organized tours of the abandoned Canol (Canadian Oil) camp across the river. The Americans undertook the Canol project during World War II to get oil from the Norman Wells field across five hundred and ninety-eight miles of muskeg and mountains to a refinery at Whitehorse in the Yukon Territory, to fuel the Pacific fleet. To do this, five thousand U.S. servicemen built a four-inch pipeline west and a supply depot to service a new road.

With the completion of the pipeline and the end of the war in 1945 the entire project was abandoned and all the buildings, vehicles and materials left to be sold by Imperial Oil. There were streets of Quonset huts and warehouses jammed with parts and equipment. One building held nothing but chains for vehicles, another tires and another tack for the horses flown in for the officers, horses which were now running loose somewhere in the vicinity. Two huge nose-hangars stood empty on the airstrip. Neatly lined up in one field were countless new radiators for the Caterpillar tractors, while in other lots stood rows of Jeeps, weapons carriers, trucks, drag lines and buses. One huge thousand-seat mess hall had a gaming room off one end equipped with crap tables and other gaming devices. Here, tacked to the bulletin board, was a list of all the female kitchen staff with their monthly VD ratings after their names like combat decorations.

Outstanding in all of this was the large two-storey log building put up for the officers, which boasted a huge fireplace incorporating in it a stone from each state in the Union. On the days

off I took groups across the river in *Nayuka* and then, using a
Jeep, drove them on a tour of all these buildings, sometimes
going as far as mile thirty-six on the Canol Road to the Carcajou
River pumping station. If nothing else, those tours taught some
Canadian Air Force men a lesson in the wastefulness of war. Too
bad the American taxpayers couldn't see what had happened to
137 million of their tax dollars.

My work at Norman Wells was exciting and not without its
rewards in the spiritual field. I would have liked to have spent
the entire summer there, but my youngest brother Thomas had
engaged himself as a deck hand on the mission supply boat and
I had permission to join him. He wanted to see firsthand this
country that had so captivated his two brothers. Alphonse and I
were on our way back up river when we met the *Sant'Anna*
around Bear Rock and I jumped ship to leave my companion to
continue on alone to Fort Norman.

Stepping on board that venerable old diesel tug pushing its
precious one-hundred-and-fifty-ton barge of supplies for the
Arctic missions was like stepping into the last century. I was
immediately surrounded by French-speaking religious in cassocks or wimples, the everyday costumes of the Oblates or Grey
Nuns, unchanged since the 1800's. Right next to my brother to
greet me was a living legend, Bishop Gabriel Breynat, O.M.I.,
who had retired in 1943 and was now making his farewell visit
to many of the missions he had founded in the last century. And
whom should I spy out on the fantail peeling spuds but "My
soul!" himself, Brother Henri! The entire boat and barge was full
of heroic characters, as though calculated to add just the right
background to this historic voyage. For once I was in the right
place at the right time.

The *Sant'Anna* was more than just a supply boat: it was a
floating monastery observing all the canonical hours,* regulated
by the ship's brass bell and serving as a water-borne cathedral for

---

* The canonical hours are the prayers mandated by the church for its
clergy and religious to be prayed at designated times during the day.

the daily pontifical mass celebrated by His Excellency. I had no sooner met everyone on board when Brothers Sareault and Dabrowski up in the wheel house brought us into the dock at Norman Wells to take on fuel. Soon we were on our way again downstream under the midnight sun as Thomas and I leaned on the rail and talked of the family and of our plans for the future.

The next morning after mass and breakfast we glided through the picturesque Ramparts section of the Mackenzie River under a warm, cobalt sky. An hour later we were nosing the barge into shore at Fort Good Hope and were met by Father Alexis Robin, a veteran of over forty years at this post, and his assistant Brother Roger Mahé. All hands, including able-bodied passengers like myself, pitched in to unload the year's supplies for this mission. The Sisters walked up the hill to visit the most famous of all the churches in the Territories. Brother Joseph Kearney had started its log sills in 1865 and when he died there in 1918 it still wasn't completed. Its colourful interior wall decorations made it the most impressive building along the entire length of this great river.

At that time a travelling magician by the name of Nemo was visiting Fort Good Hope, accompanied by his wife and a pilot flying the same old Sikorsky Amphibian aircraft used by the famous African explorers Martin and Johnson. We all crowded into the mission common room that evening to witness a thrilling magic show. When Nemo tried to leave the next morning, however, his aircraft didn't have power enough to break clear of the river's glassy surface and get airborne. He was forced to taxi all the way to his next port of call, Arctic Red River, about two hundred miles farther north.

When we pulled into that settlement the following day Bishop Breynat's successor, Bishop Trocellier, also arrived in his little scow, *Notre Dame de Fatima,* piloted by Brother Petrin. So we again found ourselves gathered with the natives, crowded into this mission's common room that night to watch Nemo in action. Bishop Trocellier was astounded when the magician removed his wrist-watch without him being aware of it. Amazingly,

Nemo could do this despite the fact that he had two bandaged fingers, caused, he said, by bailing the leaking hull of their Sikorsky the day before. When they took off the next day to fly over the mountains into Alaska we wondered if they would make it.

As the *Sant'Anna* continued north and approached the Arctic Coast the temperature dropped. Only two rooms on board were heated: the engine room, so noisy one couldn't carry on a conversation, and the galley, where we congregated to listen to old Bishop Breynat tell stories of the North he had known. Soon the steep banks of the Mackenzie fell away as we entered its flat delta, a maze of a thousand small lakes and channels with no navigational markers. Our two Brothers handling the wheel, however, knew from experience how to steer us safely up the Peel Channel where, out of the rain and fog, loomed Aklavik. The waterfront was crowded with the Eskimos' schooners and there were Eskimos themselves in parkas, just as we had always pictured them. We had suddenly entered an entirely different kind of North.

On the bank to greet us were a half-dozen Oblate Fathers and Brothers, plus a dozen Grey Nuns with a hundred and fifty children from the hostel. No doubt the forty-some tuberculosis patients from the hospital would have been there too, if they had been allowed to leave their beds. In spite of the bad weather, a warm welcome awaited us as we neared the shore. Soon the gangplank was lowered and the *Sant'Anna's* passengers streamed down into the welcoming crowd to begin a three-day visit.

Although this large mission complex had a lot of interesting features, like its huge permafrost ice cellars, I was more fascinated by the Eskimo people themselves who were in town from their winter trap lines to trade their furs. They immediately impressed me as a very happy and outgoing race of people, far less reticent than the Indians. They all seemed to be fluent in English and everywhere I went I was invited to partake of a cup of tea or any food they had on the table. I had found the Indians reluctant to do this unless I knew them well. My own explanation for this was a gut feeling that the Indians were very conscious of their different lifestyle, especially in the preparation of food, while the Eskimos didn't seem to care. If it was good enough for them, it was good enough for a white man. I like that attitude.

I walked over to George Peffer's trading post and he showed me drawers full of the cash he was using to buy white fox pelts. I paid a visit to Canon Montgomery, brother of the famous English General "Monty." He graciously toured me through the Anglican hostel and hospital, ending up in his cathedral that featured a beautiful, large painting of a native Christmas scene behind the altar. Unfortunately it was completely destroyed by fire years later. When I related this visit to my fellow missionaries I got some disapproving comments, which surprised me. Apparently there existed a deep-seated rivalry between these two missions that bordered on hostility. I was told that if the people saw me visiting the "opposition," they might conclude that we had capitulated. Apparently my fraternal overture was slightly ahead of its time.

Our arrival in Aklavik anticipated by a day the official visit of Canada's Governor General, Lord Alexander of Tunis, who was touring the Arctic in a Canadian Air Force Canso, or Catalina Flying Boat. The local Administrator, L.A.C.O. Hunt, was in a dither trying to get some four thousand feet of boardwalk built in time to cover the quagmire left after melting snow and incessant rain. When the distinguished guest arrived, however, he was driven around town in a Jeep and never used the new sidewalks. The spectators did, nonetheless, and I stood with the crowd, camera in hand, across the street from the one-room shack marked RADIO STATION CHAK, where the local dignitaries presented him with gifts of furs and native sewing.

As this was not her last port of call, not all the freight brought down river by the *Sant'Anna* was off-loaded at Aklavik. We still had freight for Tuktoyaktuk on the Arctic Ocean, from which point it would be carried east by the mission schooner *Our Lady of Lourdes*. As we backed off the beach at Aklavik not only was our barge floating higher, but there were many empty bunks as some of the missionaries, including the old bishop and all of the nuns, had left the ship. In a haze of rain we zigzagged through Schooner Channel and finally got back on the broad Mackenzie. It was smooth sailing down past the reindeer station until we reached the open waters of the Beaufort Sea at Kitigazuit. Here the ocean, driven by a west wind, was running an angry sea and the rain turned to driving snow. It was only the 16th of July. The Brothers prudently decided to run into shore to tie up and wait out the bad weather.

Within the previous twelve months three six-hundred-foot towers had been erected in a triangle several hundred miles apart to test a new navigational system called Loran. As luck would have it, we had landed within a mile of one of these stations manned by 120 Royal Canadian Air Force radio technicians. The Commanding Officer was most hospitable and gave us a tour of his new installation. He quite candidly admitted to us that he was experiencing some trouble from a few of his men who were making and drinking alcohol in spite of regulations. In the kitchen he pointed to a tell-tale ring mark on the stove top that fit exactly a brass fire extinguisher hanging on the wall. Someone had ingeniously converted this cylinder into a portable still, filling it with mash, putting it on the hot stove after hours and then drawing off the spirits through its rubber hose. The C.O. was sure he could catch them red-handed and expected to administer a stiff military penalty.

Our host also mentioned that the Governor General had stopped at the base, but that he had unfortunately forgotten to bring the mail for which they had been waiting over two months, an unpardonable sin in the North. The C.O. confessed that morale was low on the base as a result. Anyone could understand that: no spirits followed by no mail! Just how low we couldn't guess until a week later when we heard that all the windows in his quarters had been smashed by rocks and he was forced to evacuate his wife and children, the only family on the base.

The following day the Brothers unhitched the barge from the front of the *Sant'Anna* and put it on a long tow-cable behind. With this arrangement we were able to cross the open stretch of ocean and get safely into the harbour at "Tuk." The flat horizon here on the Arctic coast was broken only by a few pingos* farther inland.

The settlement was strung out along a protected gravel beach dominated by the Hudson Bay Company store and warehouse, the police barracks and the mission church and mission warehouse. The few Eskimos around had set up tents for the summer and tied their sled dogs to long chains laid out on the muskeg.

Father Jean Franche, the resident priest, gave Thomas and me a tour of his buildings, showing us the huge polar bear hide in the sanctuary of his church, a yard-long section of mammoth tusk in his attic, as well as an old whaling dart gun no longer used. His team of huskies seemed to be huge compared to sled dogs up river and looked as if they might have had some St. Bernard bred into them.

Thomas and I joined the Brothers unloading the barge into a large warehouse. Brother Auguste Josset, the engineer for the forty-ton *Our Lady of Lourdes,* was on board his boat riding at anchor just off shore and ready to transfer this freight to the missions along the Arctic Coast as far east as Cambridge Bay and Bathurst Inlet.

As soon as we got our barge unloaded, Thomas and I ran around the settlement with our cameras like tourists. The more I saw, the more I wished I could be assigned to an Eskimo mission like this. The land was treeless, covered with gravel and practically flat to the horizon. I could imagine how desolate it would look in winter, yet it possessed a peculiar charm hard to describe. The native people were unusually outgoing and hospitable and welcomed us into their tents. In short, I liked Tuk so much that I

---

* Pingos are a phenomenon of the severe and prolonged Arctic cold which, by exerting extreme pressure, forces large cone-shaped mountains, consisting mainly of ice and gravel and covered with moss, to rise above the otherwise flat land.

wished I could stay, but the sea was calm and the Brothers were anxious to get back into the protection of the river, so we shoved off, empty at last.

Because of the contrary current, our return voyage upstream on the Mackenzie was slower in spite of our shallow draught. When we reached the Sans Sault rapids above the Ramparts we were barely moving ahead until the Brothers attached an outboard motor to the transom to give us a little extra push. All too soon we were nearing my home base at Fort Norman. This trip left me with a new-born desire to go farther north in the Vicariate, to work among the Eskimos. I hoped, too, that my youngest brother Thomas, who had experienced this adventure with me, would himself catch the spark and volunteer for this North country. He didn't, however: I wasn't to see him again until his ordination in Washington six years later when he asked for and received an assignment – to Brazil!

5

GREAT BEAR LAKE

By the last week of July I was back in the mission at Fort Norman observing punctually all the canonical hours as if nothing had happened, as if I had never crossed over the Arctic Circle nor seen the Eskimo lands under the midnight sun.

I plunged into the daily routine with renewed vigour, especially my study and practice of the Hareskin language. I hadn't really stopped this study during my absence, as I carried my notebook dictionary with me.

Mission life was far easier in the summer: no need to worry about feeding a fire. I had moved upstairs into a spacious room and Brother's well tended garden was producing all the fresh food we had lacked during the winter.

This was the season for visitors, most of them travelling on the river. They were a welcome diversion, except for one who put us on our toes, so to speak. This was the Oblate Provincial, Reverend Father Jean-Louis Michel, O.M.I., Vicar of Missions, an ex-army officer coming on his yearly inspection tour to insure that we were living according to the precepts of our Holy Rule. We were being especially vigilant so as not to give reason for a reprimand, but I slipped up and immediately drew fire. I had doffed my cassock in order to join the local boys for a game of softball on the town flat. When it finished I had loitered about two minutes too long before getting back into clerical garb. Such conduct, I was informed, would not be tolerated.

The Provincial (whom Brother Henri referred to as "Le Cap-itaine") took advantage of his visit to drum up candidates for the boarding school at Fort Providence. Delivering the sermon at the high mass on Sunday, he dispelled a vicious rumour to the effect that no children were being sent from this settlement because the hung fish being fed to them at the hostel were rank. "Nonsense!" he thundered in Hareskin, which he had mastered during his early years at Fort Good Hope. What he didn't realize, however, was that the reason no children from Fort Norman were cur-rently attending either that hostel or the one at Aklavik was that the local Pastor, Father Denis, was dead set against it on the grounds that all his problem parishioners were former residents of these venerable institutions. The school at Providence had been in continuous operation since 1867 and there were quite a few old grads living at Fort Norman. Those who come back from Providence with any education, argued this missionary, show an aversion to the trapping life and, while assuming an air of supe-riority around town, turn out to be loafers, brew-hounds and trouble-makers. Needless to say, he didn't voice this opinion in front of our distinguished visitor. Still, this studied assessment sounded alarming to me. I wondered what the result would be now that the government had built a day school right in Fort Norman?

With the freight delivered to Fort Norman Mission by the *Sant'Anna* came about five hundred board-feet of spruce shiplap from the Brothers' sawmill near Fort Smith, destined for my project at Willow Lake. One of the locals by the name of Paul Wright volunteered to help me, so we loaded up the freighter canoe and ascended the Bear and then the Willow Rivers. He handled the nine-horsepower Johnson in the stern while I stood in the bow with a long pole, as the water in September is very shallow. It was amazing how we navigated that fast water barely deep enough to float us.

We unloaded the canoe in the deep grass in front of the run-down log cabin and began a week of renovations that trans-formed it into a neat and efficient outpost mission. I had always

Pilot training in a WACO F-7, 1940.

The D.C.-3 that took me to Norman Wells, the northen terminus for Canadian Pacific Airlines. It was December 1948, and the temperature was 44 degrees below zero (F). I continued on to Fort Norman the next day with pilot Mike Zubko in his Waco biplane.

The Fort Norman Mission, built of logs, was an outpost since 1859.

Inside St. Teresa Church, Fort Norman. The paintings were done on the walls using powdered paint from France mixed with local fish oil. This church was torn down in 1962, but six of the windows and the two statues went into the Colville Lake church in 1964.

St. Teresa (of Avila) Church at Fort Norman, 1949.

Bringing in a load of firewood, 1949. As soon as I learned to drive dogs at Fort Norman I would spend most afternoons getting firewood or hunting ptarmigan.

Main street of the Imperial Oil Co. townsite at Norman Wells, Winter 1950. I had come down by dogsled to the Wells from Fort Norman as chaplain for Imperial Oil.

The R.C.M.P. sled dog yard at Fort Norman, adjacent to the Mission. These sled dogs got loose in a pack a few years later and ran through the town, encountering and killing a four-year-old boy.

A young Hare Indian holds a snowshoe rabbit.

The Spring goose/duck hunt. Father Denis and I camped overnight on Windy Island two miles across from Fort Norman.

Brother Médard Latreille, O.M.I., spent many years at Norman Mission and cultivated a very successful garden.

The Quonset hut chapel at Norman Wells, across from the RCAF mess hall, 1949.

Splitting a birch root at Fort Norman, 1949. To make the handles of a toboggan we use the natural bend of a birch root for strength.

At Canyon Creek. During 1949-50 I often travelled from Fort Norman to Norman Wells in this 22-foot freighter canoe, always stopping to visit the Tourangeau's here, 12 miles south (upstream) from the Wells.

The completed Mission St. Therese at Fort Franklin, just before freeze-up, August 1950. The mission was boarded up in 1997.

In 1949 there were 174 Hare Indians living at Fort Franklin on Great Bear Lake. I used the old log Mission here until I built the new one in 1950.

During the first year at Fort Franklin only three aircraft visited me, including this De Havilland Beaver on skis. Teacher Roy Gravel stands to the left.

On Great Bear River headed for Fort Franklin, 1950. During the building of Mission St. Therese (Little Flower) at Fort Franklin that year, I made five round-trips to Fort Norman for supplies. On my last trip I brought up the Norman Mission's dog team.

Re-canvassing the freighter canoe, a V-stern 22-foot Peterborough.

Goldfields' last winter, 1953.

The Mission and Church at Goldfields. We skidded both these buildings over to the new Uranium City on the ice. The church, right, later burned to the ground.

Baptizing two Chipewyan babies at Goldfields. These Chipewyan people came into Goldfields from Fond du Lac (100 miles east on Lake Athabaska) in the summer for casual work.

Philip Stenne and I working to get Mission Saint Bernard closed in before freeze-up, Summer 1952.

Down by the shore of Lake Athabaska in front of Mission Saint Bernard, painting a water-colour sketch. Local Cree natives watch, fascinated.

Completed Mission Saint Bernard, 1953, with sled dogs and fish house.

At Johnson's trading post on the Slave River between Fort Chipewyan and Fort Smith. I examine one of the blocks of frozen milk he sold.

loved carpentry. When I was seventeen I had thrown the bed out of my room at home and put in double bunks which I made from pine trees I had felled. In the scholasticate I was appointed to the position of house carpenter. The heaviest part of my baggage coming into the North had been a wooden box of carpenter's tools. Now I had a chance to use them and I lost no time putting down a floor and building a set of bunks and an altar inside the cabin, while outside I built a stage for storing fish and put in solid posts for tying dogs in winter. The finishing touch was a cross nailed to the peak of the roof.

I was amazed at how much satisfaction I got working with my hands like this. The reason was evident: I could see the results immediately. More important tasks like studying the language were slow to show results and were not rewarding. When we shoved off to return to Fort Norman, that little cabin behind us filled my heart with pride; I couldn't wait to return by dog-team and occupy it.

On the 9th of September the Brothers from Aklavik came up river with their boat the *Immaculata* and its barge, a miniature version of the *Sant'Anna*. The purpose of this yearly visit was to pick up a load of potatoes from Norman and Good Hope for the hostel and hospital in Aklavik in exchange for cash to help cover their expenses for the year. It was a fortunate arrangement, for the once-a-year donations at Christmas were not enough to support them for even a month. Bishop Trocellier was urging each mission to work at something to help meet its own running expenses.

I took advantage of this trip to return to Norman Wells and the hustle and bustle of that busy little town. Its storage tanks were just about full and the photo detachment had photographed pretty well all the Western Arctic from the air. The boys of the Signals Corps, however, had added something new, the low-power radio broadcasting station CFNW, 1240 on the dial. It was located six miles up river at their beam station. They suggested I put a religious message on the air Sundays, so I began going up there by boat once a week to broadcast a half-hour

sermon. The missionary life held many surprises and unexpected opportunities; it was getting hard to predict what I would
be doing from week to week.

Those American Quonset huts were often referred to in the
North as "igloos." A few of them found their way across the river
from Canol. Sections of the half-moon-shaped structures could
be bolted together easily to any desired length. There was one
very long one near my chapel which had been used as a curling
rink until a better one was built and this one abandoned. It
occurred to me that the people of Fort Norman would welcome
such a shelter since they had no facility for indoor winter sports.
The Imperial Oil Refinery manager was only too happy to donate
it for such a worthy cause.

Now that I had it the problem was how to get it to Fort Norman. First it would have to be completely dismantled, no easy
task if I had to tackle it alone. When I discussed this project with
Commander Woods he saw no difficulty as he had plenty of air
crew only partially busy. Before I knew it the whole building was
neatly piled in stacks and the nuts, bolts and wiring boxed and
ready for shipment. All I needed was the ship. After a phone call
to Frank Broderick, President of Northern Transportation Company in Edmonton, a giant barge was put at my disposal for a
free lift to Fort Norman.

At this juncture I sped ahead to Fort Norman to call a meeting
of the Community Club to discuss the project and insure the necessary volunteers to off-load the material. Where I had met with
nothing but cooperation at the Wells, I now found myself up
against innumerable objections from those who should have
been most eager to see the project succeed. The upshot was that,
when the barge did arrive, no one showed up to help Brother and
me to unload it. Nor was it ever rebuilt. The sections lay in the
field between the mission and the barracks until the elements
completely destroyed them years later. Whether they were used
or not, I'm sure the good Lord rewarded the charity of our neighbours to the north, while teaching me the lesson that unsolicited

gifts are not always appreciated. No doubt we are allowed to fail now and then to keep us humble.

That fall at Fort Norman I was to experience my first freeze-up in the North. Although not nearly as spectacular as break-up, it was a seasonal weather mark that abruptly put an end to summer and signalled the onslaught of another winter. In anticipation, we set about all the tasks that must be done at that season; like getting all the vegetables into the root cellar under the kitchen floor, the potatoes in bins, the carrots buried in boxes of sand and cabbages hung from the ceiling. Then we cut up the driftwood gathered after the ice went out in the spring, and re-banked the mission buildings with dirt.

In late October all the small lakes were frozen and there was enough snow to use the dogs in harness, so Brother and I went out to Taketue and set the net again. By mid-November the Mackenzie was running loose pans of ice that had formed in backwater eddies up river. As the days wore on and the sun swept a steadily lowering arc in the southern sky, the ice floating by on the river got thicker until it covered the surface from shore to shore. On the 21st it stopped and froze together, signalling the end of freeze-up. About a week later we were down on its surface with long ice saws cutting and hauling ice, our winter's water supply, which we stacked outside the back door. With the completion of this job I was free to do a little travelling again.

Loading up the cariole and harnessing the dogs, I took off full-speed out the back road and over the bank of the Great Bear River, where the trail pitches down at a breakneck angle onto the frozen river. There were no more hazards the rest of the thirty-five miles to Willow Lake, where about thirty natives who had been camped here since open water welcomed me. Although I was enjoying the comfort of my new cabin, one thing disturbed me: in the summer I had given a new gill net to Sheriah on the promise that he would hang some stick fish on my new stage for my dogs, but I found the stage empty and Sheriah was camped at Whitefish Lake another twenty miles north. The next day I went on to his tent and camped with his family, returning the following day with a good sled-load of whitefish which fed my team for the week I stayed there.

The return trip to Fort Norman went smoothly enough with the dogs running well pulling an empty sled, so after a while I sat in the cariole and watched the miles slip by. The sun disappeared and the moon came up on a calm night with ice fog filling the low valleys.

Nearing home, we slipped down onto the frozen surface of Great Bear River and were half-way across when Fox, the lead dog, suddenly stopped. I thought that he had tired and wanted to quit, so I got out of the sled and walked up to him with the whip in my hand. He was crouched on the edge of open water! Deep and dark as it was, the white steam just above it made it invisible from a distance. The Bear had opened up during the time I was at Willow Lake. I cautiously retreated, called the leader to me, and had him follow me as I walked down along the shore and out onto the Mackenzie, making a wide, three-mile detour to avoid crossing the Great Bear River entirely.

I owed my life to Fox that night. Other lead dogs would have plunged right in and swum for the other shore before I could have gotten out of the cariole. The Bear is deep at this point; I doubt I could have touched bottom, and with the ice so thin along the edges, it would have kept breaking off had I tried to pull myself up onto it, soaking wet. If I had given up the struggle, the swift current would have carried me down and under the thicker ice of the Mackenzie. All the elements that night were right to lull the novice into a false sense of security: the balmy air, the moonlit landscape, the cheerful ringing of the harness bells and the comfort of the cariole, which in an instant could have become my coffin. Suddenly I had a new respect for sled dogs in general, and this lead dog in particular. With these thoughts racing through my mind I broke out in a nervous sweat. For twenty-two years following this incident I drove dogs in every kind of weather and terrain, but I believe that this was my closest brush with death.

The Mounties in Norman, like all the detachments of the RCMP in the North, had a crackerjack team of sled dogs, two teams in fact, because the member of the Force on patrol always had a native special constable travelling with him. The latter's job was not limited to the patrols. He fed and cared for the dogs and kept them exercised and in top running form. I happened to be visiting the barracks next door to the mission one evening when Corporal Gordon Brown was busy in the kitchen baking bannock and beans which he would put outdoors immediately to freeze. He was preparing trail grub for a patrol to Fort Franklin on Great Bear Lake and planned to leave December 9th with Special Constable Alfred Lennie. This looked to me like a golden opportunity to get inland and see the famous Bear Lakers myself, with the permission of my superior, Father Denis, of course. When I broached the subject to him the next day he was only too willing to let me absorb the punishment of a trip that usually took him three days – on snowshoes mostly – and left him lame for a week. I had the idea that if I could increase our dog-power I might be able to ride most of the way, so I purchased two older dogs the next day from Jack Hardy for twenty-five dollars apiece.

As planned, the three of us pulled out of Fort Norman on the 9th of December in the dark, Alfred in the lead with the corporal following and myself bringing up the rear. This was the first experience my dogs had of following other teams. The sight and smell of all those other canines just up ahead excited them and they pulled like mad. In fact, the first three of my dogs were so close to the back of the Mountie's sled that they kept getting their harnesses mixed up and I had to apply the brakes to keep them in line; when I let up on the brake the dogs up front would get tangled again, I would have to turn the toboggan over on its side to stop the team and then walk up and fix their harnesses. As a result I had the brake on most of the first twelve miles before we stopped to make fire for our first mug up of tea.

In little over half an hour we were on our way again, but my dogs didn't seem as anxious as before to overtake the teams ahead. A few more miles and the police teams gradually pulled ahead and out of sight. I didn't see them again until we pulled into their noon lunch fire. Before I had eaten they left, but I wasn't worried about following them as their trail was fresh in a couple of inches of loose snow. Nevertheless, I ate as quickly as I could because I knew how short the daylight was at that time of year. When we resumed the chase it wasn't long before one of my newly acquired dogs started playing out, flopping down on the trail and bringing the whole team to a halt. I took him out of harness and let him follow behind, hoping he would keep up, as he had only himself to drag along. Yet soon there was no sight of him. Thinking that he had simply decided to bed down somewhere along the trail behind us and get some rest, I thought no more about it. Some weeks later someone brought me his collar and told me that was about all that the wolves had left of him. At the time, however, I had no idea we were being trailed by wolves and I doubt that we could have done anything about it even if we knew.

By three o'clock it was dark again and I hadn't seen my companions since noon. The second dog I bought played out and I had to let him out of harness as I had his brother, but he followed closely behind. This wasn't all that difficult at the speed we were now making and perhaps he sensed the menace following. At any rate, the team began to stop altogether at any little rise in the trail and I was obliged to get off the sled and start running behind, cracking the whip whenever they looked like they were about to stop. After about ten miles of this I was ready to drop too, but I couldn't, as the only tent we had was up in Alfred's sled. When the moon finally rose we were simply walking and I was praying that those guys up ahead would quit for the day and camp. At one spot they left an encouraging message written in the snow. It said, "Not far." Still, it sure seemed far; when we dragged ourselves into their camp it was 9 p.m. and they were already asleep in the tent. Unhitching my dogs I chained each one to a tree and distributed frozen fish, then I re-lit the fire in the tent stove, cooked my own supper and ate in silence as my travelling mates fell back to sleep after a short greeting.

I was anticipating a deep, dreamless sleep myself as I finally got into my sleeping bag, but the troubles of the day pursued me into the night. In spite of the youthful spring in my twenty-nine-year-old legs, the hours I had been on them running that day had overtaxed them and a series of painful muscle spasms kept jerking me awake during the night. They are often called charley-horses, but in this case charley-*dogs* would be more appropriate. As I lay there that night, reviewing all the events of the day, I determined simply to raise a first-class string of dogs; otherwise I would be endlessly repeating the miseries of that day.

Around 6 a.m. Alfred was starting a fire by candlelight, bringing in snow to melt for morning coffee and in general rattling pots and pans to indicate that it was time to rise and shine. It seemed to have been an awfully short night and I felt like doing anything except tackling the second leg of our journey to Great Bear Lake, but remembering the long American tradition of toughness and perseverance goaded me into action. I might be on my knees, but a "Remember the Alamo" spirit would force me to fight to the end of the trail which, in this instance, was Fort Franklin.

After breakfast of rolled oats and bannock we struck the tent and harnessed up in the dark, using flashlights. Thinking Fox deserved a break after working in the lead position all of the previous long day, I put him in the number four position and put N.T. in the lead. This was a mistake, I quickly learned, for when the police teams moved out and before I could untie my sled Fox bit through the traces on both sides of him, allowing my first three dogs to take off without me. Evidently he didn't like the demotion and quickly changed his position from number four to number one. I soon caught up to Corporal Brown who had stopped and was holding the first half of my team. After some temporary splicing with rope from the sled wrapper I was again on my way behind my full team. I soon noticed, however, that my dogs had lost the zip that they had had the previous morning. There was no need to use the brake at all today as my companions pulled steadily ahead and out of sight. Evidently the long run of the day before had left them as stiff as me and I hoped that they wouldn't play out, forcing me to run behind them again.

When I caught up to the corporal and his special constable, they were just finishing their lunch around their noon fire. As I moved in, they moved out, assuring me that I would have no trouble following their fresh trail to the lake. It would have been nice to stretch out and luxuriate before that warm fire and linger over my noon meal, but the fear of going on alone along a strange trail in diminishing light drove me to get on the way again as soon as I could. To make matters worse, I hadn't covered many miles before a light snow began to fall. When I came upon their afternoon tea fire they were long gone, so I didn't stop.

As the light decreased, the falling snow increased and the trail became less distinct. We were moving ahead at a slow dog-trot while the muffled tinkling of the bells did little to dispel the gloom surrounding us. What I wouldn't have given for a fresh team of dogs or at least to have seen the cheerful blaze of a camp-fire up ahead, but no light relieved the darkness. Even the moon was hidden as we plodded along, mile after weary mile, in ever-deepening snow.

Then around supper time the black spruce began to get smaller and their numbers to thin out and the stretches of open tundra grew larger. I reasoned that we must be approaching the windswept shores of the big lake. We passed a rather large Quonset hut half-buried in snow. I thought it must belong to the Northern Transportation Company which operated boats in the summer connecting the Mackenzie River with Port Radium on the east shore of Great Bear. At last we ran beyond the trees alto-gether and the trail was blown out. Fox began to wander so I stopped him. Perhaps we were already on lake ice. Was Fort Franklin to the left or right? It was supposed to be only four miles away, but I couldn't distinguish any lights or sound to direct us. They said that there was open water all winter long around the inlet of the river. How close were we to it? In this darkness we could run into it with no warning.

As I sat on the edge of the sled and rolled a cigarette to pon-der my predicament, the dogs dropped in their tracks and curled up, apparently content to spend the night right there. As much as I wanted to complete that last four miles and get into a heated cabin for the night, the risk that I would take to do it didn't seem worth it. Finally prudence won out and I turned the dogs around to backtrack to that Quonset hut. I dug down to the door with my snowshoes and found it unlocked. Inside there was all I needed: a huge barrel stove, some firewood and a spring cot and mat-tress. This was as far as we'd go this day. I dragged my gear from the cariole, lit a candle, built a roaring fire and thawed some sup-per, thanking God for the protection of this old hut. After eating I threw my sleeping bag on the cot, blew out the candle and climbed in to sleep thirteen uninterrupted hours.

Late the next morning I was awakened by the sound of voices outside. I got up and went to the window to see a group of natives talking together, looking around in the snow for tracks, pointing in various directions, while about a dozen dog-teams were drawn up behind them. My dogs were completely drifted over with snow and invisible, and they were still so played out that they didn't even get up to bark at the intruders. So the posse, evidently out looking for me, didn't know I was in the hut till I opened the door and yelled at them. Then they all crowded in to shake my hand, showing genuine relief that they had found me alive, for when I didn't show up the night before rumours spread that I must have gone into open water nearby. Now we all formed a triumphal procession across that last four miles to the settlement.

Great Bear Lake is a mighty body of water: in fact, with its eleven thousand square miles it is the biggest within Canada and even has its own tide. It straddles the Arctic Circle and stretches from a heavily timbered south end up into the edge of the Barren Land toward Coppermine. The natives who have inhabited its shores for at least the last five thousand years are closely related to the Hareskins living around Fort Norman and go by the name of Bear Lakers. I counted 174 of them living there at that time. Sir

John Franklin, the British explorer, had built a fort at the site of the present settlement in 1824 and passed that winter there, but the North West Company operated a trading post at the same location since 1799.

If Fort Norman was remote and isolated, Fort Franklin was desolate by comparison: no road, no mail, no electricity, no school or nursing station, no white people, just the Hudson Bay trading post run by a Métis and surrounded by a dozen rough log cabins and a scattering of tents. A school had been started the year before, but it was boarded up for the winter. Near it stood the weather-beaten log cabin put up by one of the missionaries some twenty years earlier. It was to this "mission" that I was taken on my arrival. After digging a huge snow drift away from its only door I stepped down into a dark room about fourteen by sixteen feet that contained a small cast iron box stove, a few rough benches and a tiny altar clinging to the corner wall. A door in the back wall led into an eight-foot lean-to addition containing a cook stove and a bed. Outside and mounted on two poles nailed to the corner logs was a ship's bell. Twenty feet away there was a small log warehouse containing an axe and a Swede saw. If one word could describe the whole setup, it would be poverty.

Church mice are notoriously poor and I moved right in with some of them to share their life for the next month. Not that I was disappointed in what I found there; after all, Father Denis had not painted a rosy picture. Still, there was not one pleasant surprise; everything was stripped to the bare necessities. That's the picture that stays in my mind of a mission outpost in the North. It was bound to be an interesting adventure. I chained up my dogs and moved in.

First things first: I needed a fire immediately and some of the Bear Lakers were right there with an armful of kindling. The dogs needed to be fed and another native appeared with a sack of herring. The temperature in that little mission might have been perpetually chilly, but the cooperation I got from the people was heart-warming. In fact, someone brought me fish for the dogs every night I was there. As they needed exercise I started going every day for at least one load of firewood. There was hardly a tree within sight of the Fort and to find dry wood I had to go at least three miles. Try as I might, I simply couldn't melt the ice on the inside of the mission's windows and I couldn't keep a fire going all night. As long as I stayed in my feather robe I kept fairly comfortable. The trouble was that the mice must have felt cold and tried to share my warmth during the night, for they scampered over my sleeping bag looking for an opening. Charity stopped right there. The temperature hovered around forty below, and the wind off frozen Bear Lake seemed to blow night and day, leaving drifts so hard one could walk over them without leaving a trace. Fort Franklin was an exposed place to begin with, but that constant wind made it even worse.

Following the same custom as at Fort Norman I offered a mass every morning early and it was well attended. Then I cooked some breakfast and did the chores; took the dog-team for a load of firewood which I then bucked up with the Swede saw, walked out on the lake to the community water hole for my two buckets, said my breviary and studied my grammar. A visit from Chief Francis Eya was part of this daily routine. From him I heard a report on the daily happenings in the community. After-noons I found time to walk around visiting and practising the language. Occasionally I stopped in at the store to pick up a few items and chew the fat with Fred Loutit, the trader.

Fred came from mixed native and white ancestry around Great Slave Lake and had been at Fort Franklin for the past eight years. He lived alone, not by choice but through circumstances which he was ever on the lookout to change. An introvert and a hypochondriac to boot, he found it difficult to visit around or make new friends. There was, however, one ray of hope on Fred's horizon. He discovered in his yearly ration of water-glassed eggs that some of them bore the names and addresses of the farmer's daughters out in Alberta where they were pro-duced. Fred wrote to these girls and, if he got an answer, he would visit them with matrimony in mind when, every few years, he got out to civilization. So far his efforts had not borne fruit, but he had some splendid prospects lined up for his next trip outside. I'll bet his district manager never realized how important that yearly supply of hen fruit meant to this trader. One didn't joke about eggs to Fred.

As Christmas approached I became aware of the problem of fitting everyone into the mission's small room for the popular Midnight Mass. I decided to say the three consecutive masses allowed at Christmas and divide the people up into three groups, each group assigned to a different mass. The idea looked good on paper, but its execution failed when everybody showed up for the first service and stayed right through all three.

It was standing room only, wall-to-wall and out the open door. And I had to be careful where I put my feet when turning from the corner altar, as the children covered the floor under me. All the faith in that great expanse of wilderness was distilled into that one roomful of fervent Christians whose prayers that holy night must have penetrated the vault of heaven. I felt a sudden realization of my usefulness as the Lord's instrument in orchestrating this humble song of praise on the anniversary of His birth. Later years saw me presiding over much larger congregations in more elegant surroundings at this midnight service, but I doubt any of them approached the genuine fervour of this Christ-mass.

A few days later we reached the century's half-way point, ushering in the New Year, 1950, with a barrage of rifle fire directed at the starry sky. I stayed on until we had celebrated Epiphany, the feast of the Three Wise Men, on January 6th. Then on the morning of the ninth, a month to the day since leaving Fort Norman, I harnessed my team and headed back.

Luckily I had a companion for the trip: Jimmy Cleary, known locally as Egoneetsi, a knowledgeable veteran of the trail who drove a splendid team of six huskies. All that day he broke trail ahead of my team, which seemed to have learned to harbour their strength as we never got separated. By nightfall we had reached the half-way point, a height of land dividing Great Bear Lake from the Mackenzie Valley called Nadanatli, where I had camped with the police on the trip out. This time it was much colder, however, and we carried no tent. Egoneetsi showed me how to construct a fire using full tree-length dry poles that could be pushed in together gradually to keep the fire going all night, and how to dig down to the moss with snowshoes and cover this sleeping pit with spruce boughs while the excavated snow was piled up behind to reflect the heat back on us.

With this arrangement we slept warm outside in the forty-below temperature, getting up only once or twice to push the fire logs together. The following day we got into Norman in fine shape. Neither of us had gotten out of our sleds the whole way. I was amazed at the ease of this trip compared to the ordeal going out, in spite of deep snow on the trail all the way and the much lower temperature.

6

A New Obedience

On my return to the mission at Fort Norman I resumed the orderly life with my two companions. Progress in the Indian language continued under the tutelage of Father Denis, while I persisted in trying to converse with Brother Latreille in French.

About once a week Brother and I would go out to Taketue with the dog-team to visit the nets. Other afternoons we might work in the wood lot closer to home to cut green birch for holding the fire at night. These trees attracted snowshoe hares and Brother showed me how to set snares for them, an essential skill in this country. If a person got stranded in the bush for any reason, he could always manage to use one of his shoelaces for a snare and keep from starving.

Brother had a sense of humour that thrived on minor disasters. Once, while the three of us were sitting at the kitchen table, Father Denis asked for the food in a metal pot sitting behind Brother on the hot stove. Brother picked it up gingerly in his callused finger tips and handed it to Father Denis, who as quickly dropped it with an appropriate exclamation in French, sending Brother into gales of laughter.

Two years previously the Army came through Fort Norman on a training exercise called "The Muskox Expedition." After spending a night at the mission, they left a barrel of fuel oil behind to lighten their load. Once when I was sitting in the common room practising my Hareskin on two local braves Brother woke up from his short siesta and shuffled out behind a cloud of smoke from the large pipe clamped between his store teeth and noticing a chill in the air. He retreated to the kitchen and emerged with a tin can of this fuel oil. Opening the door of the wood stove he threw the fuel in on the hot coals with a flourish. Some of it shot right through a crack in the side of the stove and across the moccasins of our visitors. The stove not only roared to life, but the line of fire quickly followed the path of oil and the two natives were startled to see their moccasins burning. While they ran outside to plunge their feet in a snow bank Brother collapsed into a chair laughing so hard he had to hold his ample stomach while tears rolled down his cheeks. I was equally amused by the humour of the situation, but our native friends apparently were not, for they failed to return. Later we had some fun kidding them about this incident, because their word for the devil is *eketsele* – burned feet.

It was now the end of January, time for me to visit my outpost parish at Norman Wells. I was joined by the RCMP and a French-Canadian trapper by the name of Henry Cadieux. We made good time until we were opposite the Tourangeau cabin and started across the river. This freeze-up had been particularly violent and acres of slab ice had frozen in upright angles resembling tank traps. We were forced to walk ahead of our teams with axes trying to break off the worst chunks, but even then our oak toboggans took hard punishment and some of the dogs were torn out of their harnesses. We were glad to reach shore and camp for the night with the Tourangeaus.

We continued next morning on toward the Wells and six miles down the road reached the Royal Canadian Corps of Signal's beam station, where a few Army signalmen were stationed. One of them, Johnny Bell, had raised four fine-looking grey huskies with an eye to eventually driving them in harness and getting a little outdoor exercise. He told me that they had already learned to pull his sled and he asked if I would mind if he accompanied me back to Norman with them. A week later I came out of the Wells alone and stopped to pick up Johnny for his first dogsled trip. It was mid-afternoon by the time he was all set to go and we started up river. The weather looked fair when we left, but as we were crossing the frozen Mackenzie at Tourangeau's a light snow began falling and the wind rose. Up to that point Johnny's team seemed to have no trouble following me closely, but soon they lost their initial steam and began to lag behind. As my stops to let him catch up became more frequent, I became aware of the responsibility I had accepted when I agreed to accompany him on his first trip.

The elements conspired against us as the snow got heavier and daylight dimmed. It was dangerous to get out of sight of my companion, as he had no lead dog and the trail I was making in the fresh snow was quickly obliterated by the wind. We had barely made twenty miles when I decided to call it quits and do the prudent thing – camp for the night. Luckily I carried a tent with me and we were able to get up off the river and into the timber where we set it in the protection of the spruce.

When we woke the following morning the flapping of the tent indicated that the wind had not died as we had hoped. Once we got down on the river to resume our trek we realized just how strong it was and how poor the visibility was in the falling snow in spite of the daylight. No matter: I felt confident we could make the twenty-five miles to Fort Norman and we started off at a good clip. With Johnny's team close behind the first ten miles were reassuring, but then they began to tire and the gap between us lengthened. It was just about the worst weather we could have picked, with a howling head wind at thirty below, blowing snow stinging our faces, and no visible trail to follow. Nor was there any protection anywhere along this route. We might just as well have been out somewhere in the Barren Lands. Indeed, the high banks of the Mackenzie funnelled the winds against us like a giant venturi. We were soon reduced to a crawl, with me driving ahead a few hundred yards and then waiting for Johnny to catch up. Darkness caught us still a long way from our goal and, as much as I hated to do it, I had to admit to my companion that we would have to camp another night.

We finally found a ravine where we could get up over the river's bank and into the spruce to set up the tent again. We were both stumbling around in the semi-darkness, axes in hand, chopping down dry spruce trees to fuel our tent stove when a curious accident befell us both almost simultaneously. Both our axe handles broke and the heads went flying into the deep snow, impossible to find. Now we were reduced to breaking up small, dry branches with our hands. And to top that off we had no dog feed for this unscheduled second night on the trail and I had to sacrifice the steak and bacon I was bringing back as a special treat. As we lay in the tent that night I tried my best to convince my young companion that this was not your typical dogsled trip, but that a combination of bad weather and bad luck had worked against us.

The morning of our third day broke clear and calm and the storm was over. When we got our teams hitched up and down on the river's surface again I was in for the biggest surprise of the trip. We had actually crossed the river the night before and camped on the east side without knowing it. Ten easy miles and we were into the Fort at last, but Johnny had had enough of dogsledding. He took his dogs back in an aircraft and never made another trip.

As for me, I couldn't afford that luxury, and after a night's rest I took Brother out to Taketue and returned the same day. The more our dogs were used, the better their stamina and speed. Besides, I was learning how to handle them. There's a lot of dog psychology involved. For one thing, being too "palsy-walsy" with your team, feeding them tidbits at odd hours and playing with them, tends to lessen their respect for you so that when you crack your whip behind them it does not produce the desired result. On one trip back from Taketue I was behind the police special constable when he stopped his team, tied his sled to a tree and proceeded to give each of them a few solid cracks across the rump, indicating to them that he was not pleased with their performance. They got the message and when we resumed I couldn't keep up with him.

On the other hand there were some drivers who were convinced that only wicked dogs worked well in harness. One such was Pat Tourangeau who kept his team tied back in the bush where they had no contact with humans and who used to beat them with a chain. He paid a high price for this treatment, however, one spring day when he was returning to his cabin in his hunting canoe while his dogs were running loose along the river bank. His children saw him coming and ran to greet him, but four-year-old Norman fell and the dogs were immediately upon him, tearing his flesh and literally scalping him before Pat could help. In fact it was Pat's wife Cecile who ran out with the .30-.30 and shot most of the dogs on her child before they quit. Norman had to be flown to Edmonton on a mercy flight to save his life, but he was left badly disfigured.

I never did understand cruelty to dogs, but I had to admit that the natives got a sterling performance out of almost any emaciated team they happened to be driving. Sometimes I watched fascinated while travelling behind such a team; mile after mile the driver would throw a short stick at each dog in turn and then retrieve it again as the sled passed it. They were kept perpetually scared and straining in their harnesses. And they were wicked too. Once a native was driving his team behind me for several hours until finally I slowed and his leader got close enough to sink his teeth into my leg. I never let a team get that close to me again.

During the next two months I made two more trips down river to Norman Wells and then in early April I set out again for Great Bear Lake to spend Easter with the people out there. Alfred Lennie again went with me and we each carried a heavy load of freight for the Hudson Bay store. Mine consisted mostly of rifle shells and cigarette papers. It was almost balmy weather compared to our trip out in December, as the sun was high and the days long. In spite of our loads we both rode all the way over a well-worn trail.

In a letter to our bishop following my first stay in the Fort Franklin mission outpost I had suggested that we put up a better building out there, and he agreed. With this prospect in view I enlisted the help of the Bear Lakers in getting a dozen of the largest trees in the area cut and skidded into place. We located a small stand of very old spruce on the crown of a hill adjacent to a lake a mile away, some of which were nearly two feet in diameter at the base. Being green, they were very heavy and we had to use as many as twelve dogs to skid one of them into town.

Following the religious services of Good Friday and Easter Sunday I organized a kind of winter carnival or sports day that took place out in front of the settlement on the frozen surface of the lake. It included marksmanship, an ice chopping contest, snowshoe and dog-team races, followed in the evening by a drum dance. It was a first for the people of Bear Lake and, although I had some difficulty in getting them to understand and participate in the events, once under way they all enjoyed them.

The Hudson Bay trading post at Franklin was supplied once a year by boats coming up the swift waters of the Great Bear River. If shortages occurred during the winter they had to be supplied from the sister post at Fort Norman and brought in by dog-team. When it was time for me to return to Norman ten teams had been hired by Fred Loutit to go and bring back 300 pounds of supplies each, so we all went together. It made an impressive convoy. I was amazed to notice that a few young bucks had apparently joined the group at the last minute like stowaways, having no equipment but the parkas on their backs. They either jumped from sleigh to sleigh or ran behind. At the half-way point on the ridge at Nadanatli we all slept in the open around a huge fire. Just before arriving at the Fort they stopped again to make fire, which puzzled me as we were so close to our destination, but I learned that they customarily changed into their best clothing and dressed up the dogs with their embroidered *tapis,* or blankets, before they made their grand entrance. I went ahead to the mission and later watched them all drive their teams into the Hudson Bay fenced compound, where they left them unattended while they went into the store. A few minutes later all ten teams of dogs rushed at each other in a king-sized pile up of snarls and flying fur that brought most of the villagers out of their cabins. Certainly everyone knew that the Bear Lakers had arrived in town.

The Brother had a welcome surprise for me. The previous summer I had acquired a large husky bitch from Aklavik and during my absence at Bear Lake she had had four nice pups, three of them males. This was the beginning of a much-improved team of dogs for the mission. Unfortunately I lost one of the males when he was six weeks old. He bothered his mother as she was eating and she snapped at him, inadvertently breaking his jaw. I was forced to shoot him and learned from the incident that pups should be weaned and separated from their husky mothers as soon as possible. This bitch, Vicky, nonetheless went on to produce many fine litters of pups and I was soon driving the ideal team of blood-brothers.

As it got warmer and the snow melted, the trails would support the dogs only at night when they froze. At this time of year two steel runners called leashes are attached to the bottom of the oak toboggans to facilitate their running on the frozen trails at night and to prevent wear and tear on the toboggan bottoms. Thus equipped, I made one last trip out to Willow Lake and returned on the first of May, at which time the trails were becoming so bare of snow it became difficult to travel by dogsled. According to my notebook I had accumulated a total of 1,247 miles by dogs since fall. I was slowly growing out of my greenhorn status.

Mail travelled in and out of Fort Norman by Norman Wells on a weekly schedule, weather permitting, aboard a Canadian Pacific Airlines' Norseman, equipped with either skis or pontoons. The mail had become very erratic recently and the townspeople were complaining and writing letters of protest, but to no avail. Then two attractive nurses were assigned to the nursing station and the situation changed dramatically; mail delivery had never been so good. Funny, but no one had thought of this effective solution to the problem before.

Another ten years in the field had expired for Father Denis and he was again eligible for a vacation to his home in France. He was replaced temporarily by a French-Canadian veteran of the North, Father Maurice Beauregard, who now joined Brother Médard Latreille and me at Fort Norman. I decided that he, as a new member of our religious community, deserved a welcoming duck dinner. So as soon as the first feathery migrants appeared I positioned myself down along the river's bank at the crack of dawn and, suitably armed with our twelve-gauge shotgun, waited. It wasn't like the previous spring over on Windy Island when we saw huge flocks of migrating birds, but I did manage to bag two mallards which I bore triumphantly back to the mission where my two companions were still asleep. I intended to carry them into Brother's room as a wake-up surprise, but in my enthusiasm I miscalculated the height of his doorway and the resulting impact dropped me to the floor like a pole-axed steer. Brother woke up in a typical fit of laughter as I lay stunned on the floor grasping my proud trophies.

Brother had the floor of the room over his kitchen covered with his seed potatoes, which proceeded to sprout. As soon as the large field behind the mission was dry enough he had it ploughed and disked ready for planting. The next chore was to cut up the seed potatoes so that each section had a sprout sticking out a couple of inches for a head start. Care was taken that the rows were absolutely straight and a measuring stick used to separate the sprouts evenly. The more I thought of the week of back-breaking work ahead of us, the more I thought that there must be an easier way of doing it. I began tinkering with an old stone boat, cutting two holes in its floor, attaching small plough-like wooden fins in front and two more behind, the idea being that this contraption pulled behind our tractor would allow two men to sit on it alongside boxes of sprouts which could be placed in the ground through two floor openings. The fins in front opened a furrow and those behind closed it again. We used it and it worked! In fact we planted the whole field in a day while the three of us sat down. I felt like a budding Cyrus McCormick.

Following another break-up and the passing of Streeper's "banana boat," we again went up river and gathered our yearly raft of firewood, but this year on top of the logs we added bags of sawdust from Cleve Cinnamon's sawmill. Our idea was to use it to preserve ice through the summer for drinking water.

At that time Father Denis returned from his two-month furlough in France, carrying a precious bottle of French cognac. This he placed ceremoniously on the kitchen table in order to introduce us to an after-dinner drink he called *pause-café*. After our first meal together he demonstrated just how a touch of the powerful liquor was to be added to a cup of coffee. Brother, however, got his directions all backwards and added a dash of coffee to a cup of cognac which so infuriated our superior that he removed the bottle to the safety of his room, thus ending our experiments with *pause-café*.

It was now the right time of year to set the annual barrel of mass wine, over which Brother presided with loving solicitude. The dried muscatel grapes were delivered annually by the *Sant'Anna* and came in twenty-pound boxes. These were dumped into an oak barrel half-full of clean water and placed upstairs in a warehouse where it was kept warm by the long, sunny days. Brother went up there several times a day to stir this mash with a paddle and after twenty-one days the liquid was ready for bottling. Church regulations on mass wine are very strict: no sugar can be added, and the alcohol content may not exceed thirteen per cent. The superior got suspicious after sampling this batch and sent a small bottle of it out to the University of Alberta for analysis. Evidently he failed to identify exactly what he was sending, as the report back suggested that his horse may be diabetic!

"Summertime and the livin' is easy" is especially true of the North. The mission was warm again and I could move upstairs to my summer bedroom where I was out of the traffic. Under the midnight sun the garden in the side yard soon produced lettuce and radishes and our meals became more varied and flavourful. My formal lessons in Hareskin ceased, for I could now carry on a fair conversation as well as deliver a sermon in the language. French was the common language of exchange among my three companions, and I was no longer ignorant of the trend of the conversation going on around me. So, all things considered, life was a lot easier as I entered my second summer at Fort Norman. The trouble was, the more acclimatized I got, the more I realized that it couldn't last. There were now three priests living where normally there was only one. One or two of us would have to go, but which, and to where? This uncertainty prompted a sharp lookout up river, from which direction we were expecting the arrival of the man who held our destinies in his hands, Bishop Joseph Trocellier.

Our anticipation mounted as his little motor scow, *Our Lady of Fatima*, piloted by Brother Petrin, hove into view one day in July and pulled into shore. We priests could hardly contain our feelings of suspense as the bishop proceeded casually with his pastoral visit. Father Denis had made no secret of the fact that he had offered himself for the new foundation and permanent posting at Fort Franklin. Father Beauregard didn't seem to have any preference, while I prayed that I wouldn't be sent anywhere south of where I was.

We each had our private interview with His Excellency. During mine he told me how pleased he was with my progress during my first year-and-a-half in the country. I think he was taking his time to size each of us up and make up his mind where we could each best serve his Vicariate. He kept us hanging until the eleven o'clock high mass on Sunday when, during his sermon, he announced the new obediences to the whole population: Father Denis was to take charge of the mission at Fort Providence, Father Beauregard was to take over this mission at Fort Norman and Father Brown was to proceed to Great Bear Lake and build a new mission at Fort Franklin!

There it was. Everyone knew at once and after the mass we exchanged congratulations. No mention had been made of Brother Médard Latreille, as he was considered a permanent fixture at Norman and was perfectly happy with that. I would have been happy to have him go with me to Franklin, but I realized, too, that a Brother skilled in carpentry would be more helpful. To fill that gap the bishop told me that he was lending me Brother Maurice Larocque from the mission at Fort Simpson to help get me started. Apparently this whole idea of building a new mission at Bear Lake had not been planned very far in advance. In fact no material had been ordered for it, but the bishop advised me that he was having lumber destined for a new church at Fort Wrigley sent on down to Norman to be taken up the Great Bear River by the Northern Transportation Company. I was anxious to see the plan for the mission at Franklin, but there was none; the bishop told me to make the plan myself. I appreciated his confidence in me, but this looked like a big order if not an impossibility for someone so inexperienced in construction. Anyway I had my orders and immediately got to work with pencil and ruler to work something out. Before I had anything to show him, however, the bishop got away down river.

"Father Beau," as he was affectionately called, would now have not only the Fort Norman Mission to look after, but the parish at Norman Wells, not to mention the outpost at Willow Lake. We decided to go down to the Wells together in the *Nayuka* so that I could show him our Quonset chapel and introduce him around. En route I kept working on my plan for the new building at Fort Franklin. While at the Wells one day we talked with Wing Commander Roy Woods who commented on the trouble he was having from all the smoke in the air from recent forest fires. He was about to send a Canso aircraft to Fort Good Hope to pick up a crew of fire-fighters and he invited us to go along. This gave us the opportunity to catch up with the bishop again. I was particularly anxious to show him the plan I had made and get his approval. It showed a two-storey frame building thirty feet wide by sixty long, topped by a steeple. One side of the main floor would be the chapel, twenty feet wide and running its whole length, while the side facing the lake would be divided into a common room, kitchen, office and bedroom. The upstairs would contain a storeroom and a spare bedroom. The bishop gave it a cursory glance and pronounced it "excellent," with the proviso

that I have enough lumber to do it as planned. He wasn't sure
how much he was diverting from Fort Wrigley.

I had expected that we would go over every square foot of
my plans, cancelling or at least revising many of my lines, but
here I was walking away with a carte blanche permission to do
what I could with whatever material I received. I was reminded
of my Dad's comment to guests when he was showing them the
log bunks I had built in my bedroom when I was seventeen: "Yes,
Bernard built them out of his own head and had wood left over!"

Father Beau and I ran down the hill to reboard our aircraft
and fly back to the Wells, not anticipating the ride we were in for.
The pilot had lowered the nose wheel once he was on the water
so as not to damage the hull of the amphibious Canso when he
nosed into the riverbank at Fort Good Hope. When he backed off,
however, there was so much mud stuck in the nose wheel well
that he couldn't retract the wheel fully and we were forced to
take off with it stuck partially down. Both of us were up in the
pilot's compartment and the spray of water shooting up through
the open hatch drenched us as we tried to plug it with our jack-
ets. Once airborne, the geyser quit, but, with a full load of fire-
fighters and a glassy river, that takeoff run seemed to go on for
minutes. Now the captain radioed ahead to Norman Wells to
stand by with fire-fighting equipment: he would be forced to
land on the gravel runway and wasn't at all sure that his nose
wheel wouldn't collapse on touchdown. Father Beau and I got
busy with our rosaries and, thank God, we made a safe landing
amid a cheering crowd led by the Wing Commander, who stated
publicly that no aircraft of his could possibly crash with two
chaplains on board!

When we got back to Fort Norman we found Brother
Larocque had already arrived from Fort Simpson. A slightly built
French-Canadian, Brother Larocque was as quiet and retiring as
the Latreille brothers were fun-loving extroverts. It didn't take
him long to size up the plans and make a mental note of the material involved. While he gathered up what tools the Norman mission could lend us, I purchased a twenty-two-foot freighter

canoe and a nine-horsepower Johnson outboard from one of the natives. Our lumber had already been transferred from the *Sant'Anna* to the *George Askew,* a stern-wheeler that plied the lower half of the Great Bear River for the Northern Transportation Company. Brother and I soon followed in my canoe, loaded to the gunwales, with a local native hired as pilot.

All my earthly possessions were in a trunk on board, but my most precious baggage was the memory I carried of my first two years in the North. I had learned to like both the country and its people and would have been content to go on living at Fort Norman had the bishop so decided. The fact that it had been my training ground both in learning to cope with northern living and in acquiring two languages meant that this post held a special place in my heart. I was grateful to Father Denis for all the hours he had spent patiently explaining the complexities of the Hareskin language, and I would miss the humour of Brother Médard that brightened the dark days. Perhaps if we had had some sort of farewell banquet I could have put these thoughts into words, but as it was we simply packed up and went our separate ways. There was no one on the bank to wave us off as we pushed out into the current of the Mackenzie and a little lump in my throat told me that the first chapter of my life in the North had just ended.

7

BUILDING
AT FORT FRANKLIN

The Great Bear River, about seventy miles long, empties Great Bear Lake into the Mackenzie River. It is fairly straight, clear and fast, with nine miles of shallow water running over mostly flat limestone at the half-way point commonly referred to as "the rapids." The lower segment of the river tends to be wider and therefore shallower, with a less distinct channel, while the section above the rapids is narrower and deeper, with a much swifter current.

In order for the Northern Transportation Company to get supplies to its Crown affiliate, Eldorado Mine on the east side of Bear Lake, the Company had built a portage road around the rapids and maintained a fleet of trucks there supervised by Andy Brass. It also maintained an airport named Bennett Field after Bill Bennett, President of Eldorado. It was strictly a summer operation getting the mine supplied, mainly with diesel fuel, for the coming winter, and taking out the thousands of small bags of uranium concentrate on the back haul destined for further refining at Port Hope, Ontario. A substantial steel ship, named *The Radium Gilbert* after Gilbert LaBine who discovered the mine, plied the two hundred miles of open water on Great Bear Lake connecting the mine with the river boats. Besides this activity there was a Colonel Yukamin with a crew of Army Engineers constructing a road to connect the portage with Bear Lake, a project rumoured to cost a million dollars, but never completed or used.

It was into this beehive of activity that we pointed the nose of our canoe on the 18th of July and slowly pushed our way up to the foot of the rapids the first day. Emptying the boat and pulling it out, we set a tent and camped for the night while I enquired about the possibility of getting a truck to take us across the portage the next day. The following morning, after Andy helped us across the portage, we resumed our voyage above the rapids. Now we were seeing this beautiful river in all its rugged glory, careening off rocky points, twisting and turning in the summer sun, its clear depths moving with schools of arctic grayling, its placid eddies reflecting the tall spruce overhead. We were heavily loaded and our guide had to take advantage of every slack backwater behind the bars and little points to keep us advancing. Out in the centre of the stream we would have made no progress at all. Toward the end of the day as we approached Great Bear Lake the trees along the bank became more stunted and twisted and the temperature dropped noticeably. Some of the banks were solid with ice that would last all summer. Finally we passed the Quonset hut where I had found shelter the winter before and then the Northern Transportation Company dock and then we were out onto the lake itself. Fort Franklin was clearly visible four miles to the left. In no time at all we were across the bay of Keith Arm and I was moving into the mission cabin.

We were visited immediately by seven carpenters who had been sent in by the Department of Public Works to finish the two-storey school they had begun last summer. As they had a cook as well as a good supply of grub, they invited us to take our meals with them, a welcome and unexpected stroke of good luck.

I was free to put up the new mission anywhere I thought suitable, because the land was not yet surveyed nor did we have any lease. The fact that the school was now going up on the east end of the settlement, a few hundred yards farther out than our present site, indicated that the town would probably expand in

that direction. I would have preferred to build in the heavy timber at the west end of town where we would have been on better
ground off the permafrost, but it now appeared that such a site
would be practically isolated. Brother Larocque was pleased
with the huge logs we had cut and hauled at Easter. The spot
where they had dropped when the snow melted seemed to be as
good as any on which to begin construction. However, the
Northern Transportation Company had off-loaded our lumber
some three hundred yards away, and this meant that we would
have to spend the first week with our canoe hauling this material
up to our building site. Chief Francis Eya rounded up five capable workers who were willing to help us at a salary of $125 a
month, and we got to work.

The foundation for our building had to be those twelve
thirty-foot spruce trees which we flattened on the top side with
axes. As we were building on permafrost, it wouldn't have
helped to pour cement footings under them, which we didn't
have anyway, so we simply levelled them with some gravel and
flat stones. On top of these mud sills went the four-by-six-inch fir
timbers I had taken from the ill-fated Quonset curling rink. Once
we had an insulated double floor laid we had a nice flat platform
to work on and the walls went up quickly under the expert
supervision of Brother Larocque. Besides the pesky flies, the
weather gave us the most trouble that summer: it rained on us
every working day but seven. We could carry on in spite of the
weather, but when we ran short of nails and certain other vital
materials it became evident that I would have to make a trip
down to Fort Norman in the canoe.

Several of the Bear Lakers jumped into the canoe with me to
visit friends down there and we had a dandy roller-coaster ride,
not stopping at the rapids, but going straight through in five
hours. En route I made a lucky hit with my .270 when I shot a
large sandhill crane in the neck and killed it. The natives told me
they never kill this bird, called a *deleho*, because its death would
bring on a three-day rain. I replied that, with all the rain we had
been getting, they wouldn't notice it. Brother Médard was

delighted with it and not only cooked it, but invited Bud Boyce, the Game Warden, to join us for this special treat of "Bear Lake goose." All declared it to be delicious. It was.

It didn't take me long to find the material needed at Franklin and I engaged a river pilot to return with me. At the appointed hour the following morning this chap failed to show up, so I decided to go it alone. Aside from shearing a few pins en route, especially at the lower stretch of the river, I made it through to Bear Lake without incident. Like so many disappointments in life, the guide's absence turned out to be a blessing in disguise: I made five trips down to Norman for supplies that summer and never needed a guide.

When we got to the peak of the roof the question of the belfry came up. I showed Brother a picture of one in a photography magazine I was reading that had a little of the Byzantine onion design about it, a tiny cupola at the top of which I could imagine a beacon. Brother started the wheels of his computer-like brain and with only his steel square to go by, cut out every piece of wood for that tower on his table saw on the ground. Not only that, but when assembled on the roof every piece fit perfectly. This amazed me and made a big impression on the professional carpenters working on the school. They immediately donated enough copper sheathing to cover it. Gleaming in the sun like solid gold, the spire of the new mission church was indeed a beacon in the wilderness, a sight any missionary would be proud of.

I was up on the roof one day when a stranger walked up to the building and, doffing an incongruous brown derby, introduced himself as "Mr. Roy Gravel, age fifty-three, your new teacher at your service." I had met many characters in the North, but Mr. Gravel would soon top them all. He moved into the school immediately, even though it was unfinished, and joined us at table to share with us in a most candid manner the amazing vicissitudes of his past life. Our meals were now spiced with true-life episodes not unlike those of a soap opera. If we gained one character in town, we lost another when the Hudson Bay Company suddenly replaced Fred Loutit with a young white boy named Bob Williams. So where before there had been none, now there were three whites in Fort Franklin: Gravel, Williams and myself.

When I made my last trip by canoe to Fort Norman on the 16th of September I brought back that mission's five sled dogs: two older dogs plus Vicky and her three pups. Suddenly I needed a good supply of fish for dog food and, because I could afford little time from the critical job of getting the mission closed in before freeze-up, I decided to hire one of the Bear Lakers, equip him with nets and place him somewhere to fish for me. John Takaz agreed to take on this job and suggested the best place for a fall fishery would be at a bay called Klowahtah, forty-five miles out along the south shore of the lake. We picked the first flat calm day, which happened to be the 22nd of September, and set out in my freighter canoe loaded with Johnny's family, his dogs, tent and a small hunting canoe.

Keith Arm of Great Bear Lake has few islands and the only one on our route was down the lake about thirty-five miles. Although it is marked "Manitou" on the chart, Johnny told me that its real name was Gorabee and that a monster by that name had drowned there when he attempted to swim the lake. The island had formed over his carcass. He added that Gorabee's home in the nearby rocks still existed, but as it was inhabited now by bears no native would dare go near it. I don't think Johnny would have made a stop there had he been in charge of the boat, but as I was manning the kicker, I pulled into shore, much to his consternation. He wouldn't even step on shore himself, but, seeing that I was determined to see Gorabee's home, insisted that I carry the rifle.

I had no trouble finding the entrance to the cave in a limestone outcrop some two hundred yards up from the water, hidden behind a few scraggly spruce. Its opening was approximately the size of a normal cabin door, but inside it opened into a room about sixty feet long by fifteen wide with a ten-foot ceiling and was completely empty. I could visualize the place being used as a safe haven by prehistoric cave men; there being so few caves in this country, this one must have been found and used by them.

That fall I wrote to anthropologist Dr. Richard S. MacNeish of the National Museum in Ottawa about this unusual cave and he came down the following summer to investigate it. After borrowing my canoe and a few shovels he hired some men and went down there. He returned a few days later, however, empty-handed. The floor of the cave which would contain the artefacts he was interested in was now covered with tons of rock that must have fallen from the ceiling during the ages, and he had neither the time nor the funds to dig it all out. He added, however, that he thought I was the first "European" to see this cave and he intended to give it my name. Well, most explorers in the North get a lake or mountain named after them, but I was quite willing to settle for a hole in the ground. Yet I was to be denied even that honour. The following year I was in the Yellowknife library looking over the Journal of the Franklin Expedition, especially the map they had drawn of Great Bear Lake in 1826. The cave was clearly marked!

Johnny and family appeared to be genuinely relieved to see me return to the canoe unharmed. I could not understand how an age-old story such as this could still be exerting an influence on these people in the mid-twentieth century.

I left Johnny and his family off at Klowahtah equipped with four gill nets and sixty large trout hooks. Once a week I went back to get a load of fish and when I finally moved him back to the settlement on October 17th he had taken a total of 2,650 herring and 105 trout. Although this was a good start on my winter's dog feed, I still had to set nets for herring near the mouth of the river after freeze-up.

While Brother and I were using every scrap of material we had to get the mission closed in before the cold weather set in, the Department of Public Works crew were putting the final touches to the interior of the school and had plenty of material left over. They not only gave me enough bricks to build a chimney, but enough lumber to add a ten-foot extension for storage.

They had installed at the school a five-ton Lyster diesel engine attached to a generator, which the teacher was supposed to keep running. Mr. Gravel, however, acknowledged a complete ignorance of anything mechanical. Indeed, he protested that he had been hired to teach, not to fill the shoes of an engineer, and absolutely refused to accept responsibility for keeping that huge engine running. Therefore, by default, I was approached with the proposition that if I would accept this responsibility a line could be strung over to the mission, giving me power also. I jumped at the offer.

In the meantime Brother Larocque had received a letter from his superior at Fort Simpson informing him that he was to return as soon as possible to continue his work with a crew building St. Margaret's Hospital there. Although we now had the new mission building sealed on the outside so that it could be heated, it was practically an empty shell inside; I was hoping he might be allowed to stay on and continue helping me. In fact I had written the bishop suggesting this, but having no answer in reply, I had no choice but to let him return to his post. The Public Works crew had engaged a boat to take them part way down the Great Bear River where they were to be picked up by an aircraft at Bennett Field. When they left on October 12th, Brother Larocque left with them. Two months later, when I got the first batch of mail following freeze-up, there was a letter from the bishop giving me permission to keep Brother with me for the winter!

Now I was alone again in the little log cabin doing my own cooking and looking forward to the day when I could move into the new mission next door. One of the irritants I never got used to in the old cabin was the mice. To discourage them I had brought back a cat I named Charlie-ho on my last trip from Norman. He was probably the first cat the natives had seen in Fort Franklin and they were very wary of him, calling him a *nontaja*, or baby lynx. If he didn't actually kill many mice he certainly kept them below the floor boards and off my bed at night. And then came the day we were surprised by the visit of a short-tailed weasel who emerged from a mouse hole in his white winter pelage, a magnificent ermine. To Charlie-ho he, however, must have appeared like a huge albino mouse who had chased him recently in a nightmare and he retreated to my lap completely demoralized. Actually I was glad to see this professional killer, as I knew he could pursue mice right into their dens.

I had boasted about Charlie-ho's hunting ability to the natives and they were impressed. One such was the widow Guykazo, who lived in a tent with her four children a hundred feet from my cabin. They all slept together in a bed of spruce boughs on the floor, covered by a huge feather blanket, and the mice bothered them at night so she asked to borrow Charley-ho. I lent him out on the condition that they keep their sled dogs well tied while he was in their employ. Two days later I walked over there in the evening to see how he was doing. They were all in bed and gave me only vague answers as to Charlie-ho's whereabouts, but I could hear a muffled "meow" coming from inside a covered fifty-pound Klim can. Lifting the lid I peered down into it with the aid of my flashlight and there was Charlie-ho, in water up to his neck!

As I pulled him out and dried him off, Guykazo spilled the whole sordid story. Apparently the first night Charlie-ho had kept them awake running over their sleeping bag chasing mice. The second night the mice were laying low and, with no activity, Charlie-ho felt the fall chill creeping in as soon as the fire went out. So he tried to crawl under the blankets with them, which scared them out of their wits. The eldest son, Bekoya ("The Brain"), got up and put this "lynx pup" into the empty Klim can, covered it, and went back to bed. Charlie-ho's "meow" now sounded like the roar of a lion in the empty can, so Bekoya got up again and proceeded to dampen the sound by pouring a bucket of water on him. Charlie-ho went back to the mission with me.

I now spent my days alone over in the new building. The cat kept me company as I built a partition upstairs for a bedroom and then a few shelves, to which I would give a coat of varnish before returning to the log cabin at night. I installed my

Electrohome radio up in the new building as soon as I had a shelf built for it and it was powered by one of those large A-B battery packs that lasted a year. It had an effective short-wave band and the best station was the American Armed Forces station AFRTS coming out of Los Angeles, to which I kept it tuned all day as I worked. One evening I couldn't find Charlie-ho before I returned home, so I had to leave without him. The next day I had trouble keeping my station tuned and also noticed water on the floor under the battery, which I presumed was getting old and maybe leaking. I dried it up and re-varnished the spot as well as the shelves.

All that day I had not located Charlie-ho and began to suspect that he had slipped outside and fallen prey to the roaming huskies. The third day I was again up in that room, working with the radio blaring, when it went off the station. I re-tuned it and stood there looking at the dial, wondering what the trouble could be, when I again lost my station and I thought I could actually see the dial move! Suddenly I got a creepy feeling that made me blink and wonder what the devil was wrong. I re-tuned AFRTS and got down close to watch the needle. Nothing happened. Five minutes later when my back was turned I not only lost my station, but the BBC suddenly came on. This had never happened before. I pulled the radio out from the wall and out jumped Charlie-ho! I could hardly believe it. Apparently, with the battery removed from its niche in the back of the radio, the cat had curled up in there. When I pushed it against the wall to varnish in front of it I had unwittingly trapped him inside – for three days! All the tubes were covered with hair. The amazing thing was that he never uttered even one little "meow."

In the meantime my neighbour in the brown derby, the school teacher Mr. Gravel, had started his class of first-graders full of enthusiasm, of which he certainly needed a generous amount, for none of them spoke any English. He was riding high on a wave of initial enthusiasm so characteristic of many civil servants who come North, his head exploding with a thousand ideas of projects for the people. Typical of them was his feather-marketing scheme. He had read somewhere that the milliners of Paris paid high prices for feathers and was horrified to learn that most of the feathers plucked locally were scattered to the four winds. He intended to put a stop to this needless waste immediately and sent out word that the feathers of all birds plucked should be sent to him for safe-keeping and eventual sale. Later, to prevent loss of feathers in transit, he offered to pluck the birds himself in a special room upstairs in the school designated "the feather room." When Colonel Yukamin had closed his camp at the end of summer he sent tons of grub over to Franklin to be distributed by the teacher. Thus began the weekly handouts called "rations" every Friday, and it was soon noticed that the feather-producers got the lion's share of this booty. The feathers in the feather room got deeper and deeper over the next two years until Mr. Gravel left, at which point a small ladder was needed to scale the plywood barrier put up over the door to contain the fluffy mass inside. Unfortunately he was never successful in making a deal with the Paris milliners. His successor inherited a lot of feathers.

Baby-sitting the diesel generator at the school turned out to be a more time-consuming job than I had anticipated. For one thing, its fuel tank had to be refilled every eight hours and when it was allowed to run out, the jets had to be bled in order to get it started again. It was bolted to a concrete slab directly connected to the school's cement foundation, with the result that when it was running normally the school had a rhythmic vibration not unlike that of a huge ship at sea. As long as he could feel that steady throbbing the teacher knew that all was well, but when it stopped he was soon pounding at my back door.

I solved the fuel problem by installing a forty-five-gallon drum in place of the ten-gallon one it had come equipped with. The panel of dials proved an irresistible temptation to Mr. Gravel, however, who loved to change the ohm setting whenever he thought the voltage was low. I would notice it immediately over in the mission, as my lights would get bright, then dim again. The result was that he gradually burned out all his bulbs and started borrowing mine. Finally we got down to my last bulb and he was reduced to using a gasoline light while his huge electric plant, strong enough to light the entire village, rumbled on, hour after hour, powering only the small electric blower in his oil furnace and my one light bulb. In spite of seven thermostats distributed throughout the school, all of which he had turned up full, he complained of the low temperature and was convinced they weren't working. So he had me disconnect them and put in a single switch on the furnace that turned the heat on full-throttle. Once it was on I don't think he ever turned it off.

All Hudson Bay posts were equipped with a telegraph key which the managers operated daily using Morse code. In this way they were advised of changes in fur market prices or possibly a frost in Brazil which would necessitate an immediate markup in coffee prices. Mr. Gravel got a message out advising the Department of Education that he was out of light bulbs and we were amazed to see an aircraft land on skis loaded with nothing but bulbs. This was an event, for we got only three aircraft during the entire year.

In no time at all the school was ablaze with light and so was the mission, but soon the whole process began repeating itself; Mr. Gravel fine-tuning the ohm meter and gradually burning out all the bulbs until he put us both in the dark again.

Shortly after that the generator committed suicide when the set screw on the fan at the end of the exciter loosened and cut through the end of the armature wiring. I thought maybe he could keep warm by burning wood instead of oil in his furnace, so I converted it for him, but without the fan to circulate the heat throughout the building only the furnace room was warm. The only alternative was to take the small oil stove from the stout house out behind that had heated the rations and move it and the rations upstairs into the living room. We had no flue to which we could connect the chimney, so we removed a pane of glass from the window and stuck the chimney outside. Egg crates were piled to the ceiling on either side of the room and a dozen desks were lined up in the centre while Mr. Gravel moved his bed into the kitchen just off his new classroom.

Everything worked like a charm until one night a terrific wind out of the north-east blew directly into the stove pipe which was sticking horizontally out of the window, causing a mild explosion that drove the damper into the wall across the room, filled the school with smoke and changed the paint scheme from white to grey. Yet these minor setbacks didn't quench the enthusiastic Mr. Gravel, who carried on with his classes by the light of a gas lamp, bundled in an overcoat, a sporty pair of earmuffs added under his brown derby.

After these trials, however, it occurred to me that Charlie-ho would make an ideal companion for our teacher, especially during his long evenings in the feather room. So when Mr. Gravel's birthday came around I put a large red ribbon on the cat and presented him to the teacher as a precious gift. He was received with open arms. The following week I was informed that Charlie-ho was thriving on the canned lobster found in Colonel Yukamin's grub supply and demonstrating genuine affection for his new master.

"It's uncanny how our temperaments are synchronized," Mr. Gravel confided to me one day. "He senses my every mood. When I've had a good day and feel in a playful mood, we chase each other around the rooms, and when I'm down in the dumps he retires to the top of the egg crates and lets me brood in silence. Next to a wife he's the best companion I could have!" I congratulated myself on having brought these two characters together. One evening, however, when I was cooking supper there came a knock at the door and when I opened it Mr. Gravel shoved Charlie-ho into my arms with the announcement, "Here, take him, I'll explain everything later."

The following day I got the whole, sad story. "Something strange has happened to the finely-tuned rapport between us," confided my neighbour. "We have fallen out of sync. I had a discouraging day with the kids and Charlie-ho insisted on playing with me, and when I threw off this depression and felt like a romp with my companion he hid himself and wouldn't have a thing to do with me! We just couldn't go on living together like this. One of us had to go."

After digesting this tale of domestic strife and feeling like a marriage counsellor, I tendered what sympathy I could and promised I would study Charlie-ho and try to figure out his problem. Actually what I did was to pawn him off on Bob Williams, who quickly objected to him for an entirely different reason. Perhaps because of the stress he had been under at the school for the past few weeks Charlie-ho lost control of his bladder during his first night at the Hudson Bay manager's quarters and left an ugly stain in the middle of the new beige rug. The young manager, thinking only of the reaction this spot would trigger from the district manager on his next inspection trip, took it as a personal insult and before he had regained his composure took the poor culprit outside and executed him with a .30-.30.

Charlie-ho was gone but not forgotten as Fort Franklin's first cat.

8

PRACTISING MEDICINE

Ten days after Brother Larocque left I had the upstairs bedroom in the new mission completed and began sleeping there, although I was still cooking and eating in the old log mission. It took me another month to complete the new kitchen. What gave me the most trouble was the large kitchen cabinet with its built-in sink and row of drawers, particularly difficult for a novice cabinet-maker. The fact that it is still in use after more than forty years is surprising.

This carpentry work was as fatiguing as it was confining and I would have preferred to be out of doors driving the dogs. When a man is still in his twenties he has enough energy in his legs to make him want to run it off now and then, almost needing to release it in a burst of speed. As soon as there was snow on the ground I was often drawn to the window to watch a team of dogs run by. How I would have loved to join them, but the work facing me inside was pressing and I realized that I would have no one to help me. Besides the bedroom and kitchen, I needed the chapel area completed in time for Christmas.

Early in November Great Bear Lake was frozen over. By mid-month some daring hunters had crossed to the south shore over five miles of ice and spotted an advance herd of caribou a few miles inland. Chief Eya gave me all the details and invited me to join a mass hunt scheduled for the following day. The temptation was too great to resist and I immediately got busy preparing my gear. Yetsa's daughter Rosie had spent most of the summer embroidering a new set of seven moose-hide harnesses for my dogs, so this was all ready and Albert Menako had sewn a new moose hide on my new oak toboggan. I had just to add a few ropes and rings. By midnight I put the sled and harness outside ready to go in the morning.

I had never participated in a caribou hunt and looked forward to this adventure with keen anticipation. I was not to be disappointed. At first light the settlement came alive with the chorus of eager sled dogs being put into harness. As we fell into line on the trail leading across the lake, there were over twenty teams strung out leaving a trail of ice fog in the forty-below air. After covering the first five miles across the thin ice of the bay, we hit the south shore in a tight group, every team nose-to-tail with the next, moving ahead at a fast trot. We began to climb slowly through a partly open parkland of small spruce, heading directly into the sun which was rising at an oblique angle behind the haze on the horizon.

The first sign we got of the herd ahead was the change in attitude of our dogs, raising their heads to sniff the air and quickening their pace. It was another mile before we could actually see the cloud of vapour up ahead indicating caribou beneath. Soon we were close enough to see the quarry, a vast herd of thousands of animals covering a wide muskeg where they had been feeding.

Now the fun began. As there was practically no spruce of any size to tie the sled head rope to, the trick was to tip the toboggan over on its side, creep up and sit on its head, rifle in hand, and try to prevent the dogs from dragging you ahead. You shot over their heads, hoping that you wouldn't hit one accidentally as they jumped and barked in their harness.

Some of the hunters stopped short and began to fire immediately while others wanted to get into closer range or couldn't stop their teams and kept their heads low as the shells fired from behind raced overhead at the targets. It was a wild, chaotic scene, surpassing anything I had imagined, with over a hundred crazed huskies filling the frosty air with their howls while twenty high-powered rifles spat out fire and the poor caribou raced about in utter confusion. The strange part of it was that I alone couldn't fired a shot!: in turning my sled on its side, my rifle, still in its case, got caught between the sled's backboard and a "nigger-head,"* snapping the stock in two just behind the trigger guard. When the firing died down there were still plenty of animals within range of my telescopic sight and I wondered to myself if I could fire by holding the two sections of the broken stock together. I couldn't go back empty-handed. No matter the risk I just had to try it.

First of all I found a small spruce to tie the sled to and then, by cradling the barrel in a branch, I fired. Although the stock jack-knifed with the recoil, the bullet sped true to its mark and the caribou dropped. I quickly dispatched three more, two of which were hobbling on broken legs. With the help of my dogs I skidded all four carcasses together and began the less exciting work of skinning and butchering.

My hunting companions were spread out all over the muskeg doing the same thing, as the surviving members of the herd continued digging up and feeding on the caribou moss at a respectful distance. I tied the head rope of my sled to the rack or antlers of a large bull I had killed, thinking that this would restrain the dogs, but when a pair of yearlings ran by at close range they lunged after them, dragging my bull behind, and I had to drop my knife and jump on the bull's back to stop them. After that I tied them in a circle with the lead dog's trace snapped to the sled.

In an hour's time everyone had his toboggan loaded with meat with the hides tied on the top prepared for the triumphal trip home with the first meat of the season. As I pulled out with my load I could see several wolves creeping up on the kill site from the outer muskeg. I learned later that some of the hunters

---

* The unfortunate term *niggerhead* is used commonly in the north to designate the clumps of moss that stick up a foot or two all over the muskegs. They usually measure about two feet across and may be formed by frost heave.

had killed more animals than they could take away and intended to return for this meat the following day, but a sudden, violent west wind took all the ice out of the bay and by the time it had re-frozen the wolves had cleaned up everything. The lesson that should have been learned was not to kill more than you could keep, but I was to learn that those who live off the land are not necessarily conservationists. A case in point came up about two weeks later when Sonny Naedzo asked me if I would go with him to bring in the meat of a dozen caribou he had shot about fifteen miles away. I figured that my dogs needed a good thirty-mile run if they were to get in shape for the trip to Fort Norman, so I went with him. We had gone about half-way when we ran into another bunch of caribou. Sonny opened fire on them and soon we had two sled-loads of meat right there. Sonny never did go back for the animals he had originally shot.

I had just gotten into the mission after this trip when some-one came to tell me that old Lucy Trakazo was sick. When I asked what kind of sickness, they said she couldn't pass water. I imme-diately began to think of what I could substitute for a catheter which I didn't have. If I could only locate a piece of plastic tube it would work. I had heard that in similar circumstances the natives had successfully used a swan's hollow wing bone. Before I could locate something, however, another person ran in to say that she had died.

This wasn't the first death I had had at Franklin. During the past summer twenty-one-year-old Jimmy Tucho was running a slight temperature and complaining of a sore throat. I began injecting him with a daily dose of 2 cc's of penicillin at the mis-sion. I had been warned not to engage an aircraft unless it was a case of life or death two years before, when I had stopped at Edmonton en route into the country. Dr. Faulkner at Charles Camsell Hospital, who had charge of Indian and Northern Health Services, had told me that aircraft med-evac charters were very costly. I had this warning in the back of my mind as I con-tinued to treat Jimmy, who showed no sign of improving. Finally I could wait no longer and, although my patient didn't look at all near death, I had Bob Williams send a message to pilot Pappy Hill at Norman Wells. He lost no time in flying over in the CPA Norseman and landing out in front of the settlement on floats. Because there was no dock and the shore rocks could easily damage the floats, he waited a couple of hundred feet from shore. We took Jimmy out in a canoe, but before we could get him into the aircraft, he died.

Before I had left home to come North my uncle the doctor gave me some practical advice regarding most of the first-aid problems I might encounter in the North. He also gave me a copy of the latest *Merck Manual* (a handy medical reference work for diagnosis and treatment). Another friend, Jane Hasselwander, gave me her student nurse's dissecting instruments. Before I left Fort Norman the nurse there gave me a box of medicines and bandages she thought I might need at Franklin. Nonetheless, I found myself up against a bad health situation that would have taxed the skills of a bona fide medical doctor. I don't think that it is exaggerating to say that the natives of Fort Franklin at that time were riddled with tuberculosis. I noticed this right away in winter by the amount of blood spat along the trails in town. The worst cases had found their way out to the Charles Camsell Hospital, where they had died, and this reinforced the conviction that a visit to hospital was a one-way trip. Perhaps if some curable individuals had been evacuated first and then returned cured, it might have encouraged others to submit themselves for treatment before they were terminally ill.

Assisting at a childbirth in the role of midwife was a challenge I didn't look forward to, but it was inevitable. One night I was awakened to go to the cabin of Sonny Naedzo whom I had married to Georgina Cleary the previous October. During the next hour she delivered a healthy baby with little help on my part. After tying and cutting the umbilical cord I waited patiently for the placenta to be expelled. The book said it should come out in about fifteen minutes, but said little about how much pressure should be used on the cord to help in the process. After a half-hour I became worried and exerted more pull on the cord. It was amazingly tough and I had no fear of breaking it, but I was apprehensive about pulling out more than just the placenta, if that were possible. I think I was sweating more than Georgina when it finally emerged an hour after the birth.

In mid-winter I was successful in getting a Dr. Gray to fly down from Aklavik Hospital with a portable X-ray machine. He landed in a De Havilland Beaver aircraft equipped with skis and we set up the X-ray in the Hudson Bay store, as it alone had electricity. I acted as interpreter for the doctor as he gave Chief Eya a little pep talk on rounding up everyone in the settlement for their first X-ray. It was after supper when they began coming in to stand in line, stripped to the waist, to get their picture taken, after which I was charged with the task of giving them shots for small-pox and diphtheria. By midnight we had processed 75, but 100 had failed to show up and the doctor was very perturbed and vented his dissatisfaction at me saying, "What's the matter with these people? Don't they realize TB is decimating them? The government has gone to a lot of expense flying me down here for this clinic, but I can't hold this aircraft here another night. How are we going to get them in here?"

Although I was doubtful about the outcome, my only sugges-tion was that the two of us go about the village pounding on doors and urging the laggards to get up to the store. After this midnight invitation we went back to work and by four in the morning our total had risen to 126. Yet I realized that those who were spitting the most blood did not show up. Others believed the rumour that it was that devilish X-ray machine itself that gave a person tuberculosis. Most of the 50 who never came to the clinic reasoned that if they did have the disease they might as well die right there among their family and friends than off in some strange land.

Because of this reluctance of the natives to go outside for help, I wrote several letters to Dr. Faulkner requesting a periodic visit from the nurse in Fort Norman. Finally Miss Beckham flew in for a trial visit. She was a sight: an Englishwoman of generous proportions, hidden behind a mask of white powder and red lipstick, a combination guaranteed to scare the living daylights out of a group of people who had seen few if any white women and who had no knowledge of these aids to beauty. I escorted her about the village to see my current patients and she was a sensation wherever we went. The adults were as tongue-tied in disbelief as if I were showing off a winged monster from Mars, while the children scrambled screaming under the beds. Poor Miss Beckham couldn't understand the reception she was getting and I found it difficult to be candid with her and simply mumbled something about the people not being used to visitors. Unfortunately her visit accomplished very little and she never returned. In one way I couldn't blame her. No one wants to waste her time without accomplishing anything, especially the professional person.

On the other hand, you can't blame the Bear Lakers either. To be confronted with such a formidable specimen of an alien race takes some getting used to. Perhaps if I had been able to remove her makeup and perfume and rub a little fish oil on her face so she smelt "right" it might have helped. I don't suppose there was anything we could have done about her curly red hair. She and Dr. Gray were certainly dedicated and capable members of their profession, but they just didn't understand the people they were sent to help.

When December rolled around and we hadn't had any mail since summer I decided to run in to Fort Norman with the dogs. Sonny Naedzo went with me. Both our teams were in good shape and they needed to be, because the snow was deep and no one had broken a trail yet this winter. I carried a small tent and we pitched it both nights, leaving it set the second night for the return trip. Brother Médard welcomed me back at Norman with his customary good cheer and Father Beauregard was pleased with the sled-load of fish and meat I brought. It took me a few days to read all my mail and then I had to answer the important ones, for there was no telling when I'd get the next chance to send mail out. Furthermore, it was time to get the Christmas cards on their way.

One thoughtful woman in Edmonton had sent me a parcel containing a head of lettuce and three tomatoes which arrived frozen solid. I considered them a complete loss, but Brother Médard insisted he knew of a technique to thaw and save them. When his process failed and they turned black he made a salad out of them anyway and put them on the table to watch our reaction, which provoked his typical gales of laughter. I had missed his humour at Franklin and it was good to be back in an Oblate community in spite of the regulatory bells, the early rising and the frosty windows. Yet deep down I was no longer at ease there because I kept thinking of my Franklin mission, of the plans I had for celebrating Christmas with my people there and of those who were critically ill. Before returning I got a good supply of medicine from the nursing station. The return trip was the best I had made – thanks to a splendid performance from my seven huskies – except for a frozen chin, the result of forty-below temperatures.

I had just gotten back into the mission after unharnessing my dogs when someone ran in to announce another death in the village. This time it was the oldest member of the Betsedea family, Cecile's mother Yahon. If this weren't enough to cast gloom on this family, I soon learned that Rosie Yetsa had succumbed to tuberculosis while I was away. Neither death was any surprise, and I had given both the Sacrament of Extreme Unction (since revised as the Sacrament of the Sick) before I left. It was particularly tragic in the case of Rosie because her parents wouldn't accept any medicine for her – not to mention evacuation to a hospital – so her doom was sealed. Nor did the future look any better for this family: four of its living members were spitting blood.

My long days of carpentry resumed as I continued to put up partitions and hang doors in an effort to have the chapel ready for Christmas. I hired Johnny Neyalle to help handle the four-by-eight sheets of plywood, which speeded up the work considerably; it also helped that I no longer had to go over to the old mission to cook my meals. When the big feast rolled around everything was ready. There would be no more trouble trying to stagger the congregation for the three Midnight Masses: now there was plenty of floor space even though we didn't have benches, and the barrel stove threw all the heat we needed. I had hung accordion doors across the altar end of this large room so that with them closed the room served as a rec hall. We brought in a spruce tree and trimmed it. Underneath I put a pile of presents I had gotten from the States in the mail at Fort Norman.

On Christmas afternoon after the gifts had been distributed to the children I introduced them to some traditional games of my culture, like pinning the tail on the donkey (I drew a caribou), musical chairs, candle lighting, as well as nail driving, a balloon dance and a contest to see who could whistle first after eating five soda crackers. Not everything turned out as I had planned however. As a special treat I had made a bucket of ice cream, but the reaction was *"Ellagu!"* – "It's cold!" – and they held their dishes over the stove until it was melted before eating it. I had even planned on having games outside for the adults and in anticipation had put flags out on the lake for the dogsled race course and targets for the shooting events. The fifty-below temperature and stiff wind, however, postponed these events until Easter. An inside drum dance and stick game was substituted, and everyone agreed that it was the best Christmas ever.

As the last days of 1950 ticked into eternity I couldn't help but feel thankful to God for all its blessings, but especially for the new mission, so spacious yet so easy to heat. I used to shudder walking by the old log building, remembering how dark and cold it was. In preparing a year-end report for the bishop I notified him that the cost of building the new mission at Fort Franklin came to exactly $7,829.22, including the materials, the transport and the labour. Although the job wasn't completed I didn't anticipate needing any more material to finish. I sweetened my letter by enclosing a U.S. cheque for $2,000 ($2,200 in Canadian funds) from Aquinas Institute, the high school from which I graduated in Rochester. It represented the result of a paper drive they had organized for the missions.

Among the letters I had received at Norman was one from Bishop Trocellier dated early November, in which he told me that a "good American" in Toledo, Ohio, was giving him a four-passenger Aeronca aircraft. He then went on to describe a trip he made to Rochester on which he visited my parents and noticed on the wall of my room my pilot's licence. As I was the only missionary he had who was trained to fly, he added, "If you are able to pilot that machine you may have it and then get away from dogs." Now I had to write him: Thanks, but no thanks. I had enough of flying to realize that it was not as much fun as driving dogs and a lot more dangerous.

The bishop did receive the aircraft and sent another missionary to the States to get licensed in my place, but I never regretted my decision. At that time, in that place, dogs were the best means of transportation.

Now that the new mission at Fort Franklin was built it was time to give it an official name. I had great devotion to the Carmelite nun, Thérèse of Lisieux, who had not only been canonized by the Church but named Patroness of Missions. Since the parent mission at Fort Norman carried the name of the "big" St. Teresa of Avila, it was fitting that the new daughter mission on Bear Lake be named after the French St. Thérèse, who was affectionately known as "The Little Flower." The bishop granted my request and it was official: Mission St. Therese.

9

TRAGEDY
AND TABOOS

Gone were the leaden skies, the endless fall of snow and the dark days of November and December; we were now into the clear, bright days of January. The atmosphere was clean and the air sharp as temperatures stayed down around forty below zero. The frozen surface of Great Bear Lake sparkled in the New Year's sun as it sailed higher and higher over Rocher Clark, a mountain on the far southern horizon. Now I no longer needed a gas lamp to see if I were sawing a board straight. The sunlight poured in through the mission's new windows, most of which faced south toward the lake.

The bluer skies were a promise of the fine weather to come with spring, when I hoped to be outside enjoying them, not still inside, harnessed in my carpenter's apron. To speed that day I enlisted help for the outside work so that I could finish the inside work faster.

First I gave a contract to Isidore Yukon and Victor Beyonnie to cut fifteen cords of firewood at eight dollars a cord. Then I hired Francis Baton to drive my dogs five hours a day, six days a week at seventy-five cents an hour, to bring this wood in from the bush and to visit my nets. Now I could devote myself entirely to the carpentry and at the same time my dogs would be working and kept in fine shape for the long hauls. Just like athletes, sled dogs must be continually exercised in order to run well.

By mid-February it was time to go into Fort Norman again for the mail. Luckily, Jimmy Cleary, who the winter before had taught me the right way to camp out at night, accompanied me, along with Victor Menago. I drove my seven dogs and had the sled loaded with a hundred and fifty herring and three hind-quarters of caribou. Vicky and her three pups were in the team now and they pulled their hearts out. I couldn't get over the pace they set and kept up, hour after hour.

That night we camped in my tent which we set at the height of land right on the old burn where there is plenty of dry wood. The next morning I left the tent set for our return trip and put thirty-five herring in a gunny sack high in a spruce. That day we ran into a dozen caribou on a small lake and they would have disappeared into the bush at the far end had not Jimmy resorted to the old trick of firing over their heads into the trees beyond, causing them to wheel around and come back down the lake toward us. As they passed broadside both Jimmy and Victor opened fire on them with no effect. When they got down to the other end of this lake Jimmy was able to turn them once more with a shot into the timber ahead of them. I had not fired at first because of the small calibre of my rifle, a .22, while my companions carried the standard .30-.30. When I saw no hits after the first pass, however, and they were coming back again I decided to give it a try. So all three of us joined in firing at them when they passed the second time. Again, none of them dropped and this time they were not fooled by a third shot over their heads to turn them. They kept on going up and into the bush as we looked stupidly at each other.

Then Victor thought he saw one of them go down in the deep snow off the lake, so we drove our dogs up there and, sure enough, we found one dead caribou. As we butchered it there was lots of speculation about which of us had hit it, but when a .22 long slug was found in the heart, speculation ended. The lowly .22 calibre rifle had proved more effective than the big guns. This fresh kill not only provided the ultimate in open-air cooking, a side of ribs for our lunch, but we all had fresh meat to carry with us into Norman, where we arrived at 7 p.m.

Brother Médard was especially grateful for what meat I had brought with me, for it had been a particularly hard winter to get meat, even rabbits. As I visited around the settlement during the following week I picked up rumours that caribou were in the area of Cleve Cinnamon's sawmill, some forty miles south on the Mackenzie. One thing led to another, and four local hunters eagerly joined me with their dog-teams for a caribou hunt in that area. It took a very short day to run up there with empty sleds and camp at the mill with Cleve and his crew who had killed caribou recently on the muskegs ten miles east across the river.

The following morning saw us crossing the frozen Mackenzie and then climbing a precipitous trail up a one-hundred-foot-high cutbank, and then on across country for an hour or so until we ran into the first fresh tracks. Then we tied our teams and proceeded on snow-shoes, each in a different direction. It wasn't long before I spotted three bulls about a mile away in partly open country, walking slowly in my direction. I hid myself in a little island of spruce and waited nearly half an hour until they were so close I couldn't miss. Before leaving Bear Lake I had timed one of the natives out there while he skinned and butchered a young caribou – just over seven minutes. Now I kept track of my own time as I tackled these three bulls and it came to fifteen minutes each. There was room for improvement.

My trip back to the sawmill with my sled-load of meat was highlighted by our descent of that precipitous cutbank to the river. At the top of the bank I stopped and wound the heavy head rope around the load and under the sled, a manoeuvre called a roughlog. It afforded little breaking power, however, and it taxed all my strength to keep the sled from running over the dogs and breaking some of their legs.

Our return trip to Norman turned out to be something of a race. On the trip up two days before we had made fire on an island about half-way. Now one of the Fort Norman natives by the name of Ekokoolay, who was particularly proud of his team and often bragged of their speed, suggested that I go ahead and break trail to the fire spot and then he would take over from there. I agreed and took off in the lead, breaking trail in about four inches of snow that had fallen since we had come up. I got to the fire spot well ahead of my four companions, made a fire, boiled my tea and pulled out again just as they were coming up. Ekokoolay was yelling and waving at me to stop, but I paid no attention. He didn't even stop at the fire but swung right onto my trail determined to overtake me. When we passed close to some cutbanks he fired his rifle in an attempt to excite his dogs into thinking caribou were near, but even with this false encouragement he couldn't overtake me.

Far from having to encourage my dogs, I was worrying about them working so hard that they'd drop, especially the bitch Vicky. Once in a while when I'd stop for a rest, she would be panting so hard she looked like she would choke to death. I got into Norman before sundown, bells jingling and all seven tails waving triumphantly in the air, about four miles ahead of Ekokoolay and his comrades. He never again mentioned his dogs to me. For the first time I had a team of dogs I could be proud of. No longer would I be forced off the trail into deep snow to let faster teams pass or even get into camp at night after my companions were asleep, not to mention the charley horses that plagued me when I was forced to get off the sled and run for miles behind. On the other hand, having a good team did not make me any more popular with the natives; in fact, it seemed to rub them the wrong way, especially when I overtook them and they were forced off the trail to let me pass. Driving dogs was one of their specialties and for a newcomer to show them up took more humility than they could muster.

I made the return trip to Franklin alone in a day-and-a-half without getting out of the sled. When I arrived I was surprised to find the town practically empty. With the exception of the two whites and two old, crippled and blind couples, everyone had moved to the caribou muskegs eight miles south, where they were now living in fourteen tents.

After three more weeks devoted to the carpentry, I decided I needed a break and, driving over to the huge tent camp, moved in with the family of Arsene and Cecile Tetso. This gave me the opportunity of observing the people in intimate surroundings day and night, and my education in their way of living took a giant step forward.

The whole purpose of the tent camp was to be near the huge herd of caribou which had been feeding on the moss of this muskeg ever since our fall hunt. The men of the camp went out daily with their dog-teams, shot and butchered a few caribou and then returned to camp with their sled-load of meat. At this point the women took over to handle the meat and hides, most of which was temporarily thrown up on stages to keep it out of the reach of loose dogs, especially at night. With over 150 people crowded into tents, surrounded by 200 sled dogs, it was a lively scene.

As crowded as the tents were, there was always room for one more and during that first night in Arsene's tent we had to move over for a visitor from Fort Norman, Joe Dillon, a notorious rascal. He claimed that he had made the trip in thirteen hours, stopping only once to make fire, and this we could readily believe, because Joe's wicked, long-legged huskies were famous for their ability to cover ground in record time. The RCMP were aware of this, too; I happened to be visiting the barracks the winter before and watched the police entice Joe to part with five dogs by laying out 250 one-dollar bills on the table. He would never part with the huge bitch that produced these teams, however.

Joe was the darkest complexioned native I had seen and might have had some Negro blood in his veins. He told me of an incident when he was working as a guide on the Canol pipeline where the American Forces included a thousand black men whom their white counterparts often called "Midnight." Joe picked up the term and one day, when he greeted one of them, saying, "Hello there, Midnight," the black man, eyeing Joe's colour, replied, "You's about a quarter ta twelve youself!" Joe got a big kick out of it.

For a few years Joe was persona non grata at the Wells, accused of stealing equipment, but later he was re-hired to work at a salvage operation he had suggested. Joe had convinced the refinery manager at Imperial Oil that they were losing a lot of empty barrels off their dock during unloading operations. He offered to retrieve them for a dollar each. In order to do this work Joe installed himself and his wife Kapa in a tent a half-mile down river. It was soon apparent that far more drums were being lost than had been realized and Joe was busy from morning till night with his freighter canoe. Then one day the dock foreman happened to see an accomplice of Joe's "accidentally" kicking a barrel into the river and the scam was uncovered.

Another time at Fort Norman I had asked Joe if he knew of any old tent stove I could buy. The following day he brought me just what I needed and wouldn't accept a cent. I smelled a rat, but it was weeks before I heard a native talking about losing the stove from his tent across the river.

Joe threw his bedroll on the spruce boughs next to mine and snored peacefully that night as I recalled some of these incidents. True or not, the following day Joe proved himself to be quite a man in my eyes. We had decided to hunt together, harnessed up at first light and were off at breakneck speed in a crackling forty below. My team followed Joe's out of camp and all I could do was hold on to the handle bars as the small spruce raked our sleds and broke one of my mitt cords. Up ahead, there was Joe sitting nonchalantly inside his cariole facing backwards while, with bare hands, he proceeded to whittle a toothpick with his axe. Joe's performance could be compared to Gene Autrey's riding hell-bent-for-leather from a band of dangerous, mounted Apaches, arrows whistling all around him, while he sat backwards in the saddle rolling a cigarette. I was impressed.

In twenty minutes we entered the broad, open muskeg full of grazing caribou and Joe outlined his plan to drive a bunch of them right past me while I waited, concealed behind a clump of spruce. Joe carried out his drive perfectly, but when I raised my rifle to fire I couldn't pull the trigger and all the animals ran safely by me. Joe pulled up and we had a look at my gun. When I had broken the stock of this .270 earlier in the winter I had put an old stock on it without test-firing it. The trigger hole lacked about a quarter of an inch of clearance. It didn't take me long to make this adjustment with my jack-knife and we were successful in securing nine caribou with it before we returned to camp.

With our meat safely stowed up on Arsene's stage we retired to his tent for the night. And it was a night to remember: to my eyes it looked like something that might have happened in pre-historic times. We watched the children dig live warble fly larvae out of the fresh caribou hides and gobble them like jelly beans, while Arsene's ancient, toothless mother sat close to the candle cracking leg bones with the back of an old butcher knife to get at the marrow.

At the end of March I got an unexpected visitor in the person of Brother Henri Tesnière, flown in from Aklavik on orders from the bishop to help me finish the inside carpentry. Unfortunately he was about five months late and I had completed everything except the quarter-round moulding, which he finished in less than three days. Although he offered to spend the balance of the winter with me, he had instructions to proceed to Fort Smith to work on the construction of the new St. Anne's Hospital there as soon as my mission was completed, so I felt obliged to send him on. My aide-de-camp Naquerichile took him and his 300-pound tool box to Norman with my team.

Soon everyone moved back into the settlement to celebrate Easter. This time we not only had all the religious ceremonies connected with this great feast day, but I was able to hold the Ice Carnival the following day. With some difficulty I was able to persuade some of the younger men to run their dogs in a five-mile race out around the flags I had stuck in the snow of the bay, while the older men raced the clock to chip down to water with their ice chisels. Most of the afternoon, however, was occupied shooting at targets, a life-size caribou at two hundred yards for the men, using their .30-.30's, and a ptarmigan for the women, who shot with a .22. In the evening I awarded prizes to the winners. This was followed by a drum dance in the mission common room.

As the old log mission was now unoccupied, Joe Dillon asked to use it temporarily. I let him have it on condition that he didn't make any brew while he was in there. One day I could hear Joe's wife Kapa singing her drinking song, "You are my sunshine," so I made an excuse to go over there to look for something I had left in the attic. There I found a ten-gallon keg of simmering firewater. Joe feigned surprise and blamed it all on Kapa. Soon after, he returned to his home at Fort Norman and I got new tenants in the old mission, Arsene Tetso and his family.

Arsene needed a roof over his family's head because his little five-year-old boy John was sick. He had started getting headaches in the fall and would wake up at night crying. I kept a record of his pulse and temperature for a week and wired all the symptoms to the doctor in Aklavik. He replied that he suspected spinal meningitis and advised me to get the boy to Fort Norman for evacuation to hospital as soon as possible. When I discussed this with Arsene the first thing he did was to ask the boy if he wanted to go to the hospital. Of course, the boy said, "No!" This reply seemed to settle the matter for Arsene, but I was more insistent, trying to convince him that it was a matter of life or death. I offered to take the boy into Norman myself and to keep him with me until he left, but I could not get the father to agree. They left to spend the winter in the bush. When I camped with them at the big muskeg while caribou hunting, the boy seemed to be improving. I saw him out playing without a hat and running to the neighbour's tent bare-footed. After Easter, however, little John was worse again, and when they moved into the old mission house I was acutely aware of his suffering.

He began throwing up his food and was soon so weak that he lost all desire to play. His mother Cecile kept him in bed with no objections from him while I tempered my needle-and-penicillin visits by making sure I had some little gift with me which I let him search through my pockets to find. When he was more or less free from pain he would entertain me by playing a miniature drum his father had made him and singing one of the dance songs in imitation of the elders. Yet most days he would just lie there holding his little head and crying, *"Se kwi eya! Se kwi eya!"* – "My head hurts! My head hurts!" As the weeks dragged on and his condition deteriorated, his poor mother reflected his pain and tried in vain to alleviate it. Having already lost three of her six children, she was no stranger to sickness and death.

As the disease progressed and little John got worse, they took him from his wooden bed and placed him in the middle of the cabin floor, where I would invariably find him surrounded by visitors. Finally he began having fits or seizures that caused his muscles to twitch, while he ground his teeth and muttered incoherently. The good women of the village stayed by his side day and night holding his little hands and feet during seizures and putting a stick wrapped in caribou skin between his teeth so he wouldn't break them. I looked in vain in my *Merck Manual* for any medicine I could give him in addition to the penicillin, but could find none. Evidently tubercular meningitis was impossible to cure under these circumstances.

We did persevere in prayer, too, hoping for the miracle that never happened. I realized that his days were numbered, and yet when his time expired and the women ran to tell me, yelling, "Negille! Negille!" – "He's not breathing! He's not breathing!" – I felt a sudden pang of grief I hadn't felt with the other deaths we had experienced. I rushed to his side and felt for a pulse that was not there, but I could only watch helplessly as his mother kept rubbing his little limbs and calling him back through her tears. He was gone. Finally she raised her voice in that heart-rending chant of grief, the keening peculiar to her race, mournful and desolate. I think all of us standing by died a little that day with young John Tetso.

That afternoon Arsene came over with a notched length of spruce pole to indicate his son's length and together in silence we built a pine box. I suppose I could have told him that his son might still be alive if he had let me take him to the hospital the fall before, but what was the use now? The next day was a clear, warm Sunday in May. After the eleven o'clock mass we put the small casket on Arsene's sled and pulled it up to the cemetery. There on that peaceful knoll covered with caribou moss and sheltered by some huge pines we took turns digging down four feet into the soft sand. After I had blessed the grave and said the ritual prayers the box was lowered and the women, using tin plates as shovels, filled up the hole. Then Arsene and Cecile knelt by the grave's cross, praying, caressing that cross as if it were a part of their son. And above it, on a ten-foot pole, waved a small white flag which, I was informed, was put there to amuse the soul of the departed so that it would not leave the body until the day of judgement, when both would be reunited again and ascend to the Heavenly Father. All the graves had them and I thought it a rather nice custom dating back to pre-historic times and asserting this people's belief in an afterlife.

As I got closer to these people I became more aware that such old customs, superstitions – call them what you will – were still part of their lives. For example, I was on my way to Fort Norman by dogs the winter before, when one of the women came walking toward me with an armful of fish, suddenly dropped them, and ran back. I found out later that she had noticed the end sticks of a net set under the ice and it was taboo for her to cross any net. For a woman to break this taboo would doom that net from catching any more fish for its owner. This rule applied to nets set in open water in summertime too and, if those in a canoe could not avoid crossing a net, the women were first let off on the shore to walk until the net had been passed. In fact, almost all the taboos affected the women alone.

I had a bear skin on the floor at the door to my office and at first I didn't realize all the difficulty this was causing my female parishioners who, to get past it, had to shuffle along one side with their feet under the hide. As soon as I was made aware of this taboo, I moved it.

I was puzzled for a long time over the fact that young girls were tied to the centre pole of their tents just after they had learned to walk. I thought to myself that they were being restrained from running outside where they could be bitten by one of the sled dogs. I found out that the real reason for this was to keep them from inadvertently walking over a man's blanket or maybe putting on his cap, both strictly taboo for a girl.

One day Chief Francis Eya walked into the mission, as was his usual morning habit, and announced to me that a certain girl was having her first menstrual period. When I asked him what she would do to celebrate, he informed me that she would have to stay indoors for a month and that during this time she couldn't eat any choice food or sweets or she would be fond of a soft life all her years. Nor could she even look at a knife or she would be lazy. Just how any Hareskin woman could escape the drudgery of her race to a soft or lazy life seemed hard to imagine. Later, one of the women told me just how difficult her periods could make a woman's life. Besides having to inform the household and restrict her movement about, if they happened to be travelling she could not ride on the sled, nor even use the same trail. Instead she was obliged to break her own trail alongside! One can just imagine what this must have cost her if the snow was deep and she was forced to use snowshoes.

The women were also warned about leaving any stray hairs from their head lying about, under penalty of having to return after death to find every one of them. To avoid this they would stand by the fire when they combed their heads and put any loose hair directly into it. If the fire in the stove popped and hissed, as it often does when a pocket of sap burns, they must immediately feed the fire by throwing in a morsel of food: this was the evil spirit asking to be fed. There was a set formula to be said at the same time which meant: "Make me happy, fire, and give me a long life. Thank you."

Although these taboos made life so miserable for the women, it puzzled me that it was the older women especially who taught them to the young girls. When these girls asked me what I thought about them, I had to admit that I could see very little in them that contradicted Christianity and so they could observe them if they wished. Nonetheless, I had to add that I thought they could get to heaven just as easily by not keeping these taboos. Just keeping the ten commandments was work enough for any Christian. I could not help recalling the passage in Luke's Gospel in which Jesus addresses the penitent woman, saying, "Your faith has been your salvation. Now go in peace."

Not many of the taboos affected the men of the tribe and those that did caused little difficulty. On several occasions, however, I was asked to lend my rifle to shoot a wolf, as they believed that using their own for that purpose would jinx it for good. Being a white man, I was exempt from the effects of this taboo. Another admonition was never to strike a wounded caribou with a stick, though why anybody would resort to this means to dispatching the animal was not at all clear. If a hunter were out of shells, a blow to the animal's head with an axe, which everyone carried, would be far more effective.

Although there was at least one person living on Bear Lake who possessed a good deal of medicine power, called Inkon, I never heard of him actually performing any seances in exercise of this power. At Fort Norman I witnessed old David Yukon put on a performance the summer before. His patient, ironically named George Doctor, was suffering from torn ligaments in his shoulder and, although he had been to the nurse first, he didn't think he was healing fast enough. So he contracted David to work native medicine on him for the price of one tanned moose hide. Although David had a log cabin he preferred to practise his art in a tent where both doctor and patient sat cross-legged facing each other across the fire. David beat on a drum and chanted incantations for hours on end. One of the bystanders warned me not to walk behind David or he would automatically "eat your spirit," weakening his magic powers.

George submitted to the full treatment, paid the fee and was back at the nursing station the following day for more of the free white man's medicine. When I talked to him later, he confessed that he wasn't sure just what power, if any, David could conjure up, but when a person is in pain he will look for help from anyone. I got the same opinion from some of the youth at Franklin, who were sceptical of these old taboos, yet observed some of them just in case there was some truth in them. At least observing the minimum satisfied their more traditional parents and provided a fire escape if the dire predictions for those breaking the taboos proved true after all. This attitude reminded me of a grizzled old trapper I met at Fort Fitzgerald when I was coming into the North. Seeing my clerical garb, he was encouraged to regale me with his philosophy of life, which went something like this: "You only live once. Right, Father? So I whoop it up every time I get the chance. On the other hand, you never can tell, there might just be a hell after all, so I do a lot of praying too!"

After the death of little John Tetso, Arsene, following custom, moved his family out of the old mission cabin. They didn't seem to fear death itself as much as they feared the dead, the spirits surrounding the dead and the places where they died. I didn't mind using what little knowledge I had of medicine to help them, but those cases that ended in death – five during my first year there – were particularly frustrating and discouraging. When a few days later young Marie Naedzo came to me with a huge gash in her wrist and I was able to close it successfully with nine stitches, I felt I was accomplishing something. Soon after that Victor Beyonnie came with an axe cut in his ankle which I stitched up, but it festered later and I had to put him on penicillin shots to clear up the infection. The mission door was never locked, so if I were needed during the night for some medical emergency and I was asleep, the messenger would come right into my bedroom and hold a lit match in front of my eyes until I awakened. I learned later that this was standard procedure, because if a person is awakened too abruptly the spirit might not be able to rejoin the body in time and death would result.

About the middle of May the men of the village left town for the spring hunt of muskrat and beaver. Most took a thirteen-foot hunting canoe with them as well as some pack dogs, especially the older dogs, as they had outlived their usefulness and were making a one-way trip. Now that I had most of the essential inside work done, I turned to working out in the warm spring sun and built myself one of those hunting canoes, followed by a steel-shod runner-type sled the Eskimos call a *komatik* and the Bear Lakers call a *dechunkala*, literally "a ladder," because with its spaced wooden rungs across the top it resembles one.

When the wildfowl began flying north overhead I had little difficulty persuading the Hudson Bay manager Bob Williams to close up the store and accompany me on our own spring mini-hunt. I had new moose-hide moccasins for my team to protect them from the candling ice. With my new canoe on top of the komatik we headed northeast along the shore of the lake. With the surface snow melted down to a hard ice, the travelling was easy and the sun so hot we hardly needed parkas. Canada geese flew so low over us we actually shot some without getting off the sled. About twenty-five miles down the lake we set up our tent next to a small open lake, where we had ducks landing all night long and a midnight sun to shoot by.

Back at the mission three days later I built a few more chairs and put a new canvas on my twenty-two-foot freighter canoe. Open water was beginning to appear in the bay ice and the sight of ducks landing on it was too great a temptation to resist. One day I harnessed three dogs to the komatik and ran around on the ice near the settlement, shooting ducks in these spots of open water. I was using a lead dog named Taffy that I had bought from Victor Dolphus. When he saw a wounded duck flapping around on one of these open spots in the lake ice, he headed straight for it. I grabbed my shotgun and .22 and slid off the sled, just before it followed the dogs into the deep water. Taffy grabbed the wounded duck in his mouth, swam to the ice edge, and pulled himself out, followed by the other two dogs and the sled. They headed directly home. When I got there I found the duck sitting in my kitchen sink, still very much alive. My neighbour Beya had taken it from Taffy's mouth and put it safely inside the mission house. After that I quit hunting ducks by dog-team.

Toward the end of June, with no mail for months and old-age pensioners badly in need of their monthly sixty-five-dollar cheques, I decided to make the trip to Fort Norman. I had written the postal authorities requesting a monthly mail delivery by air, but was turned down because of our small population. Just as soon as there was enough open water along the shore I shoved off with a teenager named Onkie in my big freighter canoe powered by the faithful nine-horse Johnson. We got around the edge of the lake ice, but for the first ten miles down the Great Bear River I could not start the motor because the floating ice was so thick. Our arrival at Fort Norman coincided with the passage of the mission supply boat *Sant'Anna* heading down river and, because I had been suffering from toothaches, I decided to go at least as far as Norman Wells with her to seek the services of a dentist. Although the RCAF mapping contingent was still operating out of the Wells, they had no one capable of fixing teeth, but offered me a quick flight to Yellowknife on one of their Lancaster bombers. I not only got to ride on this historic plane, but when the crew heard that I had held a pilot's licence they let me handle the controls for a segment of the flight. My headphones were connected to the navigator on board and all I had to do was make the heading corrections he gave me.

While getting my teeth fixed in Yellowknife I resided at the log mission in the Old Town with the famous Father Alfred Gathy, a colourful character who sped around town on a motorcycle, his cassock flying in the wind. There were a lot of interesting people to visit around Yellowknife and it was a treat to be speaking my own language again. Henry Busse, the town's official photographer, showed me some of his interesting collection. Coming as I did from the Kodak City of Rochester, New York, it was only natural that I had carried a camera north with me and, although I didn't have it on this trip, I did have some of the thousand 35 mm slides I had taken while at Fort Franklin. One evening when I was showing them at the home of the mining engineer, Norm Byrne, he had as guest a young writer named Pierre Berton, to whom I sold a lot of photos later when he became Managing Editor of *Maclean's Magazine*. One day Father Gathy sent me by the mission canoe over to the Indian village on Vale Island to conduct services for the natives living there and the editor of the local newspaper, Ted Horton, sent his son with me to act as acolyte. Another day I took a walk up the dirt road two miles to the new townsite, where the only completed building was the new theatre. The new site of Yellowknife seemed to be out in the middle of nowhere and not nearly as picturesque as the original townsite along the blue waters of Yellowknife Bay. Fort Smith was still the unofficial capital of the North West Territories, but later Yellowknife would be officially designated.

After returning to Norman Wells I got a ride upstream to Fort Norman with Dolphus Norris in his roomy scow. From there I went on up the Great Bear River in my canoe, loaded with provisions. I hired a crew to go ten miles up along the north shore, and help me cut fifteen cords of green spruce, and raft them back to the settlement for next winter's fuel supply. With a team of growing huskies and eight hungry pups I had to visit my nets every day and make plans to get ahead on the dog food for the coming winter. So late in August I decided to move my fishing operation up along the north shore to a place known as Finger Bay. I invited my old friend Aunty Zole, another old crony, Natuzo, plus my steady worker, Naquerichile, to go with me.

Just before I set out, the Hudson Bay Company Beaver aircraft landed with a Mr. Scurfield, the District Manager, making the annual tour of his posts. He walked over to the mission with the mail he had picked up en route at Fort Norman and we chewed the fat for a few minutes. The war in Korea, he said, was threatening to close down so many of their northern stores that he was forced to raise the price of gas from $1.00 to $1.10 a gallon and other staples similarly. I took my unopened mail and ran down to the shore where my companions were patiently waiting in my canoe.

It was only after pitching tent thirty miles down the lake that I got a chance to open my mail. One letter that immediately caught my eye was postmarked Fort Smith and, as I suspected, it was from the bishop. What I didn't suspect was that it would terminate my life at Fort Franklin. It was a new obedience. I was being assigned to Goldfields, Saskatchewan! As I read on I learned the reason for this sudden transfer: a new mining town was soon to be built at a uranium discovery just north of Goldfields. Because it would be populated mostly by English-speaking whites, the bishop needed an English-speaking priest there to start that mission.

In view of this turn of events I pulled up my nets the following day and headed back to Franklin. Two days later I received a message from Fort Norman via the HBC telegraph that the bishop was already winging his way north in his new plane with my replacement and would arrive in a few days. I packed my trunk and put the mission in A-1 shape, even baking a new batch of bread. Seeing that I still had time, I got busy building a badly needed dock. It was out fifty feet by the sixth of September when the bishop's Aeronca float plane appeared in the sky. Father Bill Leising, another American, was the one chosen to pilot it and he was now making his first flight north. For the first time, too, a float aircraft could taxi right in to shore and its passengers step off dry-shod onto terra firma.

I led the way on a tour of the new mission and premises, proud to show how much I and my people had accomplished during the past two years on less than eight thousand dollars. His Excellency seemed pleased with this latest in his chain of some forty-odd missions throughout the North. He predicted that my experience in carpentry work here would stand me in good stead as I started my next mission on Lake Athabaska.

The next morning the bishop presided at a Solemn High Mass and conferred the Sacrament of Confirmation on twenty-two young aspirants. It was a fitting climax and the ultimate use to which this new building could be put no matter how many years it would stand. I took advantage of the occasion to say a few words of farewell to my parishioners. If my halting Hareskin carried a note of sadness in it, it was genuine. In the future I would be working with many different peoples of the North, from Crees to Eskimos, but with none of them would I establish such a close bond as I had with the people of Fort Franklin.

After lunch Bill Leising flew the bishop back to Fort Norman and brought back my successor, Father Victor Phillipe, with whom I had only a few minutes to share before my departure. Worst of all, the small cabin size of the Aeronca prevented me from taking my trunk or even one female dog with which to start up a new team. I showed Victor all the precious objects he was inheriting: not only the bright, snug mission, but the newly canvassed canoe at its new dock, seven fine sled dogs plus the new litter of six brothers, the harnesses embroidered in silk, the two sleds and the large hunting canoe, three pairs of new snowshoes in the attic and three nets set in the lake. Nothing was lacking for the new incumbent. It was lucky for him, but wrenching for me to be so suddenly uprooted.

I finally got a chance to ride in the new aircraft that had been donated to the diocese, but it was a short trip. We took off at 2 p.m. and headed for Fort Norman, where I was to catch the *Sant'Anna* on her return trip up river. We were hardly half-way when the cylinder head temperature gauge shot up into the red, indicating trouble, and we were forced to put down on a small lake which was just where we needed it. We were stymied, however, in our efforts to locate the trouble, because the aircraft's set of Snap-On tools had been stolen off the dock at Fort Resolution the week before. Our only chance of getting help was through the aircraft's VHF radio, set to the Department of Transport's frequency, and we kept calling every half-hour. By supper time we had broken out the box of emergency rations; they were very sparse and mouldy. I took a walk around the lake with the .22, but couldn't even find a muskrat. The two of us squeezed into the Aeronca's cabin and tried to stretch out on its floor, passing the night in fitful sleep.

September 8th, the feast of the Birth of the Blessed Virgin Mary, a feast important to the Oblates, dawned foggy and wet with the temperature close to freezing. We resumed broadcasting blindly on the aircraft's radio, giving our position and predicament, rekindled the fire on shore and stood around it helplessly, trying to revive our spirits. Had we known it, we had reason to rejoice, because our message had been picked up by Royal Canadian Signalman Moe Lynn at Fort Wrigley, who had a reputation for picking up distress calls. At that moment help was on the way. A search and rescue C-47 aircraft had been searching for bush pilot Johnny Bourassa east of Great Bear Lake and refuelling at Norman Wells. They got our co-ordinates from Moe and were soon circling overhead, dropping three kegs of 80/87 Aviation gas, a wrench attached to a long streamer, and a note saying, "We will continue to orbit until you take off"! Apparently they figured that we were simply out of gas. What neither they nor we knew at the time was that we had a hole the size of a half-dollar through the head of No. 5 piston. The Aeronca wouldn't get airborne for another couple of days.

They soon left us, but it wasn't long before we heard the raucous sound of a Norseman aircraft approaching from the south. It turned out to be the Eldorado machine which was just finishing up their summer's work at Port Radium and ferrying men over to Bennett Field when they got word of our trouble from the RCAF Dakota. Our rescuers were pilot Don Ferris, and engineer George Franks, who lent us his tools. When Bill Leising heard that they were on their way to the mine at Beaverlodge near Goldfields, he urged me to take advantage of this direct flight. Reluctantly abandoning my plans for a trip up river and a chance to see new areas of the North, I agreed. I left on the Norseman, while Bill got a new piston up from Edmonton flown in by Pappy Hill. Ferris flew us back to the Great Bear River where he dropped off Franks. Then, because it was too late to cross Bear Lake, we decided to overnight at Franklin and landed in the small lake just west of the village.

As we walked through the village to the mission, the people thought that the bishop had changed his mind and sent me back. I felt like MacArthur returning to Corregidor with everyone running to greet me and following us right into the mission. It was difficult to explain to them all that had happened since 2 p.m. the previous afternoon and how I was now headed east instead of west. Anyway, I told them that I would conduct one last service the following morning, but it would have to be at 6 a.m., because we had a long flight ahead of us. The standing-room-only crowd that filled the chapel the next morning was the finest tribute I could have gotten from the people of Fort Franklin.

Our long walk through town and back to the aircraft provided a chance for further demonstrations of affection: little children breaking away from their parents and running after me, calling "Yati" – "Father," and wanting to be picked up for one last time and carried at least a few steps; Rosie Baton putting down her water pails, drying her hands on her apron before shaking hands, Cecile Tatti running to give me a farewell present, an embroidered tobacco pouch. Now I was glad the Aeronca had let us down, and doubly so, for now I had room to take my trunk, and one of the dogs. So I chose the pure white bitch Trinket. At least I had a living souvenir of two great years on the shores of Great Bear Lake.

10

GOLDFIELDS

Sunday, September 9th, 1951: a grey, dull, rainy day over Great Bear Lake, the weather perfectly in tune with my feelings as we taxied out and took off from Fort Franklin. I occupied the right front seat of the Norseman, with pilot Don Ferris at the controls to my left and Trinket crouched on the floor behind me, next to my trunk.

We headed east along the south shore of Keith Arm, flying over the legendary Gorabee Island, past Grizzly Bear Mountain, on across open water to Eldorado Mine on the east shore of the lake. We landed on Echo Bay and taxied up to the dock to refuel. There was no time to walk up to the cookhouse for coffee. In this kind of flying weather pilots tend to be in a particular hurry. Ferris was irritable and profane to boot. We filled both wing tanks and headed due south. The rain turned to snow, forcing us to fly just above the trees all the way to Yellowknife, where we again landed to refuel. Again, there was no time to visit. It was a race against the weather and the remaining daylight hours. I took Trinket out for a brief walk-around and we were again airborne across Great Slave Lake. Ferris noticed me praying my rosary and asked if I doubted his flying abilities. I didn't, but in flying weather like this a prayer for heavenly protection couldn't hurt.

At 6 p.m. we finally reached the north shore of Lake Athabaska. We could soon make out the huge headframe of the old Box Mine and, close to it, the town of Goldfields. I breathed a

sigh of relief as we touched down on the protected bay in front
of it and taxied to the town dock. The wooden buildings were
scattered between huge rock outcrops and had those high, false
fronts one associates with the western frontier. The few locals
who sauntered down to the waterfront no doubt saw something
unusual: out of the float plane came a young figure in black sou-
tane leading a white sled dog – obviously some sort of missionary. At least they weren't repelled by my clerical appearance, for
a few of the boys took my luggage and led me to the RCMP barracks. Meanwhile the pilot took off to fly over to Eldorado's
camp on Beaverlodge Lake a few miles north.

The local Mountie, Constable Bill Poole, received me cor-
dially and walked me to the R.C. Mission, a clapboard church
and rectory badly in need of paint, thoroughly abandoned and
locked up tight. We had to break the padlock on the rectory door.
Once in I was confronted by an empty barn of a place, two sto-
reys high, practically empty of furniture and cooking utensils,
draped in cobwebs with a very creaky floor. It was the exact
opposite of the bright new mission I had left that morning at Fort
Franklin. I sat down on my trunk and pulled out my pipe to pon-
der the situation. The constable dusted off a wooden bench and
sat down gingerly, half expecting it to collapse under him as he
remarked, "Understand there's been no one living here since
Father Rivet was killed some ten years ago."

Father Rivet? My predecessor, killed? Right here? This was
all news to me. Still, didn't it fit in with the general atmosphere
of the place? I couldn't wait to hear the whole story and the
young Mountie pieced it together as best he could from what the
remaining old-timers had told him. The old missionary in his
seventies had had a clique of enemies in Goldfields, men dead set
against him. Some say that it was because he was instrumental in
getting a couple of prostitutes run out of town. Whatever the reason, they hatched a grisly plan to get rid of him. One of their
accomplices acted as a lookout upstairs, right above where we
were sitting. He sat by the window, munching sandwiches, waiting for the priest to return on that ill-fated night. Then Father

Rivet completely disappeared from the community. Nobody had seen anything. Nobody knew anything.

Some six weeks later a group of Boy Scouts on a picnic three miles east of the town discovered his body at the foot of a cliff. There followed some sort of a frontier inquest and trial but it was mostly hush-hush. Names of some prominent men in town, including the doctor, were mentioned. It seemed as though a lot of people knew more than they were willing to tell. Father Rivet's superior, Bishop Breynat, never pressed the case. He simply closed up this mission and never even mentioned it in his published memoirs. This was the gist of what the constable told me that first night, but later in cleaning up the house I came across an interesting set of notes obviously written by someone following these events who had been doing some private investigating. This prompted him to ask the following questions:

Why were Botten and Hargreaves seen coming from the bush (in the direction where the body was later found) at four in the morning when they should have been coming off their eight p.m. to four a.m. shift at the Consolidated Mining and Smelting (Box) Mine?

Why was Cox, the manager of the local Bank of Montreal, seen running from the mission around midnight of that same night?

Why did Sam Hargreaves report to the policemen Ball and Lowe that the Father was missing at four in the morning?

Why were the scouts told by their director, Rev. Mr. Heather, on the day of their picnic, that if they looked in a certain section of the bush they would find something?

Why was the found body left wrapped in a piece of canvas on the point two days before an autopsy was performed by Dr. Brownridge?

Why would Police Inspector Desrosiers tell the two Catholics serving on the jury that he wanted a verdict "death by exposure" returned when the trial was held?

Why was a certain page torn from the Father's diary?

Why? Why? Why? Plenty of questions, but no answers. Had I inherited an unsolved murder? Now, ten years later, would it be advisable for me to raise the issue or even ask any questions? I decided it would not. I also decided I wouldn't eat at the haunted mission that night. So the constable and I walked downtown and had supper at Hap Cave's restaurant. Later I borrowed a sleeping bag and a flashlight from the barracks and returned to the darkened rectory. I did not sleep well that first night.

The following morning the blue waters of the bay sparkled under a bright cobalt sky and my world looked rosier. I put on my cassock and cross and walked down to Steve Yanik's hotel and ordered breakfast, which was cheerfully served by a girl known as Bubbles. Everyone seated around that counter seemed friendly and eager to tell me about their town. I soon found out that there were three restaurants, plus a bakery. There was also the usual Hudson Bay Company store, plus two free-traders with their own stores. McMurray Air Service ran a charter service out of the town, featuring four-place Stinsons. There was a resident geologist and a mining recorder, a game officer and a radio operator, a post office and a pool room that doubled as the local theatre.

Although the town had been built on gold, I soon learned that this mineral was passé, having been supplanted by uranium. The radioactive mineral was the new topic of conversation and, not only that, there was talk about moving Goldfields holus-bolus over on the ice in winter ten miles to a new townsite to be called Uranium City. With all this information under my hat and a good breakfast under my belt, I lit my pipe and walked out.

Meeting two Chipewyan Indians outside, I tried out my Hareskin language on them with discouraging results. It was obvious that I would now be faced with learning a new dialect. There were also some Crees in town whose language was absolutely foreign to me, but luckily they did speak some French.

Noticing some pots and pans in a window I wandered into Alec MacIver's General Store and was pleasantly served by his wife Del. When I walked out half-an-hour later I was laden down with most of the vital items missing at the mission, like an axe, a gas lamp, a basin, pots and pans and some basic grub. I returned to my empty quarters and began a general cleanup. That afternoon, to get the dust out of my lungs, I went for a walk around the west end of the bay and came upon the one-room school house. I was invited in to meet the thirty-four children in attendance by their charming teacher, Miss Evelyn Lamontagne. Before I knew it I was at the blackboard drawing pictures of animals and cowboys or anything else my attentive audience requested, and the ice was broken.

As the days wore on I gradually met everyone in town including the average number of characters. One of the most unusual was a displaced Englishman named Gus Hawker, who operated one of the trading posts. He told me that his native wife deserted him in Fort McMurray and he was raising their six kids alone. Four of them he had named after months of the year; April, May, June and August. June was only thirteen at the time, but three years later when she turned sixteen, Gus married her! Just how he managed this legally I never heard. One year he made *Time Magazine* when he took a dozen beaver hides to Buckingham Palace and presented them to the Queen in the name of all Canadians. His store was an absolute mess, with everything thrown helter-skelter, the floor littered with mixed grub and hardware, and his money thrown in cardboard boxes. He claimed to be a member of my flock, but, like a lot of other nominal Catholics in town, I never saw him in church.

Another day I discovered a Mrs. Livingstone living alone in a house hidden among the rocks and trees. Her husband was a prospector and was seldom at home. To keep her company during his long absences she had acquired about two dozen cats which she kept inside, fearful of the sled dogs roaming the town. She had opened a trap door into the attic and had a special ramp built so the cats could use the upper floor as their play area. I sat there drinking tea with her, her pets constantly going to and coming from the attic. Only the aromatic smoke from my pipe overcame the heavy scent of cat gas in the air and I marvelled that a person could live in such an atmosphere.

According to Gordon Carruthers, who ran the pool hall and sold beer on the side, Goldfields was an unusually thirsty town: it took a minimum of 700 cases of beer a month to quench that thirst. The effects of this addiction was particularly notable on Saturday nights. On one of these a group of inebriates got hold of the good constable and threw him in a mud hole. One midnight I answered a knock at the rectory door and a Mrs. Montgomery asked if I would accompany her to the church: her husband was on a drunk and in that condition he often felt religious. Sure enough, we did find him slumped over one of the benches. So if old John Barleycorn brought out the worst in some townsfolk, it brought out the best in others.

Constable Poole and Game Officer Chick Terry were making a trip over to the new Eldorado uranium mine site and invited me along. As we portaged the freighter canoe from Lake Athabaska some three hundred yards into Beaverlodge Lake we passed the cemetery and my eye fell upon the grave of Father Rivet. I said nothing to my companions. What was the awful secret that lay buried there with him? There was no answer to this question, but it disturbed and troubled me. My gloomy thoughts were soon chased from my mind by the bright, warm sun lighting up the colourful fall foliage. Chick picked off a half-dozen ducks with his twelve-gauge as we motored east into Beaverlodge Lake.

The Beaverlodge townsite was fronted by a long, sandy beach and the new homes were being constructed among the trees without disturbing them. Unlike the old townsite of Goldfields, there were no rocky outcroppings among dilapidated buildings. We pulled our boat up on the beach and walked up to the administration building. I was lucky to meet and have lunch in the "Blue Room" with some of the top men in the Eldorado hierarchy, including the President, Bill Bennett, the District Manager, Dr. E. B. (Gil) Gillanders, the Mine Manager, Robert Sexsmith, and the President of the Northern Transportation

Company, Frank Broderick. Also present at the table were a Mr. Merrit from the U.S. Atomic Energy Control Board and a Mr. Gooding from Saskatchewan Natural Resources. Our conversation centred on the building of the new townsite, to be called Uranium City, five miles west of the mine site. Following the meal I had a private meeting with Bennett and Gillanders about my role in serving the mine as chaplain and I was urged to begin at the earliest moment, possibly working out of the Goldfields mission as accommodations were at a premium at this stage of the Beaverlodge operation.

Back at Goldfields I continued to get acquainted. It was the rare walk through town when I didn't run into some inebriated character who didn't profess to be a good Catholic. I got into endless discussions on faith and morals and the meaning of life every time I took a meal at the hotel. Often I ate with the many native families who were drawn into town during the summer to take casual jobs.

Perhaps in their home settlements the natives were faithful to their religious obligations, but here on their "vacations," so to speak, they were slow to respond to the church bell. Nevertheless, I persevered in ringing for morning mass and afternoon rosary. If success for a man of the cloth were to be judged solely by attendance at services, he could easily become discouraged. Yet we all know that God's work can be accomplished in mysterious ways, despite appearances. So, who knows, I argued to myself, maybe I'm having a good influence without realizing it.

An old pilot-friend from Norman Wells, Red Hammond, flew me and Trinket along the north shore of Lake Athabaska and landed us on the bay in front of the sprawling mission at Fort Chipewyan, where I was soon welcomed by its numerous staff. This mission, founded in the middle of the nineteenth century, was still in its golden years and growing, with a complement of 4 priests, 5 Brothers, 14 nuns and 150 children in its boarding school. I was absorbed into its vast structure without causing a ripple, just another figure in clerical garb. For me this was a relief after my conspicuous role at Goldfields.

I was conducted to the newly built rectory, a frame building, huge by northern standards, with a typical barn roof containing a beehive of rooms measuring a scant six by ten feet, one of which was assigned to me. That evening our religious superior treated the Oblate community to a "*Gaudeamus*," or celebration, of home-made wine and maple sugar in the recreation room in honour of my arrival. In my broken French I tried as best I could to express my appreciation.

If there was any doubt in my mind that I was back in a formal house of our congregation, it was dispelled the following morning when the 4:50 wake-up bell echoed up the stairwell and stridently summoned us to morning prayer in the chapel at 5:15. There would be no more sleeping in until 7:30 as I had been doing the past two years at Franklin. Now my day was strictly regulated: no if's, and's or but's, just follow that bell. My recent freedom had made me forget how "caged in" the bell made me feel, but now I detected in my subconscious some empathy with Tennyson's lines, "Theirs not to make reply, Theirs not to reason why, Theirs but to do and die." Perhaps it was not that dramatic. Between that morning wake-up bell and the one at 8:45 p.m. calling us to night prayer, there were another dozen bells summoning us to a particular place for a certain activity. And there was plenty of activity besides the spiritual.

This mission, like all the others in the Mackenzie Vicariate, was practically self-supporting. It had a large farm under cultivation and at one time got the prize for the best wheat in Alberta. It had an active fish camp on the lake fifty miles east, a wood camp fifteen miles to the west and of course a good team of horses. What particularly impressed me was their dog-team neatly caged in their individual corrals. They were huge animals, bred from stock in Tuktoyaktuk. Three were pure white. My Trinket was in heat, so I had a perfect mate for her.

The day after my arrival I was down in the potato field helping with this important yearly harvest. We were all there: Fathers, Brothers, Sisters, hired hands, even the school kids. It was a gala event and we made short work of the spuds. It was a good thing too, as a quick freeze-up on the 15th of October froze the ground as well as the lake. Many of the natives, having come by boat from their outlying trapping cabins, were still in town and now were caught. So they began building small log cabins just west of the mission and a veritable subdivision sprang up almost overnight. They called it "the United States"!

Old, abandoned buildings are fascinating to me and the old mission that had been abandoned when the Oblates moved into their new one and which had stood out in front since the last century proved especially interesting. It was full of the stuff with which one could start a museum. Most of the small rooms were furnished with handmade beds and chairs with seats woven from babiche. Many old steamer trunks were full of personal items from the past; old photos and even tintypes. On the top floor I discovered a stack of old muzzle-loading rifles. I emerged with simply one brass candle holder, but the superior, Father Mousseau, promised me I could take whatever I wanted and I decided I would certainly get those guns as soon as I had a permanent mission. When I returned the next year to get them, however, the entire building was gone and I was told the guns had been thrown into the dump and buried, along with everything else. Canadians in general seem to lack interest in preserving the past.

Fort Chipewyan is one of the oldest settlements in the North and consequently steeped in history. Alexander MacKenzie himself left here in 1789 to explore the great river named after him. Sir John Franklin and many other explorers followed in subsequent years. The population was about one thousand, half of Chipewyan extraction and half of Cree. Many of them were Métis. Almost all the early French-Canadian voyageurs passed through this Fort, along with a few Iroquois paddlers, and a few of them settled here. The French influence is evident in names like Marcel, Voyageur, Bourque, Vermillion, Lepine, Gibbot, Boucher, Poitras, Desjarlais and Tripe de Roche.

The Hudson Bay Company had always maintained a large establishment at this post and the principal origin of her recruits in the Orkney Islands or Scotland was also evident in names like Fraser, Flett, Wylie, McKay, Simpson and Stewart. Old Jack Wylie showed me the original contract on parchment that he had signed with the Bay when he was recruited in Scotland as a boy. He had signed on for two years for very few pounds sterling. His boys were now producing a fine example of the Chipewyan skiff, dynamiting out tree roots for the ribs of these boats so that they would have the natural curve.

The Chipewyan language had the reputation of being the mother tongue of the various Dene dialects spoken to the north of us, such as the Beaver, Yellowknife, Dog Rib, Slavey and Hare. Because I had a pretty good working knowledge of the latter, it was not too big a task to learn Chipewyan. I lost no time in soliciting the aid of Father Picard as my instructor. We spent a couple of hours together daily and I started an English-Chipewyan grammar. Afternoons I spent walking around town and getting acquainted with the residents. It wasn't unusual to be invited to stay for supper, but when I did so I missed some of the exercises back at the mission. This didn't bother me too much, but evidently it did bother the superior. I soon received a letter from the bishop in Fort Smith informing me of this complaint which he had received by mail. His advice: continue visiting the people!

In late November Trinket presented me with eight pups, the start of a new dog-team, and I was elated. In early December the Barren Land caribou had reached the Brothers' fish camp east along the lake and they went there with the hired hands to lay in a fresh supply of meat for the hostel. The children preferred this to the buffalo meat supplied by the government from the Wood Buffalo Park downstream. I couldn't join the caribou hunt as I had been assigned to preach the three-day children's retreat. Following this it was time to return to Goldfields for Christmas.

En route we flew over the small trapping settlement of Camsell Portage and I had the pilot land there so that I could meet the people. I found 102 of them, mostly Crees, a Hudson Bay store and a school in operation. In spite of the fact that ninety-eight of the residents were Catholic, a minister of the Northern

Evangelical Society of Meadow Lake and his family had moved in to convert the people. Although the mission at Chip had bought a log cabin in the village for possible use as an outpost, it had never been used and the people asked if I would come and stay with them for a while. I promised to return and then flew on to Goldfields. I would be back, and Camsell Portage was to become a large part of my life. I found one significant change at Holy Cross Mission at Goldfields in the person of Father Rudolph Perin, O.M.I., who had been transferred from Stoney Rapids to help me. It was comforting to have another human being to live with me in that spooky old house.

The new town of Uranium City was growing quickly and many buildings were being skidded over from Goldfields. Steve Yanik had his entire hotel moved over while Gus Hawker was operating out of a tent at the new town. Our plan was to jack up both church and rectory and get them moved as soon as possible. In the meantime I got Steve's brother Joe to let me use the new movie theatre in Uranium City for a Midnight Mass at Christmas. The Mounties agreed to stand at the door in their best scarlet uniforms to deter any drunks from going in. I ended up with a full house and the police said later they had prevented 150 from entering. From there I moved over to Eldorado's Beaverlodge Mine for New Year's. Since my last visit many families had moved into new homes, so it too was becoming an independent community worthy of my attention.

On the sixth of January I flew back to Camsell Portage and moved in with the family of Francis Powder, a patriarch of the community. His father, Paul Lepoudre, had moved to Camsell Portage from Plamondon, Alberta, raised twelve children and practically populated the settlement. It got its name, however, from Charles Camsell, who portaged north from this spot on one of his many geological expeditions. Later he sent me his book, *Son of the North*. During the twenties George McInnes established a fish cannery here and for a while the place was known as The Cannery. Fishing here was still excellent and most winters the Barren Land caribou migrated through the area. With the presence of the store and school it looked like a permanent community.

By living with one of the Powder families I quickly got acquainted with the whole village, but it was confusing, for sixty-five of the people all had the same last name. As they were mostly Cree-speaking, I started a dictionary of basic Cree words. Attendance at services was extremely good and I felt my presence was appreciated. They told me that a collection had been taken up around 1935 to build a proper mission, but nothing had been done. They showed me the old log cabin purchased by Father Picard as a possible mission house, but it looked terribly old and run down. I told the people that if they would help me I would immediately go out and cut enough logs for a proper building and if possible put it up the following summer.

All the able-bodied men went out with me the next day about a mile down the bay and began cutting logs. During the next ten days we cut down ninety good logs, flattening them on one side for ease in skidding. The temperature never rose above thirty-five below zero Fahrenheit and on one day it hit seventy-two below, but deep in the bush we hardly noticed it. In fact, it urged us to greater exertion. We not only cut and limbed them, but got them all skidded back into the centre of the village on an empty lot where a cabin had recently burnt down. It was an ideal location on the sand ridge some hundred and fifty feet from the lake edge. I heard from Dennis Murphy, the Bay Manager, that when the Pentecostal minister saw all our activity he sent a message to his headquarters suggesting a new assignment. Actually he was a fine fellow. I went to his cabin one evening and had supper with him, his wife and children. What puzzled me, however, was why he would be sent to evangelize a group that had already been completely baptized into another Christian faith when there were millions of pagans in the world who had yet to hear of Christ.

After a month at Camsell Portage I flew back to Goldfields and rejoined Father Perin, who was discouraged by all the drinking he found there. In fact, he had been asked to replace another priest at Fond du Lac, the next mission station east of us, during his vacation and he gladly accepted. I returned to my base at Fort Chip.

During my absence all of Trinket's pups had frozen to death outside and I was crestfallen. This discouragement was only temporary, however, as the Brothers promised to give me their splendid team for the winter. I resumed my daily classes in the Chipewyan language under the excellent tutelage of Father Picard and now included the Cree language as well, in which he was proficient. I was back in the classroom again, but I was an eager pupil. Our tight schedule was relaxed on Sunday afternoons, when a group of us would walk the three miles to the mission boat shack on a snye of the Slave River. I would pack my guitar and we would have some animated sing-songs around a red-hot, pot-bellied stove.

In early March I was sent over to the Brothers' wood camp on the Quatre-Fourches Channel in Wood Buffalo Park some fifteen miles west of the mission. Here all the wood needed to heat the various mission buildings at Chip were cut and decked by the water's edge for transport by barge in the summer. It was customary to have a chaplain there in case of accident and to conduct a morning mass for the crew. Other than that I was on my own to help in any way I could. The first thing I did was to draw up detailed plans for the new log mission at Camsell Portage.

Our cook at the wood camp was the venerable Brother Louis Crenn, who had come to Fort Chipewyan in 1899 from Brittany in France. His obedience to this mission had never been changed nor had he ever taken a vacation. He had simply followed the exacting regimen with unwavering fidelity for over half a century. In addition to being a jack-of-all-trades, in several areas his abilities were outstanding. What impressed me most were his feats with his dog-team. The Mounties in Fort Resolution had told me how he carried one of the early bishops from Chip to Fort Fitzgerald with his dogsled in one day. He told me that he never carried a dog whip and never gave his dogs individual names, referring to them all simply as "chien." Surely he had a very unusual rapport with them, as all the old-timers in Chip attested. Now, at age seventy-three, his dog-driving days were over, but he was still a very useful member of the mission staff, acting as cook at the wood camp and on the mission tugboat and working long hours in his room at the mission repairing the shoes of nearly 200 people. For me he was a living link with a past, a past I would never see, but that seemed far more interesting and exciting than the present times. During the two weeks we were together at the wood camp I had a chance to listen undisturbed to many of his stories while the rest were out felling trees. What a book he could have written, but, like many knowledgeable northerners before and after him, he recorded none of his experiences.

At the end of March Bert Burry, the owner of McMurray Air Service, flew me back to Goldfields in one of his Stinsons. I spent a week there and then went over to Eldorado, fourteen miles by ice road, in a bombardier or snowmobile. I was assigned an office in the staff house next to the clinic of Dr. Donald McMillan and we grew to be good friends. In view of the medical work I might be called upon to do at Camsell Portage, I was anxious to acquire more skill, especially in suturing wounds. In this the good doctor was most helpful, letting me do some sewing on his patients, under his direction. Unfortunately most of these wounds seemed to be to the scalp, probably the thickest skin to sew on the human anatomy. None of the patients objected, but they should have!

This staff house had some very educated and interesting men who knew a lot more than geology. Homer d'Aigle, for instance, had a great love for classical music and taught me to love the symphonies of Beethoven, especially the seventh, which he knew by heart. Another of the staff was Ben Allen, who had a room on the second floor which was dominated by a large record console he had flown in so that he could listen to his Mozart records. He considered all other classical composers inferior. When he got off work he retreated to his room, turned on Mozart and was immediately in a different world. People like Homer and Ben, who have such an appreciation for the finer things in life, are to be envied.

While I was at the mine this trip, Bill Bennett, President of Eldorado, landed in his private DC-3 en route to the Company's original mine site on Great Bear Lake near Port Radium. Frank Broderick was travelling with him and they invited me to join them. I first obtained permission to do so from the bishop in Fort Smith and from Father Gathy in Yellowknife, who regularly took care of this mine mission. Palm Sunday fell within the time of our trip, so I enlisted the help of Bill Bennett to read the long Gospel of the Passion and Frank Broderick to take up the collection. The day before the service I walked eight miles to Cameron Bay and invited a few families of Franklin Indians, who were spending the winter there, to join us for the Sunday mass at the mine and they came by dog-team. Shortly after Gilbert LaBine had staked in this area in 1930, the town of Cameron Bay became the largest settlement in the North West Territories with over two thousand men and seven airlines operating out of it. Now it was a ghost-town, with the Indians occupying the abandoned Hudson Bay store and the Assay Office.

When I returned to Goldfields I found my companion Father Perin back from Fond du Lac. He was not, however, in good spirits, for the drinking in town greatly reduced attendance at services. This was especially noticeable for him after spending some time at Fond du Lac, where the mission chapel was full every day of the week and where the missionary was called upon every hour of the day to help in one way or another. In Goldfields the people were actually in greater spiritual need. For the man of the cloth pastoring was something like prospecting. If he looked he could dig up all kinds of work. If he waited for it to come to him, however, he could easily become discouraged.

I flew over to Camsell Portage for Easter where the situation was vastly different. Fifty-five of the adults presented themselves for the sacrament of penance on Holy Saturday evening and one hundred and ten attended the mass held at the school on

Easter Sunday, including four girls and three boys who received their First Holy Communion. Afterwards I baptized two infants.

On this happy note I returned to Fort Chipewyan for the break-up. Pilot Bill Van Allen put me down safely on the rotting ice in front of the Fort. It was the last aircraft to land before open water. The next two months were to be my last at the big mission and I aimed to make the most of them. Using the well equipped workshop in the afternoons, I built a tabernacle for the Camsell mission as well as an octagonal belfry. I removed and packed a dozen windows from the old mission soon to be demolished. As soon as the lake ice melted the first barges down from Waterways off-loaded the lumber I would need to build.

On the 18th of June we loaded the barge *The St. Eugene* with my materials and equipment, including my new steeple, a tent and stove, a twenty-foot freighter canoe and eight-horsepower Johnson outboard and, last of all, Trinket. With Brother Veillette at the helm and Brother Crenn in the galley, we headed east on a calm lake just newly freed of winter ice. We continued on through the night for eighteen hours, arriving in the protected harbour at Camsell Portage early in the morning. Leaving our barge there to be unloaded, we again nosed out into the lake and continued east to Goldfields. We rendezvoused there with Bishop Trocellier who landed shortly after our arrival. I put a large wood-burning cook stove and heater on board *The St. Eugene* for the new mission at Camsell and off-loaded my canoe and kicker. The Brothers returned to Camsell to get their barge which the natives had unloaded, and returned to Chip. Meanwhile the bishop had a good look at the old church and rectory at Goldfields and discussed with Father Perin and me the wisdom of moving it over to the new townsite of Uranium City. We agreed that it should be done, as Goldfields was in its death throes and soon would be another northern ghost-town.

I now began the first of many solo trips on Lake Athabaska, going out with my canoe to the McInnes summer fish plant on Crackingstone Point. About 100 people were employed there, including many from Camsell Portage. Both lake trout and

whitefish were netted nearby and brought into the plant, where
they were filleted, packed in boxes and frozen for shipment
south. Roy Schlader and Bill McPete were in charge of the operation and afforded me their gracious cooperation in conducting
services for their workers. When I left there and continued west
I stopped at the tent camp of Albert Zeemil and Walter Blair, who
were prospecting for uranium for the legendary Gilbert LaBine.
Labine is considered the "Father of Uranium" in Canada. Not
long afterwards Albert hit a mine-size deposit of the precious ore
a stone's throw from their tent and wired Gilbert in Toronto,
"Have shot the elephant!" He was not exaggerating. It would
become the Gunnar Mine with its own processing mill. About a
year later I ran into Walter Blair in an old torn mackinaw helping
to unload a barge on Beaverlodge Lake. I asked him how he had
made out after staking Gunnar. "Gilbert gave me 50,000 shares,"
he told me. The stock was then worth over twenty dollars a
share; he could have told me that he was a millionaire. His story
was not typical, but the rush was definitely on and the country
was crawling with prospectors and rapidly being staked.

I stopped at a few more prospecting camps on my way into
Black Bay, where barge freight for both Uranium City and Eldorado Mine was being unloaded at a terminus called Bushell. I
hitched a ride the eight miles into the boom town called "U-City"
by the locals. I had been writing the CCF Government in Regina
asking for a site in the new town for our buildings. I had tried to
get the bishop to do this, thinking that his letters would carry
more weight, but he had declined. At any rate, I had repeatedly
been assured that definite parcels of land would be reserved for
various denominations. One letter had been signed by Brokel-
bank himself, the top man in the ministry concerned with development at Uranium City. I had a piece of high ground above the
townsite contour surveyed and drawn up by friends in the drafting office at Eldorado and submitted to Regina for consideration.

Now I went to see the Provincial Land Agent in town to see
if the land had been set aside for us. I was dismayed to learn that,
not only had no land been set aside for our purposes, but that it

was practically all gone. The parcel I had originally chosen and had surveyed had been picked for the school site. This agent went around town with me showing what lots remained, but they could scarcely accommodate our two buildings from Gold-fields even if they were butted up side by side. In desperation I finally took a piece of ground adjacent to the school site, most of which was down a ravine. My opinion of the CCF Government in Regina may be imagined as I continued on the remaining five miles to Eldorado. I was steaming!

The best I could do was to accept what was left of parcel "C" adjacent to the original lot I had chosen and now reserved for the school. In the following January I was back in Uranium City by dog-team and eating supper in Tom Embleton's tent cafe, when I happened to get seated at the counter next to a government land surveyor. His name was Alexander Stewart and it didn't take me long to explain to him all the troubles I had in trying to obtain a suitable piece of ground on which to locate our Goldfields build-ings. He lent me a sympathetic ear and promised to look at our parcel "C" the next day – which he did, on snowshoes.

"How much land would you need along this boundary with the school to accommodate your church?" he asked me. I replied, "About a hundred feet would do it." Without hesitation he pulled up the steel pin marking the eastern border of our prop-erty and moved it over a hundred feet. Suddenly my problem had evaporated. And to secure it, when they moved the church and rectory over from Goldfields, I had them place each building at opposite ends of the parcel. To this day the church rests on that extra hundred feet of ground.

That Sunday at my mass in the recreation room of the Eldo-rado staff house I informed the men that I would be away for the summer building a log mission for the natives at Camsell Por-tage, twenty-six air miles west. After the service a group of Irish-men came up to me offering to help, at least on weekends, if they could get there and back. This was unexpected and I promised to see if anything could be done.

The following day I went over to the new Nesbitt-LaBine Mine where shaft-sinking was in progress under the direction of Foss Irwin. Johnny Nesbitt was a well-known northern bush pilot who was in partnership with Gilbert LaBine on this new mine and he had a Beaver aircraft on nearby Martin Lake. Although Johnny was not of our religious persuasion he was anxious to help and readily agreed to take a volunteer crew back and forth to Camsell at no charge. (In later years Johnny published a book of his experiences entitled *Keep Your Nose on the Horizon*, but with characteristic modesty he neglected to mention this act of kindness.) I was elated when I went back to Eldorado to inform the volunteers. I also wrote to Father Perin at Goldfields asking him to help me with the construction work ahead.

The next day the skies were sunny and the lake calm as we pulled out of Black Bay, my canoe loaded with supplies. I rounded St. Joseph's Point and headed into Camsell Bay. I already felt pride in the thought that I was heading toward "my" mission. So what if it were nothing more than a pile of logs and lumber at this stage? In my mind's eye I could already see its steeple pointed to the sky. And it did officially bear the name of my patron saint, Mission Saint Bernard. Now it would take only a couple of months out of my young life to make it a reality.

11

MISSION
SAINT BERNARD

On my return to Camsell Portage I first had to pitch my tent and get my trunk and bedroll under canvas in case it rained. After that I sorted and stacked my building material with the help of one of the local boys. Help was scarce: most of the able-bodied males were away at the fish camp or hired out staking claims in the area.

On July 1st, Dominion Day, Johnny Nesbitt made his first trip with an overload of volunteer workers – eight of them – led by Pat Hughes. Pat was a bricklayer by trade and in charge of a kiln at Eldorado where he made bricks and cinder blocks. Like most of his companions he had come over from Dublin, Ireland. The first job we tackled was taking the old log cabin apart and moving it, log by log, to the new site. This was the building bought by the Chip Mission but never used. The skies were bright and the sun so hot that most of the men stripped to the waist as they dragged these logs about two hundred yards. The bugs and mosquitoes were not nearly so bad here as they were around Great Bear Lake, where no one ever worked outside shirtless.

The next day after mass in the school we laid out the perimeter of the new mission and positioned the sill logs on the sand. The main building measured twenty-four by thirty-two feet, including the front porch which ran the width of the building. A wing running off this to contain the kitchen and workshop measured thirty-two by fourteen feet. By the time Johnny flew in early Monday morning to pick up the men, the project was well under way. And at the last minute I got an unexpected but welcome surprise.

Philip Stenne had immigrated from France, a graduate of the Sorbonne in his early twenties. His father was a sculptor of huge equestrian statues. Philip had been working as a carpenter at the Eldorado mine, but the housing situation there in a huge Butler building containing over 200 men was intolerable to him. I could understand that. One evening I had visited the men in that building, mostly shaft-sinkers from Nova Scotia, and some of their habits were downright dangerous. For example, they would open a beer bottle by simply cracking off the top on the edge of a table and when it was empty they threw it over the partition of their cubicle to land and smash in one of their neighbours', sparking some profane threats of retaliation. So Philip offered to stay and spend the month of July helping me and I eagerly accepted.

Together we put in long hours under clear skies and the work progressed. Father Perin came over and gave us a hand for two weeks, then borrowed my canoe to go down to Fort Resolution for that mission's centenary celebration. Young newlyweds from Fort Chipewyan, Charley Flett and his bride, stopped by on their honeymoon and worked with us for a couple of weeks. Nobody could stand around watching us work for very long without having an axe put in his hands. During the month Trinket delivered some good news when she dropped eleven pups. The bad news was that nine of them were females.

Every weekend Johnny Nesbitt flew over faithfully with a plane-load of helpers which not only doubled the work Philip and I could do during the week, but also gave us a great morale boost. On one trip he urged me to fly over to Crackingstone Point with him and stake a few claims. I declined, arguing that if I took any time off the building, the mission wouldn't be closed in before cold weather. Later I realized that I had missed a golden opportunity. Any claims staked at that point, especially after the Gunnar find, sold for thousands of dollars.

I had no reason to worry about finishing the job during that summer. I was far enough along to move into the new mission the 31st of August, my thirty-second birthday. When Pat Hughes came over the following day he put in front steps of cement, the finishing touch. The building was now completely closed in and I could work on the inside at my leisure during the winter. I now felt safe in leaving for a while to visit the miners.

At Eldorado I was still using my office in the staff house, but sleeping at the home of Hank and Colleen Bloy. To show my appreciation I got out my oil paints and did a painting of sled dogs for them. I had been carrying my painting equipment ever since I arrived in the North, always telling myself that I would get back into it again, but there never seemed to be enough time. I had produced nothing in this line while at Franklin, although while I was there I had a visit from A. Y. Jackson, one of the famous Group of Seven. He was up at Port Radium at the invitation of Bill Bennett one summer painting scenes around Great Bear Lake and he encouraged me to get back to it. Later, at Beaverlodge, I started evening classes in painting for adults at the school, which sparked a lot of interest. I loved it, but I didn't seem able to get into it while occupied with mission work or on the move.

While at the mine this time I got another opportunity to visit the operation near Port Radium. A group of about forty Irishmen working there were most faithful in attending a very early morning mass before going on shift. *The Radium Gilbert* was plying the lake regularly, crossing over to the mouth of the Great Bear River opposite Fort Franklin with bags of uranium concentrate and bringing back fuel oil. Captain Allen McInnes invited me to make a trip with him and I lost no time throwing my bag on board. Henry Christofferson, marine maintenance supervisor for the Northern Transportation Company, was on board too, and his humorous anecdotes all the way across provided a lot of fun.

It was a great thrill to see Mission St. Therese again, to go down the line and pet all my dogs and remember the long trips we had made together, to look around at all the familiar objects. My successor Father Victor Phillipe and his young assistant Father Felicien Labat were hard at work adding a closed porch to the chapel end of the building. Soon the natives were flocking to greet me with warm embraces reserved for their own kind, a special mark of affection. I thought I had pounded my last nail in this mission, but the next day Father Phillipe had me cut a new window into the outside wall of the sacristy. Mr. Gravel came to visit and I asked him if I could send him another cat. When I left I took one of the pair of snowshoes I had left in the attic.

The trip back across the lake in *The Radium Gilbert* was uneventful until we neared the east shore. We were proceeding in a dense fog at half-speed when suddenly a sheer granite cliff loomed up in front of us and Captain McInnes telegraphed for full-speed astern. His ship, although beautifully furnished, lacked any radar to aid navigation.

Back at Port Radium I heard about a group of some forty natives who were employed at a bush camp cutting spruce for underground timbers. Although many of the Bear Lakers had been trained to work underground and were good at it, they found this work too gruelling. So they ended up at Hunter Bay about forty miles north of the mine, cutting lagging timbers. Captain McInnes's brother captained a smaller, wooden barge named *The Radium Bear* and was making a trip to the natives' camp to take on a load of timbers, so I went with him.

I knew most of the people at this camp from Franklin, so I decided to spend a couple of days with them and then have them bring me back to the mine by canoe. Everything worked out as planned until we ran out of gas about half-way back. There were nine of us in a twenty-two-foot freighter canoe. We tore up the floor boards and made paddles out of them. We hadn't planned to camp out and the second day we were completely out of grub. The first day we expended all the shells in our only .30-.30, with the exception of one, vainly trying to shoot four otter. The

Philip Stenne en route from Camsell Portage to Fort Smith, with Spider Island in the background.

Simon Bashaw, here at Camsell Portage about to return to his traplines, was the last trapper I saw wearing those traditional leggings.

Standing before the only painting I did during my four years
at Camsell Portage.

In front of the old St. Anne's Hospital, Fort Smith, 1953. These Oblates are walking back to the adjacent Mission, after a conference.

Mission "Our Lady of Seven Sorrows" at Fond du Lac, 1953. Fr. Charles Gamache, O.M.I., stands on the porch with his flock of Chipewyan natives.

The completed Santa Barbara church at Uranium City, 1963, built by Burns & Dutton,
Contractors, on the site of the burned-out church. It was still standing in 1997,
but had no priest.

The *Sant'Anna* departed from Belle Rock near Fort Smith for the Arctic Coast twice every summer.

Bishop Breynat points to my future.

"Noon tea fire" (oil on masonite, 16" x 24")

"The camp at Wokatue" (oil on canvas, 24" x 30")
A caribou-hunting camp 20 miles west of Colville settlement.

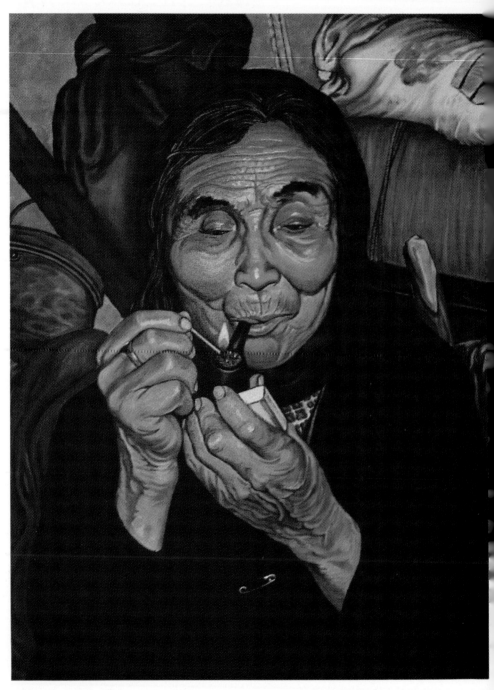

"Ahson" (oil on canvas, 18" x 24")
The word means *grandmother* in Hareskin. Her name was Verona Pascal.
One of my tasks as the local medic was to remove and clean her glass eye weekly.
She died at Colville in 1980.

"Woman threading needle"   (oil on masonite, 24" x 29")
This is Therese Coezi, still living at Colville Lake.

"Racing the storm" (oil on canvas, 22" x 28")

"Ketaniahtue" (acrylic on canvas, 20" x 24")

"Sunset teepee" (oil on linen, 24" x 32")

"Evening chores" (oil on canvas, 20" x 24")
A woman using a Swede saw at Colville Lake.

"Margaret's huskies" (oil on canvas, 24" x 30")

"Classic Iceberg" (oil on canvas, 30" x 40")

"Breaking trail" (oil on canvas, 16" x 20")

remaining shell was used successfully the second day on a common loon. We immediately went ashore and built a fire. I was amazed how good that loon tasted. Finally we found an old fuel cache and got the kicker restarted.

Port Radium had no airstrip but used the old gravel strip at Sawmill Bay about thirty miles south and ferried passengers back and forth in *The Radium Bear*. In winter they landed the company DC-3 on the ice right in front of the mine. Over at Sawmill Bay there was a wrecked Dakota just off the runway with a large notice painted on it advising: "CAUTION, THIS COULD HAPPEN TO YOU!" I saw a similar wreck on the new strip at Beaverlodge after Alf Kaywood had flown me back south.

One dark, rainy night the following week the Eldorado DC-3 piloted by Jack Love circled overhead with a full load of men from Port Radium mine. They were unexpected: there were no lights on the new gravel strip still under construction. Two of us jumped in a pickup truck and went for the kerosene pots used to outline the strip in the dark. We found them all empty. While we were frantically trying to fill them the circling Dakota was burning the last of its fuel. As we put down the first three pots marking the end of the strip Pilot Love did touch down, but quickly got airborne again for another circuit. We had just put down the first light along the side of the runway when he came in again. This time he landed, but the plane was heading about fifteen degrees to the right of the runway and promptly hit a six-foot ridge of gravel. This severed the undercarriage and the plane slid some three hundred feet on its belly, stopping just short of a precipice. We rushed over to find that the props had sliced through the fuselage, rupturing the wing tanks. Gas was pouring out as the occupants scrambled for the exit in the pitch dark, lit only by the headlights on our truck. Fearing fire, we kept yelling, "Don't light a match!" "Don't light a match!" All twenty-one passengers got out unhurt. Among them I was surprised to see three of my Bear Lake Indians. This was their first plane ride and one of them said to me in the Hare language, "It must cost the white men a lot of money every time they land this flying boat."

After the engines were removed from this crippled bird Charlie Storm, the camp cook, bought it from the company for $300 and moved it just outside the mine gate. He fixed it up as a fast food diner and operated it successfully for several years. Later he moved it over to Uranium City, where he again altered it for use as living quarters and rented it out. Finally some men from the States bought it from him for $5,000 with the intention of rebuilding it. It may still be flying today.

Before returning to Camsell Portage I went over to Goldfields to visit my sometime companion missionary Father Perin to find out what he had done with my canoe and kicker. He told me he had left them over at Camsell while I was away and by way of compensation for keeping them so long had left a sled dog there for me as well as a brass bell for the new belfry. Jack Walters took me and my considerable freight there in his large inboard motor boat. It was the 18th of October and shell ice was beginning to form along the shore. I now had ten dogs to feed; one brought by Father Perin, four I borrowed from Victor Augier, plus Trinket and four of her pups. It was late to start a fall fishery, but I borrowed four nets and set them. Then I took down an abandoned log building built in the early twenties by a Swede named Eric, and using the logs built a fish house down by the water's edge. I got about twenty-five days of net fishing before I was forced to pull out both the nets and the canoe when the bay froze completely on November 14th. As soon as the ice got thick enough the caribou came and we could see them crossing near the end of the bay. The first one I got had fallen through thin ice and I shot him in the water. Soon everyone who had not yet left the settlement for their trap lines had plenty of meat.

The people were generous enough to keep me supplied with firewood so I could go ahead with the carpentry inside the new mission. I found myself doing the same kind of work I had been doing at Franklin twelve months earlier. Only this time I was a little more accomplished in building cabinets and furniture. I also built a wood sled as insurance against the day, fast coming, when my people would tire of bringing me wood. My supply of dog feed was rapidly being depleted and it was just a matter of days before I could no longer enjoy the luxury of staying home doing carpentry. Soon my time would be mostly taken up visiting nets and hooks set under the ice and hauling firewood.

In the meantime I rushed to build all the items necessary for Christmas, like the altar and benches. And it turned out to be a very holy and happy feast with the new mission absolutely filled to the walls for the Midnight Mass and not a drunk to mar the religious atmosphere. The once-a-year collection amounted to $55.79, with everyone donating. On Christmas afternoon we had Benediction of the Blessed Sacrament, followed that evening by a slide show. I had a generator from an American Sherman tank bought through war assets, and, although it produced a frightful din in the workshop, I was successful in showing about a thousand slides I had taken, mostly around Fort Franklin. I followed this with a bucket of ice cream which I had concocted with many secret ingredients and everyone declared it the best Christmas Camsell Portage had ever seen.

The New Year of 1953 was ushered in with some sporadic shooting around the village as the temperature dipped to twenty-four below zero. Philip Stenne was still in that Butler building at Eldorado mine, but he had written me asking if he could team up with me and stay at the mission at Camsell. I agreed on condition that we converse only in French, because I was determined to gain more fluency in the language. So he quit his job and on January 2nd walked the thirty-five miles to Camsell. He arrived slightly frost-bitten but otherwise none the worse for the long hike in sub-zero weather. His arrival was an answer to prayer and I welcomed him with open arms. At the time I wasn't sure just how long he would stay, as I had no money with which to pay him. As it turned out, he stayed longer than I did and is still there today!

Philip adapted easily to bush life. It wasn't too many days before he could manage our new team of dogs himself as he took over the job of supplying us with firewood. I went with him to show him how we set a net under the ice, just as Brother Médard had shown me a short time before. We shot a few caribou and I showed him how we skinned and butchered them, keeping our hands in the warm blood so they wouldn't freeze. We lowered baited hooks through the ice in deep water for the big trout. It wasn't long before he could do all these things without my help.

About this time I was content to pass the rest of the winter peacefully at Camsell and completely forget about Goldfields or the mines or Uranium City. I received a telegram, however, from the Saskatchewan Government in Regina informing me that my request for Parcel C next to the school property in U-City had been granted and that I should sign the lease with the land agent there as soon as possible. Without hesitating, and in spite of the fifty-five-below-zero temperature, I left alone with the team the next day. Having no place to stay at U-City, I went right through to Eldorado's mine on Beaverlodge Lake, now safely frozen. I had a neat little shack there next to the staff house given me by Lefty McLeod, one of Eldorado's pilots. With the cookhouse right next door I could count on Charlie Storm for scraps to feed my dogs indefinitely. The next day I drove the dogs back to U-City, where the town was booming. It was still practically a tent city, with the exception of the Saskatchewan Liquor Store which was solidly built of brick.

I lost no time in getting over to Goldfields where Father Perin was engaged in getting our two buildings jacked up, preparing them to be moved to U-City. I explained the situation carefully and the importance of putting the church on that top hundred feet of ground in order to hold it. In a month it was over there and placed exactly where we wanted it, while the old rectory occupied a site at the opposite end of the parcel. The following summer officials from Regina drew a line right through the middle of our property and ordered me to move the church back across that line! I expected this, but I held firm. We eventually won the fight and the church stayed put. No doubt about it, I was elated as I drove the dogs back to Camsell. That had been an important trip well worth the hardships involved.

In the meantime I had received a letter from Fort Smith setting out the date for the important annual retreat and a note saying that the bishop would fly to Camsell for an inspection of the new mission and take me back with him. Somehow those plans were changed and the plane trip cancelled with them. This gave me the idea of going by dogs and taking Philip with me to see the country. As we didn't yet have enough dogs for two teams we would have to double up on the same sled. It could be done and Philip was game. We packed and left on January 21st, following the north shore of the lake going west. Although we had no trail to follow, the lead dog Sandy did a good job cutting across bays from point to point. It was thirty below but calm, with a noticeable ice-haze hanging in the air. The sun was setting dead ahead of us about three in the afternoon, sending out rays in the form of a cross. It was an indescribably beautiful scene and it prompted me to stop the team and dig out my 35 mm camera. I walked out in a circle so as not to get my tracks in the picture and left Philip standing on the back of the sled silhouetted against the sun. That picture turned out to be the finest I ever took in the North and was reproduced thousands of times.

We made about thirty-five miles that day and pitched our tent on Morris Point. The following evening we got into the Brothers' fish camp at Fiddler Point. Luckily the cabin was heated and occupied by a group of hunters from the Chip mission who had just killed 100 caribou. An hour after our arrival the mission tractor arrived pulling a huge, empty freight sled called a sloop. There were about a dozen of us in that cabin and we slept warm.

The next morning the Brothers loaded all the frozen carcasses on their sled and lashed them down in preparation for the fifty-mile trip back to the mission. Philip decided to go with them and take one of our dogs which had played out. I continued with the seven dogs left and made it into Chip in seven hours. We had completed the first hundred and twenty-five miles and were about half-way between Camsell and Fort Smith, our destination. In spite of the fact that one dog died that night, it looked as if we could make it.

After resting up two days at Chip our dogs looked as though they were ready to tackle our final dash to Fort Smith. The route led us down the frozen Slave River. As there were a few trapping families living all along this route we anticipated finding our trail broken in the deep snow. In this fond hope we soon found we were mistaken. There was no trail at all. Whereas on Lake Athabaska we really didn't need a trail because the wind had blown the snow into a hard surface, here in the protected valley of the river it lay soft and deep. We had to take turns running ahead of the dogs on snowshoes. The first day we barely made twenty-five miles, were completely exhausted and we were showing signs of *mal de raquette*, that famous scourge of snowshoe travel that afflicts all the muscles from toes to hips. Fortunately we didn't have to make an open camp but moved into the cabin of Bill Moore at the mouth of the Peace River. After wading through that soft snow all day the poor dogs just dropped in their tracks and we had to drag them from their harnesses to chain them up for the night.

In the morning we were stiff and sore and the temperature looked even lower, but luckily we had no thermometer. There was nothing to do but get down on that river and continue breaking trail north, taking turns as we had done the day before. It definitely was colder, for ice formed on the bottom of the toboggan, making it pull like it was running on sand. Every few miles we had to stop, turn it over and scrape the ice off with an axe. About noon we came to the small cabin of an old Swedish trapper. We left the team down on the river and walked up the steep bank to the cabin. Once inside we were assailed by the pungent aroma of Sloan's Linament, which this old recluse must have been using by the case. It was so overpowering we couldn't really tell if we were drinking tea or not. The poor fellow was so starved for company he couldn't stop talking in his thick Scandinavian accent. He followed us back down to the river, jawing all the way. Even as we pulled away he was standing there waving his arms and shouting after us. One might diagnose this as incipient cabin fever.

We plodded on down river through the deep snow. The exertion of running ahead on snowshoes so warmed us that in spite of the intense cold we were forced to remove our parkas. Our faces, however, were picking up patches of frostbite. By late afternoon we pulled into Johnson's Trading Post and stopped for tea. This post was unique: besides carrying the usual trade items, Johnson kept a bull and three cows. He froze the milk and sold it in solid blocks which were stacked up in the entranceway to his store. He had a thermometer hanging outside and it registered sixty-two below zero. We knew it was cold, but we didn't realize it was that low. This explained why our sled boards were icing up the way they did. When we queried him about the lack of any sign of a sled trail, he told us that they had had a lot of snow recently and everyone was waiting for someone else to break it. He predicted that there would now be plenty of traffic on our trail. As Tom Champaign's cabin was only another six miles down we decided to go at least that far before camping for the night. The river takes a big bend west at that point, so the blazed trail leaves the river and cuts straight across. Our lead dog had no trouble following it without benefit of a forerunner, though there were six inches of fresh snow on it. The warm light of a cabin window up ahead was a welcome sight as our harness bells echoed through the empty bush in the darkness.

Not having met Tom before, we weren't too sure if we would be invited to spend the night in his cabin with his wife and numerous children, so we left our dogs in their harness and followed him into the cabin. Tom did all the talking and never stopped. We shook hands with his wife, but the children mostly retreated under the bunk beds. It was evident that they weren't used to strangers. As usual, there was a kettle of hot tea on the stove, but Tom informed us that he would immediately send his eldest son over to the store to pick up a few things for our supper and he took off in the dark. We sat around smoking and drinking tea for three hours as Tom regaled us with his war stories. Finally the boy came in and put a tin of butter on the table. That was it! Why hadn't he said something? We had butter out in our sled. In fact we had plenty of caribou meat as well as bannock and beans and a lot of other grub that Tom evidently did not have.

It didn't take us long to bring in an armful which Tom's wife immediately began cooking. We unharnessed our dogs, brought in our bedrolls and were soon at the table with Tom stuffing ourselves. It is common practice in the North for the women and children to wait until the men have finished before eating. Evidently the smell of that good food overcame the shyness of the children as they crept closer and closer to our table. Their big eyes were riveted not on us but on the food. Philip and I became uneasy. Apparently they were practically starving. We weren't really finished when we excused ourselves and moved from the table to let those poor kids have a chance. Without a word they scrambled onto the benches and devoured everything in sight while Tom droned on about the moose he had been tracking and would probably shoot tomorrow. In the meantime "moose tracks alone make very thin soup," as the saying goes.

The following day was the same as the last two, more than sixty below and no trail. We pushed on doggedly mile after weary mile, staying as close to the banks as possible so as to avoid any overflow or thin ice in mid-stream. As we traded places breaking trail, we looked for the tell-tale white patches on each other's face indicating frostbite. You can easily freeze parts of your face without being aware of it. Later in the warmth of a cabin it feels like a burn and acts like one too, at first turning black, then blistering and peeling, leaving a very sensitive area of skin that can freeze even more readily the next time it is exposed. Finally that afternoon we reached the Wood Buffalo Park headquarters known as The Hay Camp. They had a well-organized abattoir there and were actually in the midst of their annual round-up and kill. There was plenty of room to throw our bedrolls and no shortage of buffalo meat for our weary dogs. Even if we had to pay for it, the going price of five cents a pound would have been cheap to the big commercial meat packers who were carting it away.

We still had forty-five miles to go to Fort Smith, but it was all over a recently plowed road. No more river travel. No more breaking trail on snowshoes. It took us just five hours to Fort Fitzgerald where we stopped for tea with Lawrence Yanik. He was the brother of both Steve and Joe, both of whom were prospering in Uranium City. He had built his log house here of huge logs that had drifted out of the Peace River. I had never seen four logs to a wall before. With only sixteen miles left to cross the portage road into Fort Smith we pushed on, anxious to get there in time for the opening ceremonies of the retreat. We missed it by forty-five minutes and stopped the team right in front of the chapel as the twenty-five Fathers and Brothers filed out to cross over to the mission residence. We must have presented quite a sight standing there by our sled, covered with frost, the steam rising from us, like two wraiths from Ultima Thule. They all filed by without a word of greeting! The retreat had begun and they were all observing the rule of Grand Silence! C'est la vie.

Our return trip to Camsell Portage was remarkable only in that it was so easy compared to the trip out. This time, as Johnson had predicted, the trail up the Slave River to Chip had been kept open by the locals and we could ride instead of walk. The lake from Chip to Camsell was about the same, but the days were longer and warmer. We got in on the 26th of February, the very day I told the people I would return.

In our absence the teacherage had burned down, but the school was still in operation. After a few days, during which we set two nets and replenished our wood pile, I left alone with the dogs to visit the mines. At Uranium City I found the staking rush had accelerated and over at Goldfields I found that Father Perin had sat around the rectory as long as he could stand the inactivity and then went out and staked nine claims himself. When he confided to me that he had already been offered $500 apiece for these claims but was holding out for $1,000, the staking bug hit me too. On my way back to Camsell I picked up prospecting licences for both Philip and myself. We lost no time in going out and staking forty-two claims close to the settlement; not that we were aware of any uranium in the area, but we felt that we might just as well stake some land before it was completely gone. And we were aware of the fact that even "moose pasture" was selling. On my next sled trip to U-City I stood in line with all the other prospectors outside the mining recorder's tent and got our claims properly filed. We were now caught up in that frenzy that was sweeping the country.

At Camsell Portage we celebrated the great feast of the Lord's Resurrection with all the pomp and ceremony we could muster. The altar was beautifully decorated by the young women and everyone wore their finest. Following the late morning high mass we were surprised to see three caribou bedded down out on the ice in front of the village. At 2:30 everyone returned to the mission for Benediction, at 5:30 for a common meal and at 7:30 for bingo. No doubt about it, the mission had become the centre of social activity in the settlement. On Easter Monday we had the first marriage, when Georgina Powder was joined to Herb Mercredi in Holy Matrimony, after which we all gathered on the front porch for a group photo. This event occasioned some alcoholic toasts around town which resulted in old Ira Allen getting a few ribs kicked in. I taped him up as best I could, then got a med-evac to fly us over to Dr. McMillan, who examined him and pronounced my medical work A-1. He left my bandages just where I put them and Bert Barry flew us home again.

Philip and I had seen the country west of us, so it was time to familiarize ourselves with what lay to the east. I had heard a lot about the old mission at Fond du Lac and its resident missionary, Father Charlie Gamache, so we decided to visit him. As we would be travelling on the lake ice all the way, the proper sled to use would be the komatik, with its heavy wooden runners. So I built one sixteen feet long and shod it with steel runners. Traditionally the komatik is pulled by dogs harnessed in the "Nome hitch," that is, they pull in pairs, side by side, except for the leader. With webbing I made a set of nine Eskimo-type harnesses that have no collar, but do have individual whipple trees. In the meantime the mission at Chip sent me their six dogs, so we had two good teams.

With our best nine dogs in the new harness pulling a sled usually not seen on Lake Athabaska, Philip and I left Camsell on April 14th. Everything worked well and that night we made camp on Big Fowl Island east of Goldfields. The following day took us through the spring migration of caribou crossing our track going north to the Barrens. We shot and butchered four of them. With the sight and smell of so many caribou our dogs were incited to give their utmost all day long and we arrived at Fond du Lac early in the evening.

This northern post, more than any other, retained a flavour of the old times. Of course the 300-odd Chipewyan Indians here were all living in the log cabins they had built. Unlike any other settlement, however, they were still fencing in their yards with vertical poles similar to those I had seen in photos from the last century. Some had teepees or warehouses set up in their yards where they would tan hides. All had dog-teams.

The huge church stood by the edge of the lake and was mostly unheated in the winter. The mission building was separated from the church by the main road and contained a large chapel. Its yard was fenced in with a high, pole barrier. Once this gate was open we drove in with our team. With our load of fresh meat we got a warm reception from Father Gamache, a rotund figure in cassock, and from his wiry assistant, Brother Labonté. We unloaded our gear and were escorted to two cots upstairs.

In the kitchen that evening supper consisted of two staples on which these missionaries apparently lived most of the year. The first was a kind of stew made up of chunks of caribou and potatoes from their garden. The second was local raspberries. Both were preserved in mason jars and were delicious. Hundreds of similar jars were stored in the cellar. During the next five days we learned a lot: about living off the land, about the Chipewyans and about our host. He was a Canadian who had already spent a quarter of a century at this post. Like all our missionaries he was fluent in the local language. He was also an avid reader of world history and current affairs and well acquainted with the classics. Yet what particularly distinguished him was his inquisitive mind and willingness to test his ideas. This had led him into all sorts of experiments.

It was easy to guess that he had attempted to raise mink, as the pile of empty mink cages in the backyard attested. He had also tried foxes and marten. All these animals failed to reproduce, he told us, simply because of his location in the centre of the village surrounded by yapping sled dogs. In an isolated location they could have been successful. He also had an idea that he could possibly improve on the type of sled dog the natives were using. Toward this end he imported a pure-bred female St. Bernard and a pedigreed greyhound, the idea being that this combination might produce a fast dog that could withstand the cold. We looked at one product of this union chained out in the yard. With its pointed nose and long, woolly legs it resembled an orangutan. It was evident around the settlement that this particular experiment had been going on for years as nearly every dog in town had the long, pointed nose of the Greyhound, and even when we met these teams around Goldfields we knew immediately that they were from Fond du Lac.

Another ongoing experiment involved chickens, a good number of which kept themselves warm enough to survive the winter in an unheated hen house in the back yard. Unfortunately he had run out of proper chicken feed and had substituted dry fish. The birds, it seemed, were living well enough on this type of food, but their eggs tasted fishy. To encourage the production of larger eggs the Father made some plaster of Paris eggs of amazing sizes which he was placing in their nests to challenge them; the desk in his own room was covered with moulds. From time to time during the day he would slip out to the hen house and return with his cassock pockets filled with eggs which he would put in his sleeping bag on his bed. Just why he did this I never found out. Nor did I find out why the tea kettle was half-filled with egg shells.

Every summer Father Gamache would import two piglets on the first barge. They were kept in a log cabin out in the middle of the yard, fed any scraps the mission could spare and butchered each fall. One was always sold to the Hudson Bay manager and this paid for their initial cost. One summer when I was visiting I looked in the open window of the pig house and noticed that the two of them were standing in about six inches of water. When I notified the Father about this situation he replied that this was another experiment in making the meat more tender!

A very successful operation of this mission was its garden and we were shown how it took two years to make the proper soil by mixing moss into the sand. The potatoes this soil produced not only tasted great but they were especially suited for long winter storage. Another outstanding success of this Father and Brother teamwork was their smoked trout which I had seen for sale in MacIver's store in Goldfields.

The mission also housed the Post Office in one small room that seemed so crowded with unclaimed C.O.D. parcels that there was scarcely room to walk into it to get to the wicket. It looked to me like a place where mail could be lost for years without anyone ever noticing. Against the outside wall was a huge pile of beautifully tanned caribou hides for sale for $4 apiece. I bought several with which I later had a jacket made.

That first night Philip and I were comfortably in our cots upstairs ready for sleep when the two house cats started playing tag on the exposed rafters overhead. In the pitch dark one jumped down and hit me in the stomach. When I sat up the second one landed on my head. Apparently my bed had been their habitual landing site.

This mission at Fond du Lac had been established in 1853 and was currently just one year short of its centenary celebration. The people's long association with the church and its music was apparent when they sang at the daily services. What singing! I had never heard anything quite like it. Led by one of the male elders its sheer volume was astounding. I wished I could take a contingent of them to Camsell Portage to show the people there how a congregation could praise God in song. And apparently their pastor was satisfied that his flock was well schooled in their religion, because he never preached to them! He told me that after twenty-five years they had heard everything. And certainly they must have added to their knowledge of Christianity during their frequent visits to the mission common room where there were always a few visitors smoking pipes or chewing snuff and discussing local and world events with their knowledgeable pastor. I remember spending most of one day discussing with him Galileo's theory of a sun-oriented universe. No doubt about it, this visit to the Fond du Lac Mission was one of the high points of my first five years in the North and one I couldn't easily forget.

Our return trip took us through the continuing migration of the caribou, but the surface of the snow on the ice was beginning to melt and the temperature of the air was too warm for working dogs. We got our tent pitched again on Big Fowl Island just before we were hit by a spring blizzard of snow and rain that kept us pinned down all the following day. The storm blew itself out during the night and when we resumed our trip the third day the temperature was down below zero. Our komatik zipped along on its steel runners with little effort, even after we took on the meat of five caribou we killed. When we came to the large pressure ridge of ice off St. Joseph's Point we had to follow it for two miles toward shore in order to avoid the deepening water on either side of it. In spite of this detour we got back to Mission Saint Bernard in the early afternoon.

The following month saw us using our dogs almost daily to carry out our main tasks. Besides going to the nets, hunting caribou or hauling firewood, we went west twenty-five miles to stake another group of claims and made two more trips into U-City and area. By the 21st of May we had to leave the sled out on the rotting ice of the main lake as the bay in front of the settlement was now black and unsafe. When I totalled up our mileage for the winter I found that we had travelled 1,214 miles with the dogs, not counting all the short trips for wood and fish. It was time to hang up the harnesses for the summer.

12

THE EASIER LIFE

Spring came to Camsell Portage as usual on the wings of song, the song of all the birds that had left us for the winter and were now returning. As the sun rose higher day by day it melted the snow and released all the pungent aromas that had been dormant and imprisoned. The warm wind wafted the sweet scent of flowering lichens and pine. Even a blind man could have known that spring was in the air.

What a treat to sit out on my front porch watching the ice melt in the bay and feel the blessed heat. The dogs no longer had to curl up and hide their noses in their tails. They could stretch out full-length and rest their tired muscles, with no more travelling for a while. Too late for sleds, too early for boats; it was a time to relax, a time to be quiet and think. Which was what I was doing; thinking back over my first years in the North, comparing where I was now with where I had been over the past five years.

Already I had seen the four seasons come and go at Camsell Portage. The new mission was completed and in service. The natives' lives were enriched by it and they showed their appreciation by faithful attendance at services. We were isolated and yet close enough to get to most of the mines in a single day.

As there were far more people at the mines than there were at my home base I could say that I was ministering mostly among men working in a technically specialized world. Yet most of my time was spent with a people still living off the land and I shared part of that life, too. I could say that I had the best of both worlds. As at Fort Norman, I was still studying native languages, but I no longer had to answer to a dozen bells during my day. Without the bells I was freer, less constrained, but at the same time I had more personal initiative. More self-discipline was demanded for me to do on my own the things the bells had called me to do. After all, I was still living by the Rule Book of the Oblate Congregation to which I belonged. The Breviary, for example, still had to be said daily in its entirety, except when I was travelling. The mass, too, was a daily event, but here the steeple bell called the faithful, not me. It was my job to be the faithful bell-ringer.

I could see more similarities than dissimilarities between my two years at Fort Franklin and my current circumstances. In both situations most of my time was consumed by the manual labour of building. Whether on Great Bear Lake or Lake Athabaska, I needed a dog team to travel, so I had to keep nets in the water to feed them. All the missions were heating with wood, so I had to be continually cutting and hauling no matter where I was. So too with the hunting of caribou, our staple meat. At Franklin my people were concentrated in the one village, while here at Camsell Portage my flock was scattered, so that now I was obliged to do more travelling to reach them. The main difference between Franklin and Camsell was their geographical positions six hundred miles apart. Thus at Camsell the winters were not nearly as severe nor as long. Although I wasn't adverse to winter, still it was nice to feel the heat of spring in May instead of having to wait until July. No doubt about it, life was easier for me now than at any time before.

Eldorado had recently opened for staking all the land along the north shore of Lake Athabaska which they had reserved for two years while they had the first look at it. This was a Crown-owned company and the ore was militarily strategic material. The Crown had exercised its priority rights on that basis.

There was a rush to stake this land just as soon as it was declared open and among the first to do so was Pat Hughes and his Irish buddies. Their lack of knowledge in this field coupled with their evident zeal made them the butt of a lot of joking. I knew some of the boys working in Eldorado's map office where they kept copies of the charts used in all their airborne scintillometer work. These showed where they got the highest readings from ground radiation. Eldorado had already checked out these hot spots and found that most of them were caused by pegmatite, the uranium prospector's fool's gold. Anyway I had a copy of these maps made for me and I loaned them to the Irishmen along with my canoe or any other equipment they needed. They began to sell claims and stake others. Within a relatively short time they had quit their labour jobs at Eldorado and were into staking full-time. By the time the uranium boom had passed they had acquired considerable savings. When they announced that they intended to shift their scene of operations to Ireland they were again laughed at. Everyone knew that there was no prospecting for minerals in Ireland, but they persisted.

They got hold of the old Irish maps showing where the smithies were located near mineral deposits, probably iron ore. These became their original prospecting areas and, as luck would have it, they not only found iron, but lead and zinc and other more valuable minerals. The next thing people read in their mining newspapers was that Northgate, their company, was putting up a mill near Dublin to process this ore. And shortly after that a second mill. So the Irishmen who had been so generous with their time in helping to establish Mission Saint Bernard had been rewarded tenfold and their scoffers were left shaking their heads, silenced.

As soon as the lake was open in June I left by canoe for Uranium City and moved into the old rectory which had been skidded over from Goldfields during the winter. Father Perin had begun living in it but at the moment he was back around Goldfields looking for his skiff which had disappeared during break-up.

One afternoon I was upstairs putting up partitions to divide that area into rooms when I answered a knock at the door. I was dumbfounded to find my parents standing there, having just arrived from Rochester, New York. The telegrams they had sent ahead to inform me of this visit never reached me. As if this were not enough of a surprise for one day, in less than an hour after their arrival Bishop Trocellier walked in unannounced! He had landed at Camsell Portage in his new Norseman aircraft CF-GTM through the dense smoke of forest fires. His intention was to confer the Sacrament of Confirmation on the twenty candidates I had prepared there but he did not want to go ahead without me. Being unable to use his aircraft to get me, he had Philip bring him over to Uranium City in the canoe. We all went back to Camsell Portage the next day, a Sunday. The bishop confirmed the children with my parents acting as sponsors.

That afternoon after Benediction of the Blessed Sacrament, the smoke having cleared somewhat, I flew back to Uranium City with the bishop and his entourage and we spent the night at the rectory. This visit gave me the opportunity to show the bishop the new mission at Camsell Portage and the problems facing us at Uranium City. He agreed with me that the old frame church we had moved over from Goldfields was not going to meet our needs and gave his permission to make plans for a new one. At the same time he made it official that I was the Pastor of Uranium City with jurisdiction over Camsell Portage and the surrounding mines. The next day I went over to the Eldorado mine and using one of their drafting rooms began drawing up plans for a new church. The bishop had flown on to visit the missions at Fond du Lac and Stoney Rapids and on his return two days later picked me up and flew me back to Camsell, where Philip had hosted my parents in my absence. I had a plan of a church to show the bishop and he approved it.

Dad wasn't too impressed with my hospitality. He had flown in on Saturday and here it was Wednesday and he had seen very little of me so far. I assured him that the past few days were very unusual and that I had a great spot picked out for a fishing trip the next day. Before we could get away the following day, however, a Beaver aircraft landed on floats bringing in Gordon Moore, a mining consultant who was sent by one of the big uranium companies to look at the KAY group of claims we had staked some thirty miles west of Camsell. He needed both Philip and me to show him those claims, so the fishing trip with Dad was suddenly off. Philip and I were flying west and Dad and Mom were left alone in charge of Mission Saint Bernard.

My father was not at all comfortable being completely surrounded by Indians; he had read too much of the Oregon Trail. Mother told me that on one occasion when the mission was full of natives he had removed his hat to expose his bald head and announced, "Look! Already scalped!" I didn't realize how relieved he was when I returned two days later. As it turned out we might just as well have stayed home. We ran around with Gordon for two days with our Geiger counters but all the "hot" rocks we picked up turned out to be pegmatite and we never did sell those claims. My parents' second week proved to be less hectic and I did my best to make up for the lost first week by spending as much time with them as I could. It was a good thing I did, for that was their first and last trip to the Canadian North.

In the meantime Uranium City was growing like Topsy as the new inhabitants replaced their tents with more permanent frame buildings. To pay for their new brick liquor store, the Saskatchewan Government barged in thirty-eight tons of beer and assorted spirits. One enterprising young man named David Good began editing a newspaper called *The Uranium Times.* He also sold insurance on the side and I took out a $5,000 fire insurance policy on our old church and sent the $35 premium to the bishop. The bishop wrote back that none of his buildings in the Vicariate were covered by insurance and that he confided their safety to St. Joseph (his patron saint). So I let it expire.

Mines were springing up all over the area and I was having some difficulty visiting them with my canoe and kicker. So I had the Wylie boys of Fort Chipewyan send me one of their fine twenty-two-foot skiffs and I bought a new fifteen-horsepower Evinrude motor from Dana Spence. He had just opened a hardware store in Uranium City. The Wylies took pups in trade for their boat and the sale of the old eight-horse Johnson and the canoe paid for the new motor.

I took the plans I had drawn for a new church to a local carpenter named Slim Demgard and he estimated that he could build it for about ten thousand. Shortly after that I was over at the new FAY shaft at Eldorado where Bill McKee, foreman for Burns and Dutton Contracting, was supervising the new headframe. I mentioned that I was working on the project of a new church for Uranium City and he asked to see my plans. He asked me to let his architect draw up a proper working blueprint at no charge, so I gladly agreed. A week later he showed me the completed plans and told me they could put it up for us for $36,000. The figure seemed astronomical to me and I told him the bishop would never approve such an outlay. Bill wasn't going to take my word as final and immediately asked where the bishop lived. Within an hour we were in a chartered aircraft flying to Fort Smith. The next thing I knew we were in the bishop's office with the blueprints spread over his desk and before the afternoon was out we were back at Beaverlodge with the bishop's signature on the contract. I was amazed, delighted and slightly awed by Bill's salesmanship. He even made two costly changes to the plans for me. One was the substitution of steel I-beams under the floor to avoid pillars in the church basement and the second was the installation of another gothic window in the front of the steeple.

About two weeks later, after the 11 a.m. Sunday mass at the Uranium City church, I was walking along the shore of Martin Lake visiting some families living in tents when one of them casually remarked to me, "Too bad about your church burning down today!" This was the first I'd heard of it and by the time I got back it was just a pile of smoking ashes. Apparently it had started after one of my parishioners threw a cigarette into the moss following the service. As there was no fire brigade in town as yet, it simply burned itself out. I sent a telegram to the bishop saying, "St. Joseph let us down here today. STOP. The church completely destroyed by fire." On the following day, however,

Bill McKee had his bulldozer working in the hot ashes digging the new church basement.

As soon as the walls began to rise I realized that I needed a name for the church. About that time a Sister Mary Bernard, R.S.M., wrote me from Rochester reminding me that the patron saint of miners is Saint Barbara. Of course: what could be more appropriate? Subsequently I got a chance to fly to the original New World site of Mission Santa Barbara in California, still directed by the Franciscans. There I got the background of this saint of the early church. I decided to use the Spanish version of her name and got the bishop's approval.

Using the new skiff and kicker I zipped down fifteen miles to the end of Crackingstone Point to spend a few days at the new Gunnar Mine and also to visit the old McInnes Fish Plant a mile away. Roy Schlader at the plant always made me feel welcome and this time gave me a complete tour of the operation. They had one warehouse full of winter ice for cooling the fresh trout and whitefish and walk-in freezers to freeze the fillets once they were packed in attractive boxes which, if I remember correctly, carried the Birdseye label. Eating at their mess hall was an experience that reminded me of my scholastic days: the men ate in complete silence, although I don't think that this was a company rule. Most of the men were Icelanders who lived around Lake Winnipeg. Roy explained to me that originally their fishing boats were manned by natives from Lake Athabaska, but the arrangement proved unsatisfactory. Apparently the local boys often got wind-bound in the harbour at Goldfields, where liquor was readily available. Consequently much of the fish they brought in rotted in the nets. This was unfortunate. The natives, who knew the lake like the backs of their hands, were relegated to the status of deck hands, while the Icelanders captained the boats.

When the dishes were cleared from the mess hall I set up my equipment and used it for a chapel. On at least one occasion I conducted this service with wet feet. I was wearing moose-hide moccasins and the cement floor had been hosed down following the meal. It took time for the travelling missionary to learn to cope with his environment.

I made it my first priority to be at the new Mission Saint Bernard in Camsell Portage on August 20th to celebrate its annual feast day. And this year was special, for the saint had died on this day in 1153, exactly eight hundred years before. The forty souls remaining in town joined me in the offering of a High Mass of Thanksgiving in the morning, followed by Benediction of the Blessed Sacrament in the afternoon. Then we all crossed over the short portage behind the village to the sandy beach beyond, where we enjoyed a picnic together.

With the rectory now habitable at U-City and the new church rising rapidly, it became apparent that a priest would be needed there full-time. Father Perin had returned to the east end of Lake Athabaska to start a new log mission at Stoney Lake. The bishop realized that I didn't want to quit Camsell Portage, so he appointed one of the Oblates from the Eskimo country to fill this post, Father John L'Helgouach, who came down from Aklavik. He arrived aboard *The St. Eugene* from Fort Chip and I immediately joined him at U-City to familiarize him with the area. Once he knew his way around I was free to continue visiting the mines from Camsell Portage. This arrangement suited me fine. I never did feel comfortable in that old rectory.

Early in September I got another chance to visit Eldorado's mine at Port Radium. Not only that, but I was able to cross Great Bear Lake again on *The Radium Gilbert* and visit my old mission at Fort Franklin. There I offered a special Requiem Mass for all the people who had died from tuberculosis since I had left, and I dusted off my Hare language to venture a sermon. The local boys took me by canoe from there down the Great Bear River to Bennett Field from which point the Eldorado DC-3 picked me up and returned me to Beaverlodge. It was less wrenching to leave Franklin this time, what with a neat new mission to return to at Camsell Portage.

While I continued visiting the mines around Uranium City, Philip took Mike Powder up to Tazin Lake to stake twenty-one claims on David Island, which we named the DAV group. It had become the current rush area and we thought we might have shot our own "elephant." At least we had our iron in the fire.

What we actually had on our hands was about three dozen sled dogs to feed, mostly pups. Harold Reed, Superintendent of Game from Regina, had visited and signified his willingness to pay twenty-five dollars each for as many pups as we could produce, so we were keeping five bitches. At the time this money looked like its own bonanza. Harold was using them to restock the trappers around Walliston Lake area whose strain of sled dogs had deteriorated. We saw that we would have to put up a substantial supply of fish for these dogs in the fall when the fish were running so that we could feed them later through the winter when the catch fell off. To do this we decided to establish a fishing camp about twenty-five miles west of Camsell.

We got away finally on the 15th of October. I borrowed an extra skiff, hired Mike and Archie Powder, and loaded the boats with our tent and gear, all our dogs and fifteen nets. Darkness caught us off Lobstick Island a little short of our destination. We probed around in the dark looking for a campsite for the night. We couldn't find one, and finally slept in the open. The following morning we decided on Spider Island as our base of operations and set up our tent. We were surprised to find the shore of this island littered with new dimension lumber that must have been lost off the deck of a barge during a storm. We gathered up a valuable pile of it and then put out three nets. We were torn between getting our fifteen nets out and salvaging as much of this lumber as we could before it got frozen to the rocks along the shore. The following day we did set the rest of our nets, besides picking up more lumber. We found our island covered with low bush cranberries which were attracting sharp-tailed grouse on their fall migration south. We succeeded in picking off six of them with the .22 for our supper.

On Saturday afternoon I loaded up my skiff with fish and returned to the mission at Camsell in order to conduct Sunday services. When I returned to Spider Island on Monday the boys had over 1,500 fish, mostly whitefish, the rest trout. Our principal antagonist was the weather, which was typically windy with rough seas and freezing temperatures. They were constantly pounding the ice out of their boat with axes so that it was beginning to leak. Late that evening I pulled out for home with another full load of fresh fish, but in the failing light and high seas I clipped the end of a reef and lost one blade of my prop. I stopped long enough to cut down the other two blades to reduce the vibration, but it was far from satisfactory. I limped into Camsell in the dark, thankful to have a safe harbour for the night, but I realized that I would be forced to go to Uranium City for a new prop.

The next day I was on the high seas of Lake Athabaska in one of the worst storms of the season. With gale-force winds streaking out of the southwest across a hundred miles of open water the surface of the lake was unfit for any kind of boat travel. Once I got out far enough from our protected bay and felt its full fury behind me I couldn't turn around to face it to beat my way back. I was committed. The next twenty miles was quite a ride. My speed was scary, just slightly faster than the huge waves themselves. I would gradually edge up their windward side, cut through the spray at the peak and then plunge down the lee side like a giant surf board. Going over the crests the prop was often out of the water despite the fact that this kicker had a long shaft. To lose directional control and broach in these conditions would have spelt disaster. I finally made it, nonetheless, thanks to a lot of praying and considerable luck. I was not unscathed, however: my nice new skiff had suffered a split bottom board and a broken rib. Once into Black Bay, Bob Heron told me that he had turned back in his large commercial fishing boat. It looked as if I were the only fool out on the lake that day.

After conducting service at the Eldorado mine on Sunday, I was again out on an angry sea heading back on Monday. That same south-west wind was still blowing, though not as hard. Luckily so, as now I had to force myself directly into it. At least I had a new prop and the motor sounded normal. Still, when I gained the shelter of Camsell harbour I had split another bottom board and the boat was again leaking and covered with ice from the freezing spray. Nothing had been heard from my crew on Spider Island and I was anxious to get through to them with the supplies I was bringing from town.

I got back out into the lake late in the afternoon to face a new obstacle – blowing snow coming directly at me, reducing visibility to a few hundred feet. Twenty miles down the lake it got dark and my motor quit when the carburetor iced up. I was washed by the breakers pounding on a reef near Lobstick Point and had to jump into the water and beach the skiff as best I could. Using a flashlight I got the carburetor apart and thawed out without too much trouble, but getting that heavily iced skiff back through the surf where I could restart the motor was almost more than I could manage in the dark.

Under way again, I found my way to Spider Island where I tied up to our temporary dock at midnight. The boys were fast asleep in the tent, snug in their feather robes. They didn't even hear me come in. I was too tired to eat or even to make a fire, so I simply unrolled my own bag and crawled in. Lying there waiting for sleep to come as the tent creaked and groaned in the wind and the snow piled up against it and covered the ground, I began to wonder whether keeping sled dogs was worth all the work involved. It seemed that there was really no alternative, for the age of the snowmobile had not yet arrived.

When we peered out our tent flap in the morning we saw six inches of snow covering the ground, shore ice frozen out thirty feet, a pea soup fog covering a flat sea with the temperature at zero Fahrenheit. The prospects for continuing our fall fishery were not good. Beaten by the weather? Yes, and we had started a couple of weeks too late. Besides that we had all come down with miserable colds. When we visited the nets we got only 250 fish, which indicated that the whitefish run was over. It was no use to prolong the agony. We decided to quit Spider Island. I had tried unsuccessfully to hire a large boat to come from Black Bay to get all our fish and lumber and bring them back to Camsell in one load, but no one wanted to risk the lake in the month of November. I decided to take a good load back immediately, leaving the three boys to pull all our nets and put the fish on a hastily erected stage which would protect them from wolves and other predators. They would return with me on the next trip.

Back at the mission dock, my skiff was rigid with ice. This time, however, instead of chipping it out, I simply sank the boat and left it under water overnight. In the morning it was wet but ice-free and I congratulated myself on discovering yet another way of coping with the environment. The next day the wind was up and the temperature still down, so I waited late in the day, hoping conditions would improve. They didn't, and I was forced to pull out and to battle again an angry head wind and freezing spray along thirty miles of open water. When I finally reached our camp in the dark I was completely covered in ice and stiff with cold. The thought of the warmth of the tent had helped keep my spirits up for the last hour, but I was robbed of this reward when I found the tent cold and empty: the boys had gone! I revived my circulation by spending an hour alone, trying to pull the heavy skiff up on the shore ice where it wouldn't freeze in overnight.

The next day the seas were running so high I couldn't risk leaving the island with a full load, so I busied myself around the camp cutting firewood, chipping ice off the skiff, all the while keeping one eye on the weather, anxious to leave. The other skiff was gone; it had been leaking so badly I had to conclude that the boys had used it only to reach the mainland and from there had walked back to the village. I spent another lonely night in the tent on Spider Island before the wind finally dropped and I could prepare to leave. Breaking shore ice, I got the skiff back into the water and loaded with all our nets, plus 500 fish. Now the boat was so heavy that it was resting on rocks below and I was forced to get into the water to lift it off. This was when I noticed that my sealskin mukluks were leaking; mice had chewed holes in them during the night. Ill fortune continued to plague me: I got under way and had completed half the distance home when I ran out of gas. Luckily I stopped within poling distance of an abandoned drill camp where I found some fuel. I got back to the mission at two in the afternoon and found Philip and the Powder boys had walked in during the night.

As the lake was unusually calm we quickly unloaded and Philip immediately set out to get another load of fish from Spider Island. He didn't show up by nightfall and I was worried, but he did walk in at midnight. The carburetor had again iced up and he was forced to abandon the heavily loaded skiff across the portage a mile away. When we brought it around into the bay the next morning the temperature registered fifteen above zero and the fresh fish had frozen into one solid block of ice. We had to sink the boat with rocks in order to melt the fish loose. As the ice now extended out seventy feet from shore we were forced to call it quits and haul the boat out for good.

Spider Island had taught us a few tough lessons for coping with the wind and waves in below-freezing temperatures in an open boat where one is practically immobile and exposed to bone-chilling winds. We suffered more from the cold under these circumstances than we ever did travelling in the dead of winter with dogs. We agreed that it was less painful picking fish from nets set under the ice in winter than removing them from the same nets from a boat pitching on the waves and covered with ice. Next year we would do it differently.

The colds we had contracted in that tent on Spider Island could have been pneumonia. Even after we were back in the warmth of the mission Philip was still suffering from his, and a curious side-effect was that his ankles began to swell up. As two of the boys were determined to make one last trip to Uranium City by boat before freeze-up, Philip jumped in with them and went over to see Dr. Don McMillan at Eldorado. They returned without him, carrying a note saying that the diagnosis looked like Bright's disease and that he was being flown to the General Hospital in Edmonton for observation and tests. It looked like we hadn't heard the last of Spider Island. The thought of losing my faithful companion to a prolonged sickness was enough to depress me. I had all the townspeople joining me in fervent prayer for his speedy recovery. What else could we do?

In mid-December I left our dogs in the care of Mike Powder and flew to Uranium City, then continued over to Eldorado by road. I decided that I would go up to the mine at Port Radium and stay there over Christmas and New Year's, something I had never done before. To get there I went in the opposite direction first, flying the Eldorado DC-3 to Edmonton where I could check up on Philip's condition. He was still suffering from a severe kidney infection, but was making progress. His doctor thought that he could soon be discharged. With this good news I left him in the General and boarded one of Eldorado's DC-3's for the long day's flight to Great Bear lake. I had gotten to know the pilots and they invited me up front to view the frozen panorama out the front windows. Just north of Hottah Lake we flew over a vast herd of caribou that were being harassed by ten wolves. They epitomized the wild North and its primitive law of the survival of the fittest just as we, safe above in our comfortable travelling quarters, represented the last word in civilization. It was interesting to speculate on which world would outlast the other.

As it was close to Christmas I found the mine personnel in a particularly festive mood. Everyone had a word of good cheer and welcomed my intention of staying with them over the holidays. As usual the contingent of Irishmen was conspicuous by their faithful presence at the early morning mass. For the Christmas Midnight Mass the rec hall was crowded with just about everyone living at the mine. Mine Manager Gil Gillanders was his usual hospitable self and had me comfortably bunked in the guest house along with the pilots. When I heard that there were still a few Indian families living over at the old Cameron Bay townsite I walked the six miles over there after Christmas to get all the news in Hareskin from Fort Franklin. They had moved into the assay office and were doing enough trapping and casual work around the mine to keep the proverbial wolf from the door. George Blondin brought me back to the mine with his dog-team, although I would really have preferred to stay with the Indians.

If Christmas had a religious aura about it that engendered an atmosphere of "Silent Night, Holy Night," New Year's was something entirely different. Parties were being held every night in various quarters and the pitch of these celebrations was building as the last days of the old year ran out. To add fuel to the fire the 300 men working there were given an extra ration of liquor on the last day of 1953 to help them celebrate.

Early that evening I was availing myself of the luxury of a shower when a hand appeared before my face with half a glass of rye in it and a voice yelled, "Here, Padre, you can add your own water!" Evidently the chaplain was expected to join in the general celebration. Later in the evening I was glad I wasn't down in one of the bunkhouses when two groups started a war with the high pressure fire hoses. Although there was a Mountie in camp for the holidays, he could do little to disarm the combatants alone as they drove each other from end to end of their building with their water canons. As the water got deeper they tore the doors off their rooms to walk on. With an outside temperature of fifty below, these floors began to freeze and they were soon slipping and falling on ice. The upshot was that the entire bunkhouse had to be evacuated in the middle of the night – to another bunkhouse – where the celebrations continued till dawn.

On New Year's Day most of the camp had sobered up with the exception of a few who were suffering from delirium tremens – like Joe Leduc who was bunked in a room adjoining mine. He started pounding on my wall and yelling for me to come and help him. When I got over there Joe was wide-eyed with fear. "Help me get this highboy over against that window before that tidal wave hits!" he yelled. Not having had any experience with delirium tremens patients I thought perhaps the best way to calm him down was to go along with his fantasies no matter how bizarre, so the first thing I knew I was helping Joe move not only the highboy but the bed and all the furniture up against his window facing the lake. "Get down! Get down!" Joe yelled, "Here she comes!" And then, when he reopened his eyes he said,

"Lucky it missed us, but help me get that crocodile out of here!" Finally we got the crocodile back out the window and the furniture back in place and I eased myself out the door saying, "Let me know if any more tidal waves come along, Joe." Christmas at Port Radium proved to be anything but dull. Still I was glad I was only visiting and not a permanent chaplain at that mine.

We flew south past the Beaverlodge mine and landed at Edmonton where I hurried over to visit Philip, still in hospital. His physician told me he was going to be discharged, but he advised against his spending the rest of the winter at Camsell Portage. In view of this admonition Philip decided to return to France to visit his family and I turned over to him all the money I had to finance the trip.

When I finally landed back at Mission Saint Bernard, I found our meat and fish all gone and the dogs starving. Not only that, but King, a beautiful, pure white lead dog from the Chip mission kennel, was lame. I had left orders not to drive the dogs, but I was told that Eric Powder had been using them to haul wood for himself. We still had a good supply of fish on our stage at Spider Island, so I took off the following day with a long string of dogs, leaving King at home to recuperate.

It was late in the afternoon when I made my departure, but I wasn't worried as the moon was full and I planned on spending the night with Simon Bashaw, a Russian trapper. He had a cabin up Colin River, a stream on the mainland a couple of miles from Spider Island. I was near the mouth of this stream travelling in the moonlight about 9 p.m., when suddenly my world went dark! The earth's shadow covered the moon in a total eclipse.

Once off the wind-blown lake the snow was hip deep and I couldn't find a trail with my feet as I searched from bank to bank. I had left my snowshoes back at the mission, thinking I wouldn't need them. By the time I plowed my way to Simon's cabin I was wringing wet and there was nobody home. I took my dogs out of harness and chained them to Simon's unique dog posts which supported a circular, thatched roof, gazebo-like structure intended to shelter his dogs from the winter storms. Although individually chained they could all sleep together under this common roof. I then picked my grub packsack from my sled and entered the dark cabin. Finally I located the candle, lit it, kindled a fire in his stove and fried some caribou steaks.

Looking around at the unusual contents of that cabin reminded me of the nights Philip and I had spent in it with Simon on some of our dogsled trips. Simon rated high on my list of unforgettable characters. He said he was a White Russian and we had no reason to doubt him. When he first came into this country he had built himself such a small log cabin it looked almost like a doll house with just enough length for a bunk to accommodate his short stature and one tiny window with a single ten inch by twelve inch pane of glass. That building was still standing, although its sod roof was falling in. His present cabin was a normal size and featured strings of bells hung outside each window to scare bears away. On entering the cabin, the first thing one noticed was the floor covered with all types and sizes of empty tin cans. When I asked Simon about this, he replied that once, years ago, he was visited by another trapper who spent the night with him. Before retiring, this fellow had asked for a chamber pot so that he could answer the call of nature during the night without having to open the front door. Simon looked high and low but couldn't find one, but then and there vowed to himself that he would never again be caught short of such a basic item of hospitality. He had been saving his cans ever since. The floor was so cluttered with them, in fact, that he had formed pathways through them to get around the cabin.

Another odd item was the radio sitting by his bed. It was completely covered with wax that had dripped from a thousand candles placed on top of it to read by. Two holes were worn through this covering to get to the tuning knobs. Simon spent his long, lonely evenings reading geology books, of which he had a good library above the head of his bunk. He claimed to know where all the minerals in the area were hidden and told us his price was $200 per day to guide prospectors to them. This was a modest price to pay to locate a mine he assured us, but to date no one had engaged his services.

Simon had some interesting supernatural experiences, he confided to us late one night. I think he told these stories for my special benefit. All of the incidents occurred while he was travelling by dogs in winter and sleeping by an open fire. He said he didn't pray often, but when he did he always got an immediate response. He had to be careful. Late during World War II he had heard of his countryman Stalin and decided to pray. Immediately a beautiful figure clothed completely in white walked into the firelight and asked, "Simon, did you call me?" Without asking, Simon knew he was face-to-face with Christ. "Yes," replied Simon, "I've been reading about the terrible war in my homeland and I wanted to volunteer my services to go back and speak to Stalin about ending this conflict and bloodshed." According to Simon, Christ thanked him for his offer and promised that he would call on him if it became necessary, but he never did.

Another time when Simon was camped out for the night with his sled dogs chained around him he was bothered by a pack of wolves that were circling his camp, just out of sight. The constant whimpering of his dogs was keeping him awake, so again, as a last resort, he prayed. Immediately a beautiful figure dressed entirely in green walked up to his fire to ask if he had called. Simon asked this time if it were Christ again, but the heavenly figure replied, "No, Simon, I'm the Archangel Michael. What can I do for you?" Simon explained how the pack of wolves was harassing him. Without another word the angel beckoned to his companions who were standing just out of the firelight and together they each took hold of a wolf by the scruff of the neck and led them all away. "That's the last time wolves annoyed me," concluded Simon. And then, bringing his face up close to mine he asked, "Are you thinking I'm crazy?" "Of course not, Simon," I replied as convincingly as I could under the circumstances, though I doubt that there was much conviction in my tone. When we hit the trail the next day we were convinced that Simon, if not crazy, was certainly bushed.

Recollections like these were passing through my mind as I stayed alone in Simon's cabin that evening after supper, pulling on my pipe and wondering where he'd gone and when he'd return. And then I thought I heard the distant bark of a dog and jumped to the conclusion that it was Simon returning. I walked out of the cabin into the full moonlight which lit up the surrounding forest almost like day. It was an incredibly beautiful mid-winter evening, absolutely calm and still. I stood there listening for a repetition of the sound I had heard.

There it was again, more of a lonesome howl than a bark, but certainly made by a dog. Or a wolf? It was close, toward the lake, and not moving. There was a hard trail in the snow going in that same direction so I began following it slowly. Soon I saw another cabin about two hundred yards away, one I didn't know existed. There was a thin wisp of smoke coming out of a stove pipe. Who could be living that close to Simon? Or had Simon moved? Now I could see the source of the howling I had heard, three dogs chained out behind. I wanted to look through the window before I went any farther. Though the faint glow of a candle seemed to be reflecting from the inside, the glass was too frosted to see through. I tried the door, but it was evidently locked from the inside. An old and weak female voice asked in Chipewyan, "Who's there?" I replied, *"Yati"* – "the priest" – but she immediately rejoined with *"Ille, eketsele onte"* – "No, it's the devil!"

I wasn't going to stand outside all night arguing with her, so I threw enough weight against the door to break the file that had locked it from the inside. Well, there she was lying on the floor, a little, wizened old Chipewyan woman in her feather robe. Her head was propped up on several sacks of flour, sugar and rolled oats. To her right was a small camp stove and to her left a stack of split kindling and a few cakes of ice. After she saw me she calmed down and took me for whom I said I was.

I was able to get her story, mostly by asking questions. First of all, she was Simon's wife. Secondly, she had fallen through the thin ice of Colin River, got herself soaked, and as a result caught a cold that got worse and worse. Finally, she told Simon that the only thing to cure her would be the meat of a young caribou. So he had left to kill one, but had already been gone "two Sundays." A couple of days before, she had turned delirious and rolled against the hot stove, which burned her one leg so badly she could no longer walk on it. She showed me the burn, but I had no medicines with me and could only put some lard on it and wrap it up as best I could. She had some stick fish hanging off her stage, so I fed her dogs and she gave me enough to feed mine, too.

It was several months later that I heard from Simon about the strange circumstances of his wife living in a separate cabin. After their marriage at Fort Chipewyan nearly forty years before, they had lived together for "nearly two weeks." Then there was a disagreement over her cooking, so Simon fixed up his warehouse and she moved there. That had solved their problem; since then they had enjoyed a happy marriage. No children issued from it, but according to Simon they never had an argument and, although separated, were actually very close. "Some evenings I go over there to visit and some evenings she comes over here," said Simon. According to the Crees at Camsell I learned that they not only lived separately, but travelled the same way. In winter she followed his team with her own sled and dogs, and in summer he towed her small canoe behind his boat and motor.

The following morning I saw that the old woman was as comfortable as possible under the circumstances and tried to make her understand that although I had to leave I would send her help as soon as possible. I then harnessed up and drove the two or three miles out to Spider Island where I found that the drifting snow had built a natural ramp right up to our fish stage making it easily accessible to the foxes and wolves who had been helping themselves. I took only 150 fish because my dogs were still weak from their prolonged hunger while I was away and couldn't haul a full load. As it was, it took me six hours to get back to the mission.

I sent a telegram to the RCMP in Uranium City and they immediately dispatched a med-evac plane for the old lady and flew her to the hospital. Another flight searched and found Simon camped on a lake about fifty miles north of his cabin. He was still waiting for caribou. His wife didn't live too many months following her ordeal and died in her cabin. When the Mounties came to investigate, Simon told them to give all her stuff to the mission at Chip. He didn't want to keep any of it. They were amazed to find under the loose floor boards at the back of her cabin many new items like guns, axes, bolts of cloth, and so on, things she had bought with her own fur money and hoarded. She had been an excellent hunter and trapper. The natives at Camsell said she drifted silently through the bush on snowshoes in winter, dressed all in white canvas clothing she had made. They were afraid of her. Simon, finding life alone too hard, later moved to Chip and Philip bought his cabin and trap line.

13

FOR EVERYTHING,
A SEASON

Living alone again, I had to be out driving a dog-team on a daily schedule, either cutting and hauling firewood to keep the mission warm, or bringing in fish to keep the huskies fuelled. Besides the regular trips to Spider Island, I was also visiting several nets set under the ice nearby. The fact that I had so many mature dogs, two full teams of six each, plus the corral full of pups in various stages of development, meant that we needed far more fish than our neighbours. And this particular winter with Philip gone I had to feed his non-working team as well. These sled dogs required about five pounds of fish per night each, more if they were working or the temperature was extremely cold. I not only had to provide for them on a daily basis, but to stockpile ahead so a neighbour could feed them when I was away visiting the mines.

When I hitched up and left for Uranium City on January 26th it was forty-five below zero. King had had several weeks' rest to recuperate from his "sprain," so I put him in the lead position. He never let his traces slacken all the thirty miles to town although he began limping badly the last few miles. The next day I took him to see Dr. McMillan at the mine clinic and he X-rayed his front leg. The negative clearly showed that both bones had been broken. Neither of us could understand how he could have run so far in that condition. It was an amazing testimony to sheer grit and determination that bolstered my already considerable admiration for these great animals.

Although we put his leg in a plaster cast, just like a human, he never regained full use of it and continued to limp even after it had fully knit. So I had to retire him from the team and presented him to Leon LaPrairie who kept him as a mascot for his mine on Beaverlodge Lake. The following year I was saddened to hear that King had been mistaken for a wolf and shot.

In the meantime, life was going ahead full-steam in the "Uranium Capital of the World" and in all the surrounding bush camps and nascent mines. The staking stampede was being compared to the Klondike fifty years before, as newcomers flocked in from all over the world. Although half the residents in town were still living in tents, houses were being skidded over from Goldfields in a steady stream and all kinds of frame buildings were going up even during the sub-zero months. Gus Hawker, still operating out of a tent, claimed he was doing up to $4,000 worth of business some days. The Eldorado mine five miles away had become a small town in itself, with a population of 750. Brother Larocque was putting the final touches to the interior of Santa Barbara church with a beautiful spiral staircase to the choir loft. A second newspaper, The Uranium Era, was being published by Jock McMeekan who had quit Yellowknife for the new boom town.

In Prince Albert, five hundred miles south, the Saskatchewan Mines Branch of the government announced that dozens of prospectors had cashed in claims for amounts ranging from $10,000 to $1,000,000. I kept running into reporters from outside. Famous northern photographer Richard Harrington took pictures of me and my team and advised me to get a Rolleicord camera like the one he used. Soon afterwards, I was written up in the Toronto Daily Star, which mentioned that I had hung up a "For Sale" sign on over 100 uranium claims. The proceeds would help pay off a $50,000 debt on the new church in town.

Not long afterwards I received a telegram through the Saskatchewan Government Telegraph Office in town from some oil company in New York offering me $250,000 in cash, plus 300,000 shares of stock if I would turn over to them within ten days the twenty-seven claims Philip and I owned on David Island in Lake Tazin. This offer seemed too good to be true. I had just gotten over to Camsell Portage when it was relayed to me and I immediately harnessed up and went back to U-City singing all the way! I had just tied up my dogs outside the rectory at U-City and was inside thawing out when there came a knock at the door. A certain Mr. Watt claiming to represent a small prospecting company called Great West Uranium handed me a piece of paper and hastily departed. It was an official court order called a "Caveat" against our twenty-seven claims on David Island which we had registered as the DAV Group. The Latin word caveat means, literally, "let him beware" and pertains to anyone interested in the property, warning him not to proceed with any transaction until the party serving the notice is heard. In other words, Great West Uranium was claiming some unspecified interest in these claims for some reason they did not give. My high-flying spirits were shot down even before I could contact New York.

Now I needed someone I didn't think I would ever need: a lawyer. I needed him in a hurry, too, because I had never been the subject of any legal action and I had no idea of the consequences of a caveat. The only lawyer I had met in Uranium City was Edward Lussiere who had flown into town from Regina to organize a chapter of the Canadian Legion. I was glad at the time to let him use the basement of the new church to hold his meeting and he had told me afterwards that if I ever needed the services of a lawyer to contact him. Without delay I put the case completely in his hands. Soon he got word back to me that this caveat could not be lifted before it had gone before a judge of the Queen's Bench Court in Regina, and the earliest hearing we could get would be in nine months. One can imagine my thoughts as I stood on the back of my sled returning to Camsell.

I brightened considerably when I received a letter from one Albert Jacobs in Calgary who was also interested in claims we held. This time it involved the forty-two HAR Group of claims we had staked around Camsell Portage. A subsequent letter contained an airline ticket on Canadian Pacific's DC-3 and I soon found myself in Calgary. I was impressed with the apparent integrity of Jacobs and his group of business friends who owned and operated a company called Great Shield Uranium Mines Limited. Although they owned properties containing various minerals, they were anxious to acquire some uranium property before the bubble burst. Many companies were doing this to enhance their image and help sell stock. They were also interested in our DAV Group once we got the caveat lifted from it. The upshot of this meeting was that I flew home with 50,000 vendor's shares of stock in Great Shield Uranium. These could not be converted to cash as they were held in escrow (that is, held in trust by a third party for delivery only after fulfillment of the conditions specified).

In the meantime Philip had run out of money in Europe where he was touring by motorcycle, so I sent him $250. This money came from our sale of salvaged lumber on Spider Island. Any money I collected at the mines was going to Father L'Helgouach at Uranium City to help pay for the new church. The sale of a few uranium claims for cash at this time would have been welcome.

The day after our arrival in Regina we finally got to see our antagonists from Great West Uranium in a pre-trial discovery hearing. To our amazement their lawyer stated that his clients had made a mistake in filing the original caveat against us on the flimsy pretext that they had gotten the names of the Powder boys working with Philip mixed up with other Powders from Camsell Portage who had previously worked for them and who had signed a contract that they would not stake for anyone else for a period of three years. Would we settle out of court? Imagine waiting nine months to hear this and to have lost our $250,000 sale in the meantime. Our lawyer pointed out to them that we were not just fighting an unjust caveat, but suffered the consequent loss of sale.

Although we had already waited nine months, we still had to wait another week in Regina while the same judge heard another case. We sat in on it as it involved a conflict over staking claims in our area. The judge was constantly interrupting testimony to ask simple questions about the country and the fundamental rules for staking claims. Evidently he had never handled cases like these, but it seemed to me that he could have cut days off his hearing time if he had simply studied the rules for staking mineral claims. The defendant in this case was so certain of an outcome favourable to his case that he had gone ahead and spent thousands of dollars drilling on his disputed property. This judge, however, amazed us all by rendering a decision not only against the defendant, but contrary to Saskatchewan's own mining regulations. I had supper with this poor man following the verdict. He was a defeated man and a likely candidate for suicide. I had sat through the entire proceedings and felt strongly that it had not been a fair judgement. Besides that, I was beginning to have doubts about getting a just verdict for our own case.

When our case came up the next day it proved to be unique for this court, as neither our lawyer nor the judge himself had ever been involved in a caveat case involving mineral claims. When Great West Uranium's own lawyer admitted that they had made a mistake in their caveat the judge was forced to agree with him. In his brief, however, our lawyer had not only protested the false caveat, he had also claimed general damages of a modest $50,000 for the loss of a bona fide sale due to this caveat. At this point the judge knocked the ground out from under our case, declaring that our loss of the sale should have been termed "a particular" damage; if we wished to pursue this claim we would have to start proceedings for an entirely new action. In other words he dismissed our claim to a just compensation on the basis of one word. The only compensation we did realize was $1,600 to cover our travelling and hotel expenses. Our own lawyer, who represented a firm of nine law partners in Regina, was so disgusted with this verdict that he refused to charge anything for representing us.

As soon as the red-serge Mountie on duty in the courtroom dismissed us, I immediately walked over to the new Saskatchewan Mines Building where an old friend from Uranium City, Don Sheridan, was in charge. I told him the story of our caveat experience from beginning to end. As Saskatchewan mining regulations then stood, anyone could get a caveat injunction against any mining company or individual on the flimsiest of evidence or, as in our case, on a false accusation. Not only could such a property under caveat not be transferred or sold, the caveat effectively tied up all stock promotion work or other financing. Sheridan acknowledged the urgent need for new legislation to plug this loophole and several months later sent me a copy of the new ordinance respecting "false and vexatious" caveats such as the one we had just gotten lifted. There was now an automatic penalty attached to filing such a caveat of $25 per claim per day. If this law had been in effect nine months earlier Great West Uranium would have paid $675 per day or $182,250 for the nine months they had their caveat on our claims. As the five of us flew back to Uranium City we reflected on the low calibre of justice dispensed by the Court of Queen's Bench in Regina. One can easily imagine my reaction to an offer from this same company a few months later to act as their representative in our area.

In the end we fared little better in our association with Great Shield Uranium Mines. Philip got some money to do some trenching on our HAR Group of claims and mining engineer Gordon Moore did confirm that there was U308 present on this property, but for various reasons the company had difficulty selling enough stock to finance further work. Over time I was asked by Albert Jacobs to surrender to him my shares of vendor's stock until finally I was left with none and the company died. Chalk it all up to experience. From the outside it looked like an interesting game. We played it and lost.

More than know-how was involved in the staking and selling of uranium claims and in playing the market on the many stocks offered by the established mines in the area. Certainly Pat Hughes and his Hibernian cohorts had been blessed with the proverbial luck of the Irish. At Eldorado a group of executives had formed an investment club to pool their knowledge and funds in an effort to pick the right stocks. After the first year they found to their surprise that they had lost forty percent of their money. During the same time an illiterate immigrant hoistman at that mine had made a small fortune investing in similar stocks without the benefit of any professional advice. Simply luck.

Following the last heroic run of King to Eldorado I stayed around the area for two weeks, visiting various mines. Then I returned to Mission Saint Bernard and the simple life to wind down and regain my serenity and peace of mind. I cleaned out the rest of our fish from Spider Island, saw my wood pile grow again and joined the Crees on caribou hunts. I got the last of the cupboards built in the mission and found I could keep warm even overnight in this log cabin by stoking the cast iron heater with green birch just before retiring. The beautiful view out my front windows facing the bay more than compensated for the absence of electricity, running water and inside plumbing. I had these comforts at the mines, but was happier without them at Camsell Portage. They were nice, but not really necessary to happiness.

By the first part of April I was back visiting the mines and even flying up to visit the boys at Port Radium again. On Good Friday I left U-City by dogs and was back at Camsell before noon. The next day was Holy Saturday and in preparation for Easter a crew of women gave the mission a good house cleaning. In the midst of this activity a Beaver aircraft landed on skis in front of the village carrying four chief game wardens: Frank McCall from North West Territories, Harold Reed from Regina, Chick Terry from Stoney Rapids and Earl Shannon from U City. The women retired to their homes and I rang the bell to summon the men to a trappers' meeting. When everyone was in and accounted for, Frank McCall took the floor to discuss the question of wolves.

He told us that in 1933 there had been fourteen white trappers working out of Fort Reliance who had been taking about 900 wolves per year. Last year, 1953, about 1,000 wolves were killed in N.W.T., without any bounty being paid, while during the same period 350 were killed by Saskatchewan trappers who were paid ten dollars per wolf. Eight trappers from Camsell Portage were trapping in the N.W.T. All four wardens present agreed that the bounty was simply another form of government subsidy and did not affect the number of wolves taken. Frank cited, as an example of politics interfering with game management, the recent election of Merv Hardy as the first Member of Parliament for the N.W.T. Keeping a promise he had made during his campaign, he immediately got the game laws changed, making the shooting of beaver legal, while five cases of transgression against the previous law were still pending in Fort Smith. The Game Department had had no say in the change in regulations. Various opinions were expressed back and forth regarding wolves and beavers while I took the minutes. After an afternoon of discussion it was finally resolved that the Camsell trappers would be allowed to take 13 beaver and 50 muskrat each during the upcoming spring hunt while the community as a whole would be allowed 6 permits for moose. Following the meeting I cooked up a caribou steak supper for the group and they took off.

Easter Sunday broke clear and ten above zero. My two bells, the first a half-hour before service and the second fifteen minutes before, saw the whole village crowding into the mission's common room. When the curtains were opened, revealing the altar at the far end, they were in church. We sang a high mass to celebrate the Lord's Resurrection and the twenty-six children of school age outsang their elders. The first collection of the year (the second being at Christmas) amounted to $17.39. In the evening they returned to watch a slide show of local scenes and local people, which they loved.

While the airwaves those nights were filled with the hearings of the investigation by Senator Joe McCarthy, I much preferred to read about the North. I had a good library of Arctic books and practically confined all my reading to that subject, as I had done since high school days. The exploits of the early explorers particularly excited my imagination. In the back of my mind I entertained the thought that some day I would work along the Arctic Coast. I was perfectly happy on Lake Athabaska, but the Far North held a special challenge. Often when I would write the bishop I would end my report by reminding him that if ever he were in need of someone to fill an empty Arctic mission he had an eager volunteer in me.

Toward the end of April the warm rays of the sun had melted the drifts of snow on the main lake to a point where one could again use the sixteen-foot Eskimo komatik with its steel runners. I decided to make another trip to the far east end of Lake Athabaska and in Philip's place chose Archie Powder to accompany me. He went by the nickname "Curley" and had a special fondness for the Hank Williams tune "You Win Again," which he sang throughout our entire trip. Our first port of call was Gunnar Mine on the tip of Crackingstone Point where we stopped for lunch. Since my last visit there had been a few changes, one of which was a sign outside the mess hall which read, "This Mine Under the Atomic Energy Control Board – Authorized Personnel Only." In fact, we couldn't get into the mess hall without a proper ID card and by the time I had gotten one from the office the mess hall was closed. Curley and I drove the dogs across to the island and made a fire there.

Before camping that night on Big Fowl Island east of Goldfields we were lucky to have killed one caribou. The following day we pushed through to Fond du Lac in eight hours without stopping to make a fire. We passed a pleasant night at the mission with Father Gamache and Brother Labonté and then continued east down the centre of the narrowing lake. For the last ten miles into Stoney Rapids the shore of the lake is covered with giant arctic willows, which at the time of our passing were covered with thousands of migrating willow ptarmigan. I never saw so many congregated in one spot before, nor have I since. We passed by Stoney Village at 7:30 in the evening and then got on the portage trail to Black Lake and went for another hour before we hit the small settlement of Stoney Lake. Here I found my Goldfields companion, Father Rudolph Perin, busily engaged in building an addition to his log mission. As space was limited we decided to go on another few miles to the village of Black Lake where the old mission cabin was empty.

Curley and I spent an interesting week at Black Lake. Here we found the Chipewyan Indians to be very primitive, compared to others we had seen. For example, there was one cabin there that still had windows made of caribou skin, which had been used all over the North before the first glass was imported. Some were wearing parkas made of caribou hide and one girl wore a beautiful sable coat made entirely of marten skins. I took pictures of her. In fact I spent most of the week either walking about taking pictures or at the mission making sketches of various visitors. I now had a Bell and Howell 16 mm movie camera with plenty of Kodachrome film supplied by various friends in Rochester who worked for Eastman Kodak. The film I exposed then now holds a record of a way of life long since passed. These people were waiting for the spring migration of the caribou upon which they depended greatly, for government social assistance was still unknown in their country. As the snow was melting rapidly, most of the men of the village were busy attaching runners to the bottoms of their toboggans to protect the wood boards from the candling ice on which they would soon be running.

By the tenth of May I decided we had stayed as long as we could, given the deteriorating ice conditions we would meet before getting back to Camsell Portage. We left in a spring snow storm that turned to rain after we passed Stoney Rapids and completely soaked our winter parkas and moose-hide foot gear. Luckily we came upon a tent and pulled up in front of it. The occupant was a white trapper by the name of Fred Riddle who spent his winters out on the Barrens and was camped at this spot now to intercept some of the migrating caribou. He would put up the meat in mason jars for winter use.

During the afternoon a troop of these animals passed in front of the tent and we helped Fred shoot and butcher ten of them. In the evening around his camp stove this veteran of "the land of little sticks and silent places" regaled us with interesting stories of his life there. It was his custom to fly north to his remote log cabin with his dogs a month before the first snows came. He would spend this time gathering dry willows for his winter's fuel. One fall he encountered a huge Barren Lands grizzly rolling in fat just prior to hibernation. Fred shot him and got enough fat from his carcass to fill a forty-five-gallon barrel. At one time he had neighbours trapping out there who used to run into each other occasionally, but now he was all alone, the last of that breed.

We continued on our way the following morning in deteriorating ice conditions. In many places we detoured around black ice that was completely candled and ready to give way under any pressure from above. As usual, we dragged a forty-foot rope behind the sled which served many purposes. It was always securely tied when we were harnessing up in the morning lest the anxious dogs should give a lurch and the sled take off before we were ready. If we ran behind the sled to warm up on cold days we always held on to this rope in case we fell and could thereby drag the dogs to a stop. It served another purpose this day when we approached a patch of rotten ice going through the narrows at Pine Channel. When it looked inevitable that the sled would break through the ice, Curley and I jumped off holding this rope and circling to the side. The dogs fell through followed by the komatik just as we expected and they were able to scramble out again. If we hadn't been able to help them with that long rope, however, the dogs wouldn't have been able to pull our loaded sled up onto solid ice again. If we had not been alert we most certainly would have found ourselves floundering in very deep water.

Dog-driving, like piloting an aircraft, is not really very difficult to learn, but to do it successfully demands a certain amount of good judgement and common sense. Otherwise disaster can overtake one when least expected. It took us eight hours to get from Fred's tent to Fond du Lac, where the rain resumed just as we pulled into the mission yard. The following day was cooler, with the result that the candling ice was sharper on the dogs' feet and their pads were beginning to cut and bleed. This condition didn't seem to bother them, for they kept up a very brisk dog-trot all day, sometimes breaking into a run when we got close to a band of migrating caribou.

On day four of our trip home we entered St. Mary's Channel which cuts through the southern tip of Crackingstone Point. The ice in this area was particularly bad and we proceeded with caution past the deserted buildings of the McInnes summer fish plant and stopped on the island two miles farther on opposite Gunnar Mine. We pitched our tent here and prepared to spend the night. I had two objectives in mind. The first was to hold a service for the 150 men working at the mine under the capable direction of Manager Norm Grant. The second was to prevail upon Clementine Mercredi, whose family was camped nearby, to sew canvas shoes quickly for our nine dogs. As it turned out, I didn't get a one hundred percent turnout for the mass I offered at Gunnar Mine, nor did Clementine finish enough shoes for all the dogs. Still, when we pushed on for the final leg of our journey the next day, at least the worst-cut feet were shod.

All across the thirty miles of open lake ice there was a constant ominous creaking under our sled and most of our dogs were limping. When we arrived at the entrance to Camsell Bay there was already a wide gap of open water between the ice and the shore and we had to look hard for a spot where we could get safely ashore. Once we were back on terra firma in the village, Curley's family rushed down to pump his hand like one returned from the dead. I unharnessed the dogs, feeling grateful for their splendid three-hundred-mile effort, and chained them to the line with the assurance that they could take it easy until the fall. It was the middle of May and we had been gone seventeen days. Time now to rest and loll under the warming sun of break-up.

It felt natural to slip back into the easy routine of life at the Camsell mission. I was hardly burning any wood now, so that was no longer a problem. Although the dogs were eating less than they did in winter I still had twenty to feed. With all our nets pulled out for break-up our only source of fish was the shallow water across the portage where the jackfish were numerous. A common method of catching them was to wade around in hip boots with a .22, and when one was spotted to approach as quietly as possible and then fire off the gun under water close to him. The concussion would generally stun him so that he would float to the surface long enough for us to grab him. If we delayed he would get his senses back and take off. I fed the dogs many a day after spending an hour or two at this pursuit. When more ice melted we could resume casting with a spoon hook.

Before the month was out there was enough open water in the bay for a float plane to land. It was a couple of local boys with a load of liquor from U-City. I had to wince as I watched it off-loaded, knowing what the consequences would be: a wild party followed by a fight, shouting, swearing, someone pounding on my door early in the morning to get a cut bandaged or sewn up, some women walking around the village the next day with black eyes. The Crees were unlike the Chipewyans or Hares: they held grudges for a long time; under the influence of liquor they often exploded in anger. Every time hard liquor came into the village I was apprehensive. For this reason I refused to drink with the natives and never bought any myself.

By the fifth of June there was enough open water to launch my skiff and go down to the far end of the bay a mile away and set a net. While down there I did some casting and caught a pike so large I had to go ashore and gradually drag him up on the beach. I didn't have any scales, but guessed he was over twenty-five pounds. It was the largest jackfish I ever caught. A week later the main lake was free enough of ice to permit me to return to Uranium City and the mines. The Mercredis, still camped near the McInnes fish camp, told me they could easily take care of my dogs there during the summer, when the fish plant had plenty of scraps for the taking. So I went back and brought them all over, relieved of that worry.

※ ※ ※

The first winter I served as chaplain at Eldorado Mine I got my first exposure to Unionism. This was before the staff house was built and I was given an office off one of the bunkhouses. The office was separated by a thin partition and one could easily hear voices through it. I remember very vividly an organizer from the Mine, Mill and Smelters' Union talking to several of the workers in the bunkhouse about forming a union. He was evidently going about it by down-grading the present living conditions, telling the men that the slop they were eating was fit only for dogs, and that they should be sleeping in clean sheets and not sleeping bags. Many were Displaced Persons from Europe who had suffered through World War II and now thought they were in heaven. This organizer did his best to convince them that they were being short-changed by management. I was alarmed to hear this line of vitriolic dissension being sown among the men and began asking questions about this union. I found out that they had their headquarters in Sudbury, Ontario, and had been permanently barred from the Canadian Federation of Trade Unions. They were heavily infiltrated by Communists and used any means, fair or foul, to gain their ends.

When they started agitating at the Nesbitt-LaBine Mine the officials there attempted to thwart them by proposing to their men a company union. This move provoked the Mine-Mill organizers so much they began harrying and beating up some of the company men. Bernie Belec, for instance, could not leave the mine without a police escort. In the end Mine-Mill did get certification at this mine, but some of the votes were forged.

During the summer I was attracted to the Eldorado mess hall one night to attend a meeting called by one "Brother" Thibault, one of the Mine-Mill officials from Sudbury. I sat at the back and listened for two hours to this man calumniate the mine management people. It was vicious, untrue and calculated to drive a wedge between management and labour. It was "them" against "us," and of course Brother Thibault was one of "us." No member of the staff was there to defend management, but if I had not been in my position I would have loved to have stood and refuted some of his lies.

Shortly afterwards the mine had a visit from an official of the American Federation of Labor Union (A. F. of L.) in the person of Carl Berg. Here was a man devoid of deceit who took a good look around and observed just how well the men were being paid and treated and at his meeting told them that he was not about to promise pie in the sky if they joined his union, but that if they had a mind to unionize he would be glad to represent them. I was impressed with his sincerity, in marked contrast to the representatives of the other union.

By Saskatchewan law a mine could not really protect itself against unscrupulous labour unions. They are free to proselytize at will. As a Crown Company, however, Eldorado was exempt from this law and could have insulated its workers from the likes of the Mine-Mill Union, but it didn't. Perhaps it didn't want to encourage any unnecessary criticism from the press. Furthermore, its management at the time wouldn't believe that a union as corrupt as Mine-Mill could persuade its men to choose it as their bargaining agent. So they let it come to a vote without any hindrance and were amazed to see it ratified by a whopping eighty-seven percent!

By the time this happened Mine-Mill had gotten themselves certified as official bargaining agents for all the surrounding mines, with the exception of the Gunnar Mine. Its president and founder Gilbert LaBine wrote me and asked my help in preventing his mine from going "Communist" like the others in the area. He said he didn't care what union represented his men as long as it wasn't Mine-Mill. I immediately thought of Carl Berg and his A. F. of L. and wrote him in Edmonton. As a result he sent up two shop stewards who were signed on at Gunnar incognito to begin organizing the men. We had to be careful not to alarm the local

Mine-Mill officials who had not been able to get a foot in the door at Gunnar. One reason for this was its isolation: at the southern tip of Crackingstone Point, it had no road access from Uranium City. At the same time I began to conduct a series of talks and discussions on labour unions in general at the mine following my regular services. Of course I emphasized the importance and advantages of belonging to a union that was affiliated with the Canadian Congress of Labour. After two months the time looked right for a vote, so I wired Carl to fly up, signing my telegram "Mother"! I posted notices around Gunnar for an important meeting of the 220 hourly-rate workers at the mine, to be held Sunday, July 4th at 8 p.m. in the mess hall. Over 300 showed up.

The meeting came to order promptly and was chaired by Carl Berg who gave a brief synopsis of the labour movement in Canada in general. As soon as he mentioned his affiliation with the A. F. of L. we found that we had a contingent of the enemy in our midst. One rabid apostle of the Mine-Mill Union took the floor claiming to be one of many ex-seamen in the hall who were vehemently opposed to any American labour union in general and to the A. F. of L. in particular. He was backed up by a chorus of similar discontents who were yelling that there was no way that they would let their union dues go to an American organization, that this mine was not ready yet to vote on such a serious matter. Luckily the whole lot of them stormed out of the hall or it could have turned into a bloody brawl. They immediately started gathering signatures outside for certification of their union.

We still had a majority in the hall for certification for A. F. of L. if we could get them to sign up. It didn't look too promising. Carl looked worried. I felt weak in the knees. The moment of truth had arrived as Carl sent the voting cards out into the audience for signatures. The men brought them back one by one to the speakers at the table and they were counted. The results, fifty-one percent of the mine's total hourly-rate employees had elected the A. F. of L. Union as their official bargaining agent. It was as tight a victory as we could have won, but it was valid and completely above board. I felt greatly relieved. Carl felt vindicated. Gilbert was so happy with the outcome when he got the news that he sent me a cheque for $1,000 in appreciation for my part in the whole operation.

Two weeks later I was back in my office at Gunnar when I got an unexpected visit from another representative of the A. F. of L. Union. He was a tall gentleman with what sounded like a Russian accent. He said he had been sent out by Union headquarters to express their sincere thanks to me for helping them so effectively gain certification at this mine and with those words he ceremoniously handed me a cheque. I thanked him most sincerely saying how happy I had been personally with the outcome and looked forward to a happy and peaceful cooperation at the mine between management and labour. I couldn't wait for him to leave the room so I could look at the figure on his cheque. I must admit I was surprised when I read that it was made out for five dollars. Nonetheless, the experience was worth far more than that to me and it was a great satisfaction to see the good guys win for once.

❈ ❈ ❈

I was in for another pleasant surprise when I got back to U-City. Philip arrived suddenly without any warning. He looked great and from what he said was completely cured of his Bright's disease. Never one to write, he had not sent back much news from France, but now he told me of his adventures. He spoke of his sculptor father who was working on another huge equestrian statue in marble, of his brother who ran an automobile plant, of his sister who had joined an order of nuns who pray especially for the souls in purgatory, and finally he got to himself. He had bought a motorcycle and toured a lot of Europe. What he was seeking primarily was a wife who would be willing and able to share his life at Camsell Portage. In this quest he had failed, so he was back to carry on helping me where he had left off eight months before. We lost no time getting down to the port at Black Bay, where our skiff with its motor was pulled up, waiting to take us back to Camsell Portage. Although there were only forty people spending the summer there, they welcomed Philip back as one of their own. His familiar presence back in Mission Saint Bernard made it far less lonely for me and gave me a morale boost too, not to mention the physical help his presence meant. I immediately took him out and showed him where our nets were set.

Once Philip was settled in again I took leave to visit my far-flung parish. First of all I crossed with the skiff to the McInnes fish camp at Crackingstone Point where I spent the night on one of their barges and said a 6:30 mass in another. Then I crossed over to Gunnar Mine where the work force had swelled to 450 men during the erection of their mill. Gilbert LaBine himself happened to be visiting his mine and he explained to me that he was determined to have his own mill and process his own ore, rather than send it over to Eldorado's mill on Beaverlodge Lake as all the other mines in the area planned to do. He had a chip on his shoulder ever since Eldorado had taken over his operation on Great Bear Lake. For one thing, they had also taken his Northern Transportation system. They had promised to return it after the war, but they didn't.

Close by Gunnar on a small island there was a shrine to the Blessed Virgin set up in a tall pine tree, from which St. Mary's Channel got its name. Old-timer Father Riou told me that this shrine had been erected by Modest Ladoucer of Fond du Lac to fulfil a vow he had made to the Virgin following a safe crossing from St. Joseph's Point in a row-boat about 1890. Now I was told by one of the workers at the mine that the crew of one of the Northern Transportation barges, while unloading at Gunnar, had gone to this island for a picnic. One of the men found the shrine and had taken the statue of the Virgin from it and thrown it out into deep water in the channel. Others of the party were horrified at this callous act of vandalism and predicted bad luck for their boat. They hadn't long to wait. On their return trip to Waterways they encountered a bad storm near Bear Island toward the south shore of Lake Athabaska. The captain, in attempting to remove the barge they were pushing and put it on tow behind, had the misfortune of seeing the towing cable rake the deck of his boat, cutting all the superstructure, including his pilot house, clean off and sinking his boat. There were no survivors. When found, the barge was acting like a buoy still attached by its cable to the boat on the bottom of the lake. Subsequently I put another statue of Our Lady up in its niche, where I hope it remains to this day.

As these barges didn't go beyond Black Bay on Lake Athabaska, a new bell addressed to Father Perin's new mission at Stoney Lake was left there and I was asked to deliver it. This gave Philip and me a chance to travel to the east end of the lake for the first time by boat. At Fond du Lac we found Father Gamache building himself a new mission aided by his sidekick, Brother Labonté, and supervised by Brother Larocque, who had helped me establish the mission at Fort Franklin. When we stopped there for the night, I noticed a huge, thirty-foot skiff-shaped boat on the beach which I had not seen in the winter, possibly because it was drifted over with snow. It had been the brainchild, apparently, of a young missionary who had spent a year with Father Gamache and who abandoned it after its inboard engine failed to work. Father Gamache told me I could take it, so Philip and I tarried another day there filling in the hole in its bottom where the shaft had protruded and made it shipshape for launching.

When we got to Stoney Rapids with our heavy bronze cargo the following day we could find no way of transporting it overland the final five miles or so to Stoney Lake where the empty belfry waited. The locals told us that the rapids were too swift for a boat the size of ours to go up, but after hearing that some of the natives made it in their canoes I decided to give it a try. We made it up to Stoney Lake without touching a rock and were met by the missionary and some of his flock, who seemed quite amazed at our feat. Actually it was far easier than ascending the Great Bear River up to Great Bear Lake. We unloaded and sped back to Fond du Lac in three-and-a-half-hours. The next day we launched the giant skiff we dubbed *The Ark*, and, pulling it behind us, continued right down the middle of the lake. Luckily, it was flat calm and we got into Camsell at midnight, after running fourteen consecutive hours.

About the middle of August Philip took me in our skiff over to Black Bay and dropped me off so that I could visit the mines. He needed the boat to do some assessment work on our claims. I spent a week at the Eldorado mine and then flew in their DC-3 up to their mine on Great Bear Lake. I was again able to cross over to Fort Franklin on *The Radium Gilbert* to spend a few days with my old parishioners. When I tried to converse with the natives I noticed I was losing my proficiency with the Hare language, but they were as warm and cordial as ever and asked if there was any way I could return and live with them again. I noticed some changes around the Fort, some new buildings going up. There were changes in the people too. One of the natives produced a camera and, for a change, took *my* picture. On the feast day of my patron, Saint Bernard, August 20th, Captain Allen McInnes took me back across the lake to continue my work at the mine. While there I again visited the natives living at Port Radium, six miles south of the mine. There, in the old Land Office building, I offered a mass for them for the first time.

On my return flight south Alf Kaywood put the Eldorado Dakota down at Yellowknife to refuel and I decided to get off and visit Father Frank Ebner, one of the few American padres working in the Mackenzie Vicariate. While I was there for a few days he took me around to visit some of the interesting locals like John Anderson Thompson, a noted geologist, and Ernie Boffa, a bush pilot I had met at Port Radium. Ernie had the most northern books, outside the library, that I had seen in anyone's possession. I was impressed. Later he would have a book written about himself by another person I visited in Yellowknife, Flo Wyward. Father Ebner, who was working alone, took advantage of my presence to have me preside at a meeting of the parents of children attending St. Pat's School and to conduct a service for a group of Indian people a few miles south of town.

When I got back to Camsell Portage the geese were beginning to fly south, so it was time for our annual goose hunt in the Chip delta at the west end of the lake. We got away early enough on the 22nd of September, but had to buck a stiff head wind for eleven hours before we got into the lee of the islands at Fort Chipewyan. Because it was past supper time at the mission we stopped as we often did at the home of the Hudson Bay Company Manager, Allen Black. His wife Phyllis was a marvellous cook and perfectly willing to put a meal on the table for us at any hour.

After spending the night at the mission we crossed the lake to Moose Point and pitched our tent. Hap Cave, the former Goldfields cook, was already there with his wife Slim guiding for a party of hunters headed by Ship Shipley from Miles City, Montana. They were all great companions and didn't seem to mind our competition. In fact, we were not as effective against the higher flying birds, because they were using ten gauge shotguns with magnum shells that could bring down birds we wouldn't even fire at with our smaller bore shotguns. The snow geese had a habit of flying over this sandy point twice a day, early morning and late evening, and we had dug holes in the sand about a hundred feet apart in which to hide. The very first evening we waited as a flock came in across the calm lake directly toward us. They were right on the water and we anticipated that they would rise as they approached us, but evidently we were so well camouflaged they didn't see us and passed directly over us. They were so low we felt we could have touched them with our gun barrels. We were so taken by surprise that we failed to fire a shot!

As we sat there afterwards berating ourselves for being so stupid, Philip happened to touch the hair trigger of his sixteen-gauge double-barrel and it discharged directly over my head, a few pellets penetrating my wide-brimmed Borsalino hat. He was so shaken that he refused to use that gun again, and didn't, until months later back at our mission. One day I noticed a raven eating our fish on the stage down by our dogs and yelled for Philip to get his gun. He walked up behind me as I held the front door open a crack and – bang! – that temperamental gun discharged into the floor right behind my feet! That time we got rid of it for good. A third misfire might not have been so lucky. We did make a very successful hunt that fall, however, returning with thirty-five snow geese, four prairie chickens and one duck, some fancy eating for the Sundays of the coming winter.

On our way home we stopped at the Chi-Mac drilling camp which belonged to Mrs. Viola McMillan, President of the Prospectors' Association. The crew there had an interesting and unusual bear story to tell us. They had been throwing their garbage into a hole they dug about twenty-five feet out behind their framed cabin. A black bear began visiting this dump regularly at night and his rummaging through the tin cans woke up the whole crew. As they had no firearms, the cook decided to kill him with a concoction of honey mixed with broken glass. The bear ate all that was put out for him and kept coming back for more. When they ran out of honey and then jam, one of the drill crew came up with the brilliant idea of tying a bundle of dynamite sticks to the tree trunk right beside the trash hole with a fuse running into their bunkhouse. The next night when they saw the bear back at the dump they lit the fuse. As it burned toward him with its hissing sound he perked up and ran around in front of the cabin as if he had heard something approaching from the lake. Then it exploded with a deafening roar, knocking everything from the shelves of the cabin, breaking the back windows and lifting all the shingles from the roof on the dump side. The bear trotted back around to his feeding hole which was now a great, smoking crater. He took off, leaving the frustrated crew scrambling to cover the windows with sheets as the mosquitoes poured in.

When a person lives in the North his life is largely regulated by the seasons. In this sense he is living more in tune with nature than his city counterpart and, no doubt, it is a more natural kind of existence. The weather itself pushes him to do certain things, to undertake certain chores he might leave till later if it were a matter of his own initiative. There's a season for everything in the North and if the appropriate task is not completed in its proper time, its later completion can be infinitely more difficult, if not impossible. Our forced caveat hearing in Regina prevented us from beginning our yearly fall fishery until the 22nd of October, which we realized from our experience the year before on Spider Island was late. Anyway, on this date we loaded up dogs and nets and our recently acquired *Ark* and, towing it behind us, went east to Orbit Bay. This was on the west side of Black Bay, much closer to home than we had been the year before. Another benefit of this location was an old abandoned log cabin, which we quickly fixed up for our use. I certainly didn't want Philip to get another attack of Bright's disease by spending freeze-up in a tent. As it turned out we only got in two weeks of net fishing and had to content ourselves with 1,600 fish when we knew we needed over 5,000. Loading up *The Ark* with all our gear plus all our fish, we retreated to the protection of Camsell Bay and then set three nets near its entrance. By mid-November the temperature was down to zero Fahrenheit and Philip was using the dogs to bring in firewood.

While Philip took care of the outside work, I covered our workshop area with a smooth plywood floor over the old rough boards and then built a ping-pong table. This new indoor sport quickly attracted the youth of the village and the mission soon became the local sports arena.

The main topic around town, as always at that time of year, was caribou. When were they coming? Had anyone seen any tracks yet? Finally, on the last day of November, Alec Augier came in with a sled-load of meat from a lake north of our village and we all got a piece. Soon we were all heading in that direction with our teams and the hunt was on.

During this commotion our female sled dogs were not sitting idle in their corrals. One after the other, Kapa and Princess presented us with new litters of pups. I had always wanted a team of pure white dogs and I did have a few, but now I had the pups to make a complete set. I built a new rock maple toboggan and covered it with a new moose-hide wrapper. This was a fancy job with handles made from the natural bent roots of a birch tree.

Ski-equipped planes began landing on the solid ice of our bay, even though there was still some open water on the main lake, so I flew over to the mines for a round of visits and then flew back again to Camsell Portage for Christmas. This year, in addition to our regular decorations, I put up an outside tree with coloured lights on it that we could illuminate with our small generator. And we had an unusual ceremony – a marriage – when Billy Shot was joined in Holy Matrimony to Regina Powder. Everyone predicted a successful union, for powder and shot always went well together! Following the special rubrics for Christmas I offered two masses at midnight and then a plane picked me up the next afternoon after Benediction and I offered a third mass that evening at Gunnar Mine. When I returned the following day we continued our celebrations with a community turkey dinner followed by a Christmas party for the children that evening. During this they consumed 200 ice cream cones and broke over 100 balloons, while their parents held a dance in our renovated workshop. By the time the last well-wishers had left for home, Philip and I fell into our bunks completely played out.

We were relaxing at the kitchen table drinking coffee the next day, glad that the big holiday was behind us and with little planned for the remaining five days of the year, when Budgie Larocque walked in and joined us. Budgie was a trapper we classified as "one tough cookie." He had been raised initially by the Yaniks at Fort Fitzgerald but soon gravitated east to the Barren Lands out from Fort Reliance where he fell in with the remnants of the now extinct band of Chipewyan Indians known as the Caribou-Eaters. This tribe was almost completely dependent upon the migrating Barren Land caribou and, when they didn't come, they were reduced to starvation. Budgie told us of one spring he kept alive by jigging a single ivory lure he made through a hole in the ice to attract a jackfish. And then, when the first caribou appeared, his group was out of ammunition. Budgie, however, was determined he would get one of the animals, so he launched himself in a tiny hunting canoe with no weapon aboard. Approaching a swimming buck from the rear, Budgie grasped its horns and pushed its head under water, trying to drown it. He could hold him down just so long and then the caribou bull would jerk its head up and get a breath of air. This went on for so long that Budgie was sorry he had tried it and yet he was afraid to let go, for fear that the enraged animal, once free, would gore and upset his frail craft. In the meantime a group of his friends were cheering him on from the shore, and his pride spurred him to expend every ounce of strength he could muster. The contest lasted nearly half an hour and Budgie did win, but he was so exhausted that he fell down in his canoe, unable to paddle himself ashore. He cautioned us never to try it.

This feat of raw courage and strength evidently made Budgie the object of a jealous contest between two women of the tribe, both of whom saw him as the perfect mate. They ended up wrestling for him and Madeleine won. She was presently living in his cabin at Camsell, the mother of his many young children and a very forceful character in her own right. One day in summer Philip and I watched a powerful little episode unfold in front of their cabin which clearly demonstrated Madeleine's power of persuasion. Budgie was in their canoe, about to start the outboard motor and take off again for Uranium City where liquor often attracted him. His better half was yelling a vehement veto to the trip with the words "Budgie, you no go!" He did not seem to be listening, though the rest of the village was. She ran right down into the water with the axe in one hand and with one overhead swing brought it down on the motor's flywheel in a crashing blow that disintegrated it. As Budgie calmly surveyed the damage, he said, "Well, I guess I won't go."

In the bars of Uranium City Budgie may have been nothing more than another "drunken Indian," but out in the bush in his own element he was the consummate expert. He showed me how he called spruce hens up so close they could be killed with a stick. Another trick of his that worked amazingly well was to shake a box of matches back and forth to imitate the sound of a beaver cutting down a tree. He'd do this near a lodge and the beaver, hearing this sound, would think it was a rival beaver cutting in his pond and swim right up to Budgie.

The toughest part of trapping out on the Barrens, according to Budgie, was thawing the white fox he caught in traps. During the day he would be picking them up frozen stiff and carrying them in his dogsled till evening when he slept in his tent. As wood was scarce and the tent was heated for a very short time, the foxes wouldn't have time to thaw out. Once skinned, their fur would be as light as feathers, but carrying them, carcass and all, would add too much weight to his sled. There was only one solution: to take the frozen foxes into his sleeping bag with him at night and let the heat of his body thaw them so that they could be skinned in the morning. I could just imagine the difficulty of keeping oneself warm out on the Barrens in an unheated tent at forty below, without being surrounded with frozen fox carcasses. With that kind of a life behind him, Budgie was finding life easy at Camsell and he often helped us. He even offered to help me extract teeth. He said he had extracted his own successfully using nothing but the sharp end of a file! I preferred to use my dental forceps.

On this occasion Budgie let us in on some information about rich uranium ground he had discovered a day's dogsled journey north of the settlement. You'd think that, by now, after all our bad luck with mineral claims, Philip and I would have been permanently cured of the staking bug. Yet apparently we weren't: for the next three days we were staking the twenty "fault" claims along with Budgie near the N.W.T. border. We got back home again just in time to celebrate New Year's.

As 1954 ticked its inexorable way into eternity I sat back and reviewed its history, some of which had been pleasant, some unpleasant, all of it important in the mosaic of my life in the North. I enjoyed the routine visits to the mines, including Port Radium, and my regular dogsled trips east and west, on which I went to the limits of our area. In both activities I was saved from monotony by the interesting people I encountered along the way. The year's unique encounter at court with the highest law in the Province certainly proved disillusioning. The exposure to labour unions showed me how men could be manipulated and intimidated by dishonest elements with hidden agendas. Philip's sickness was sobering, bringing home to me forcibly just how precarious our health really is. As the events of the year passed through my mind on New Year's Eve, I could imagine myself spending another forty years at this mission, but I could not imagine any future experiences that would be much different from those of the past two-and-a-half. In my year-end letter to my superior, Bishop Trocellier, I reported as usual on the year's activities and then added two requests. First, my youngest brother Thomas was due to be ordained a priest in Washington, D.C., in June, and I asked if the usual ten-year wait for vacation could be shortened to seven in my case so that I could attend. Second, in view of the fact that both Mission Saint Bernard and Mission Santa Barbara were now well established, I again requested a transfer to work somewhere in the Far North. With this letter signed and sealed I was ready to meet the New Year and see what it held in store.

The mission was packed to the walls for the 10 o'clock high mass with which we began the New Year, 1955. I delivered what I hoped was a convincing sermon on New Year's resolutions. Afterwards we all trooped over to Francis Powder's cabin to break our fast, then back to the mission for Benediction of the Blessed Sacrament at 2:30 p.m., and finally to the schoolhouse in the evening for a dance, to which I brought my guitar.

Three days later I left with my dog-team to visit the mines east of us, which wasn't at all unusual except for the fact that Philip accompanied me with his own team for the first time. Our four-day trip from mine to mine was a warm-up before we set out again for Fort Chipewyan, Fort Smith and the annual retreat. We left Camsell going west on the 9th of January. Now that we each had our own sled and dogs, the going was much easier than it had been two years before when we were both riding the same sled. It was an easy half-day's run to Simon Bashaw's cabin, where we stayed the first night. When we got to the Brothers' cabin on Fiddler Point the next evening, we were surprised to find it filled up with the same caribou-hunting Indians we had run into there two years previously. Only this time there were thirteen of them and we experienced some difficulty securing two bunks for ourselves. (It's no use to lock up a cabin that isolated because it is sure to be broken into if anyone is looking for shelter for the night.)

The next night, after an eight-hour run, we were well housed under the big roof of the mission at Chip. We tarried there the next day to give our dogs a little rest before tackling the trail, or lack of trail, on north to Fort Smith. We hadn't forgotten our days on snowshoes at sixty-two below zero on that frozen Slave River two years before.

Previously I mentioned the two Yanik brothers, Steve and Joe, who were occupied in Goldfields and Uranium City. A third was Lawrence, who had been working as a ranger for Wood Buffalo Park and who joined us at Chip to go north with us, driving his own team of dogs. I had lent one of my dogs to Philip at Chip, so was down to four, and two of them were the big white brothers of King, named Prince and Nanook. These four dogs proved superb on this run as they broke trail in eight inches of snow, and I scarcely got out of the sled all day. They were still breaking trail for the other two teams when we camped for the night at the 30th Base Line Cabin where Lawrence had cached buffalo meat. It snowed on us all the following day, but we kept right on going and reached Hay Camp at nine in the evening. There was a big crew of forty men there working at the annual buffalo roundup and slaughter. No problem to get dog feed or to find a warm cabin where one could throw his sleeping bag in that camp.

The next night we were at Fort Fitzgerald, where I camped with Father Napoleon Lafferty at the mission and Philip took a bunk with Lawrence over at the Yaniks' log home. The local pastor, Father Lafferty, born at Fort Rae, was one of only two native priests to be ordained in the Vicariate in over a hundred years. He told me that following his ordination by Bishop Breynat he had been asked to stay at Fitzgerald temporarily, pending his first official obedience. He had been there since 1923! I got the impression that his wait there in that house, now over a quarter of a century, was beginning to affect his mind. He made no effort to feed me, although I had been travelling all day without eating. Apparently he had given up on house-cleaning too some years before. It was one of those situations that badly needed some female help.

Philip and I continued on across the portage to Fort Smith the following day, where for the next eight days I attended our annual retreat. This yearly get-together of the Oblate Fathers and Brothers was calculated to give us a break from our home missions to follow a schedule of spiritual exercises which would renew our faith and commitment. Of prime importance to the success of this undertaking was the conference delivered twice each day by the designated Retreat Master. As these were invariably given in French, I was glad I had persevered in communicating with Philip only in this language. In addition to the religious aspects of the retreat, it was a happy time to meet and exchange experiences with other missionaries from all over our vast Vicariate.

Our return trip proved anything but a piece of cake. To begin with, the trail which we had broken in deep snow going down was now filled in again, as no one apparently had travelled on it. We were forced to take turns going ahead on snowshoes in spite of our light loads. We camped the first night with Tom Champaign's family and the next with Bill Moore's at the mouth of the Peace. Leaving Fort Chipewyan and heading east on the open Lake Athabaska we faced a head wind at thirty below for three solid days, about as tough as conditions can get for dogsled travel. We were completely played out when we came again into the shelter of the mission at Camsell, carrying with us the scars of frostbite. It was the last time I would make that trip.

While I was recuperating indoors the following week, I got out my oil paints and painted a burial scene from Fort Franklin as I remembered it. It turned out to be the only painting I left at

Camsell Portage. A month later Gilbert LaBine's daughter Margaret flew in to pay us a visit and I took her out on a short caribou chase by dog-team. Some time later when I visited her home in Toronto I was surprised to see a very fine painting of the Camsell mission by A. Y. Jackson. Apparently he had flown in for an afternoon in summer when I was absent. I was sorry later that I had failed to paint the same scene myself.

The following month I relieved the pastor at Mission Santa Barbara, Father L'Helgouach, for ten days while he attended the second retreat at Fort Smith. While in Uranium City I visited Eldorado Mine as usual and other mines in the area. I spent three weeks at Eldorado and then a week at Gunnar Mine, so by the time I got back to Mission Saint Bernard, a month and a half had slipped by.

Among the pieces of mail that were waiting for me, once again, was one letter that was to alter the course of my life. It was from the Provincial Father, Jean-Louis Michel, O.M.I., who as Vicar of Missions for the Vicariate worked closely with the bishop. He informed me that I had been granted permission to attend my brother Thomas's ordination in June, following which I was to present myself at Fort Smith to receive a new obedience! Whoopee! This was the good news I had been waiting for. As much as I dreaded the inevitable pain of separation from all that I had built up again at Camsell Portage, the lure of the Far North was still so strong that I was willing to do violence to my emotions in order to follow it. Yet I was living under the vow of obedience and as such I could have been left indefinitely at this post, just as Father Lafferty had been left at Fort Fitzgerald. The thought that gives the Catholic missionary peace of mind in whatever situation he finds himself is that if he is doing what he is doing where he is doing it by order of his legitimate superiors, he is fulfilling the will of God. This thought is basic to his drive to spread the Good News and his consolation when things don't go as well as planned.

Realizing that my days at Mission Saint Bernard were now numbered, I was determined to make one last sled trip with

Philip. So on the 14th of April, with nine of our dogs, we pulled out on the steel-shod komatik and headed east down the lake. Our first overnight stop was at Gunnar Mine, where I held a service the next morning. Then we continued on our way and that night pitched our tent on Beaver Island, near Oldman River. The following day we ran into migrating caribou, shot four, and carried the meat on to the mission at Fond du Lac.

Father Gamache and Brother Labonté were now living in the new building they had put up during the summer. Though it was an improvement over the old one, it lacked the atmosphere and charm that made the old one so appealing. We were given a room on the second floor next to a larger sitting room. This room was being used temporarily to house 250 chicks that had been flown in and which could not be left out in the cold. They were living in a large pen that covered most of the floor. Their chorus of peeps didn't bother us, but the dust they kicked up did, until we got our new window pried open and our door securely shut. We were forced to admit that we would have been more comfortable sleeping in our tent, but there was always some new adventure when we visited the Fond du Lac mission.

We didn't make Stoney Rapids in a single day, as we usually did. We got a late start, stopped to shoot another caribou and camped in the open at a beautiful natural campsite in Pine Channel. The next day we passed by Stoney and went on to Stoney Lake, where we expected to find Father Perin and his new assistant, Father Dauvet. They were camped in the bush, however, ten miles to the north. We went out and spent a night with them in their tent where they were busy cutting firewood. The story we got was that Father Perin had accepted a lot of volunteer labour to put up his new log mission at Stoney Lake on condition that he feed his workers, their families and dogs. In doing this he had run up a bill in the neighbourhood of $1,500 with the local Hudson Bay trading post and had contracted to cut them seventy-five cords of wood to pay it off. Leaving these two eager beavers to their work the following day, we proceeded on to the old, empty mission at Black Lake and moved in.

Our arrival there coincided with that time of year when the heat of the sun causes the snow to melt and drop, practically wiping out the sled trails. I offered a daily mass at the mission and the main room was crowded. Each morning I took communion to a woman dying of TB in her tent. After three days we recrossed the fifteen-mile portage road to Stoney Rapids. Here the teacher, Adeline Tomyn, was kind enough to make a set of canvass shoes for our dogs. It was a good thing we had them the next day, because the snow on the lake was melting, exposing the ice which was beginning to candle and get sharp. We pulled out at four in the morning to avoid the midday heat and took nine hours to get into Fond du Lac, with one stop for a tea fire. The next night we camped at the Nicholson Mine east of Goldfields, where I again said mass for the men in the morning before continuing on to Gunnar. We over-nighted at Gunnar Mine and I held another service in the early morning before we set out to run the final leg of our trip into Camsell Portage. I hated to see the journey end, for I realized that this would be my last sled trip out of Mission Saint Bernard.

During the following two days I sadly packed my trunk with the books and clothing I could carry with me, all the while looking nostalgically at everything I would be forced to abandon. High on that list were my team of faithful dogs and the new toboggan I had recently made, with its fine moose-hide wrapper. The two boats were high and dry, waiting for open water, and the fish house held the motor, the nets and all our harness and gear. The mission itself was now completely equipped, including the workshop with all the tools a person would need. I took the .22 my father had bought me before I left home, my favourite hammer and axe, the brass candlestick from the old Chip mission and a few small personal items.

On the 7th of May everyone in the village attended a final mass in the mission chapel. When all the goodbyes were said, Philip harnessed his team, I jumped in his sled and we took off for Uranium City. I had a lump in my throat as my mission in its picturesque setting slowly faded from sight and I recalled all the memories it held. Still, there was no turning back.

As for Philip Stenne, whom I left in charge on my departure, and who fell heir to the dogs and equipment and who continued to occupy the mission, his future was to be Camsell Portage. The following year he married one of the local girls, Mary Powder, and acquired Pierre Deneroo's cabin, where he proceeded to raise a family of a half-dozen fine children. He supported himself by trapping in winter out of Simon Bashaw's old cabin and in the summer by fishing commercially for the McInnes fish plant. He has managed to keep Mission Saint Bernard in repair for the visiting priests from Uranium City. He never made any fortune with our uranium claims, but his life has been satisfying and happy. What more can a man ask in this life?

POSTSCRIPT

Is this the end of the story? Not by a long shot. Up to this point I have described incidents that took place over my first seven years in the North – 1948-1955. Following the events described above, I was posted to Aklavik, near the Arctic Coast, on the west side of the Mackenzie delta. I was serving there when Aklavik was moved by the government to "East-3" on the east side of the delta. This town later became Inuvik, and I became its first resident pastor.

My next assignment was Fort McMurray, where I was pastor, chaplain of the nearby DEW line station, administrator of the hospital and secretary of the school board. More interesting, however, was the rescue and renovation of an old Mission, the operation of a seven-acre potato farm, the keeping of sled dogs and of riding horses, and the building of an A-frame log church at Nahanni Butte, N.W.T.

In 1962 I was given orders to build a log Mission at Colville Lake, 35 miles above the Arctic Circle, and to form a satellite community of Hare Indians in an area that had been abandoned for years. I left Fort McMurray in my freighter canoe loaded with my trunk and dog-team and proceeded north down the Athabaska, Slave and Mackenzie Rivers. As my life unfolded at Colville Lake I not only built a Mission and church, but built and operated a Health Centre, a Fishing Lodge, and a Co-op store. I found myself acting as a trader of wild furs, postmaster,

returning officer and dog-catcher. One summer I was recruited
to act as the commodore of the N.W.T. canoe team as it competed
in the Canadian Centennial race. Here, too, I resumed painting
the northern scene and put up a Museum and Art Gallery.
Finally I got permission from Rome to marry and our bishop
joined me in matrimony to Margaret, a part-Eskimo girl in my
own log church at Colville – "Our Lady of the Snows."

The account of these events and many others remains to be
given, and I hope that a second volume will follow shortly. New
adventures continue to take place daily, but at age 77 I cannot
delay telling of the earlier years, or I will join the long list of those
whose tracks through history have been swept away by northern
wind and snow.

INDEX

AGMV
MARQUIS
Québec, Canada
1998

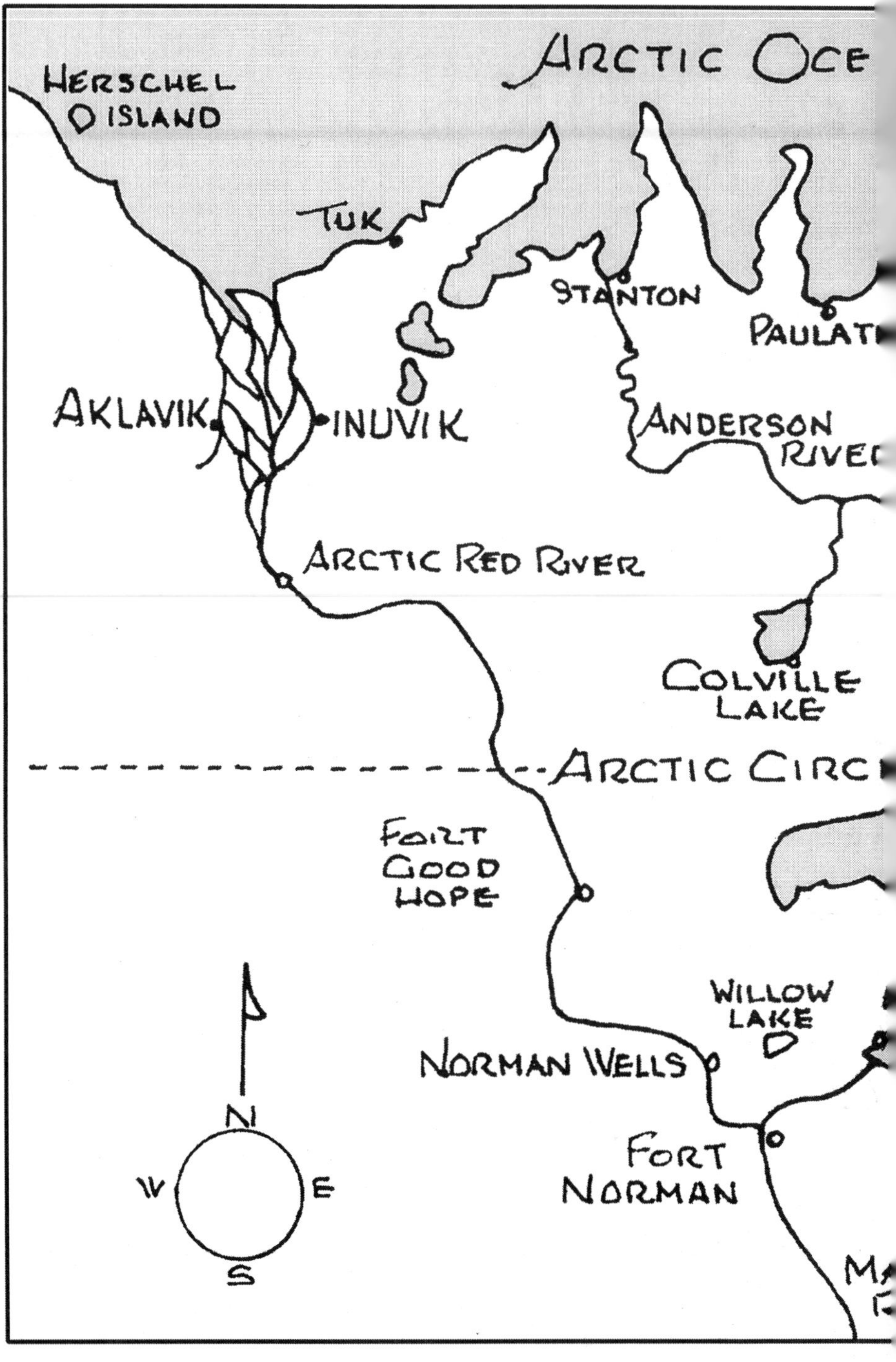
ARCTIC OCE
HERSCHEL ISLAND
TUK
STANTON
PAULAT
AKLAVIK
INUVIK
ANDERSON RIVE
ARCTIC RED RIVER
COLVILLE LAKE
ARCTIC CIRC
FORT GOOD HOPE
WILLOW LAKE
NORMAN WELLS
FORT NORMAN
N
W
E
S